Blush

A MENNONITE GIRL MEETS A GLITTERING WORLD

"Whether she is wearing her new letter jacket or biting a worm in two on a dare from her father, the young Shirley will win your affection."
—*Ann Hostetler, professor of English, Goshen College*

"Shirley Showalter is both a thoughtful historian and a balanced, inner journalist. She affirms—with detail, honesty, and humility—the need to break our own trail while honoring tradition."
—*Mark Nepo, author of* Seven Thousand Ways to Listen *and* The Book of Awakening

"Showalter's portrait of this extraordinary little girl who wants to be 'big' will captivate and enchant readers of all generations."
—*Hildi Froese Tiessen, professor emerita, Conrad Grebel University College*

"This memoir provides an authentic rendition of a plain Mennonite girlhood, so rich in sensory details that it magically transports us into that world."
—*Saloma Miller Furlong, author of* Why I Left the Amish

"Shirley's stories resonate powerfully with the tension we all live with—between our own aspirations and the expectations of others. You must read this book, and when you do, hang onto your hats and prayer coverings!"
—*Tom Beech, president emeritus, Fetzer Institute*

"She's a smart, sweetly blushing, baseball-loving, convertible-driving, taking-on-the-bishop kind of girl who delights and inspires."
—*Dora Dueck, award-winning author of* This Hidden Thing *and* What You Get at Home

"*Blush* is a collection of memories by a woman born with a knack for flirting with boundaries."
—*Suzanne Woods Fisher, author of* Amish Peace

"With spunk, candor, authentic color, and page-turning style, Shirley Showalter takes us into a girl's experience of the threshold between tradition and cultural shift."
—*John L. Ruth, author of* The Earth is the Lord's

"Like a blush, Showalter's engaging story deepens and intensifies as we discover that there is no such thing as a small life."
—*Joanne V. Gabbin, professor of English, James Madison University, and director of the Furious Flower Poetry Center*

"Shirley Showalter drew me in with the very first lines of her introduction—an audacious confession that sounds the depth of her endeavor."
—*Ervin Stutzman, executive director, Mennonite Church USA*

"Reading *Blush* is like eating the most delicious hot apple pie served with something tart, fresh, and zingy. Read it to be inspired by a brave woman willing to find her own voice."
—*Jennifer Louden, author of* The Woman's Comfort Book *and* The Life Organizer

"To read Shirley Showalter's beautifully written memoir is like stepping into a childhood as far from mine as the moon. Her story is one I longed for my whole life."
—*Darrelyn Saloom, coauthor of* My Call to the Ring

Blush

A Mennonite Girl Meets a Glittering World

Shirley Hershey Showalter

Herald Press
Waterloo, Ontario
Harrisonburg, Virginia

Library of Congress Cataloging-in-Publication Data
Showalter, Shirley Hershey.
  Blush : a Mennonite girl meets a glittering world / Shirley Hershey
Showalter.
    pages cm
  Includes bibliographical references.
  ISBN 978-0-8361-9626-9 (pbk. : alk. paper) 1. Showalter, Shirley Hershey.
2. Educators—United States—Biography. 3. College presidents—United
States—Biography. 4. Mennonites—United States—Biography. I. Title.
  LA2317.S58A3 2013
  370.92—dc23
  [B]
                            2013010204

BLUSH
Copyright © 2013 by Herald Press, Harrisonburg, Virginia 22802
    Released simultaneously in Canada by Herald Press,
    Waterloo, Ontario N2L 6H7. All rights reserved.
Library of Congress Control Number: 2013010204
International Standard Book Number: 978-0-8361-1234-5
Printed in United States of America
Cover and interior design by Merrill R. Miller

Photos used throughout this book are from family collections. Henry Hess
Hershey was the photographer for the photos of the capons in chapter 12,
page 138, and of the Home Place, page 158. Joy Rittenhouse took the author
photo, page 271, and the photo of the author on the steps leading to the arch
cellar, end of introduction, page 15.

    Portions of royalties from the sale of this book will be donated to *The
Longhouse Project* at the Hans Herr House Museum, Lancaster County,
Pennsylvania. When complete, the Lancaster Longhouse will be one of the
only interactive outdoor exhibits of Native life in Pennsylvania and one of
few similar buildings in the U.S.
    Unless otherwise noted, Scripture text is quoted, with permission, from
the King James Version.

To order or request information, please call 1-800-245-7894 in the U.S. or
1-800-631-6535 in Canada. Or visit www.heraldpress.com.

18 17 16 15 14   10 9 8 7 6 5 4 3

For Mother,
Barbara Ann Hess Hershey Becker

Her children arise up, and call her blessed.
—Proverbs 31:28

The sheltered life can be a daring life as well.
For all serious daring starts from within.

—Eudora Welty, *One Writer's Beginnings*

Contents

Foreword

Parker J. Palmer

*W*hatever you know or think you know about a country childhood, this memoir may surprise you. It's the story of a young girl with a big vision for her life growing up in the set-apart and buttoned-down Mennonite community, where aspirations like hers are often taken as signs of unbecoming arrogance, treated not as dreams to be pursued but temptations to be denied.

As a longtime friend and admirer of Shirley Showalter, I can testify that she achieved her childhood goal, and then some. She earned a PhD; became a distinguished professor of English; served eight years as the president of a fine liberal arts college; then spent six years as the vice president of a sizeable philanthropic foundation; and now, in "retirement," has written this superb memoir.

But Shirley would not want me to carry on about her many accomplishments. In good Mennonite form, she does nothing of the sort in this book. Far from it! Her memoir ends with Shirley in college, where—like most of us at that age—she is only dimly beginning to discern the trajectory of her adult life. In the epilogue, Shirley devotes exactly one sentence to her adult achievements: "Becoming a professor, a college president, and a foundation executive . . . none of these were planted in me as goals."

So what's in this memoir for the reader besides the beautiful prose, simultaneously fluid and finely crafted? In my experience, at least three important things.

First, the book offers us a textured portrayal of the Mennonite world. Many of us have caricatures of the "plain people" and their way of life, if we know anything at all about them. I know this from personal experience. I'm a Quaker, and when I get into a conversation about that fact, it often becomes clear that the only thing my conversation partner "knows" about Quakerism is "our" oatmeal. Much as I enjoy a steaming bowl of oatmeal on a winter morning, I can assure you that Quaker Oats does not come from the Quaker tradition or enrich the Quaker purse!

So if you are interested in learning something about the varieties of human life that can still be found in an America where so much has been flattened into tedious homogeneity by mass media and mass culture, read this book. It will introduce you to one of those "worlds within the world" that reassures us of the continuing human capacity to march to the beat of a different drummer.

Second, even though Shirley pushed against the constraints of her Mennonite culture from an early stage in life, she writes about her religious community with great appreciation for all of the gifts it gave her. In an age when memoirs sometimes serve as clever covers for taking revenge on whatever and whomever the writer blames for his or her struggles, it's profoundly refreshing to find one that looks with compassion on all of the factors and actors involved.

Shirley looks with kindness at even the most difficult people along her path, seeing them as the mixtures of darkness and light that all of us are. As I read her account, I laid it down occasionally to ask myself how I might remember certain people and events in my past with the same degree of charity that Shirley shows, a charity that's one of the gifts of her Mennonite formation. Perhaps you will find yourself doing the same.

Third, this memoir is an evocative exploration of a paradox that has long intrigued me: creativity and containment. North Americans do not take kindly to containment of any sort. We want to be free to think our own thoughts and do our own thing without having to color inside the lines. But creativity of any sort requires us to honor the limits of the materials we work with, whether they are paint and canvas, words and paper, or clay and slip. And as every creative person knows, there's always a gap between one's vision for a work and what that work ends up conveying—a gap that beckons to the creative spirit to try again and again to bridge it, knowing that it cannot be done.

Much of Shirley's upbringing was an exercise in containment. As I read about it, I understood more deeply the creativity she has exercised in her life as a teacher, writer, and leader. Like all creativity, hers is a balance between freedom and discipline, rooted in a respect for the ineffable mystery that the creative spirit reaches for, a mystery Shirley was taught to hold with deep respect during her Mennonite formation.

The epigraph to this book is a quote from the novelist Eudora Welty: "The sheltered life can be a daring life as well. For all serious daring starts from within." "Daring Mennonite" might seem like an oxymoron at first . . . well, first *blush!* But in the context of this memoir, the phrase makes sense. It is daring to swim upstream to the prevailing culture; it is daring to find the good in people and events that might be regarded as nothing but impediments; and it is daring to hold the tension between containment and freedom, allowing it to open your mind and heart to creative possibilities.

Shirley Showalter has dared all of this and more, not only in writing this book but in living her life.

—Parker J. Palmer is the founder of the Center for Courage and Renewal and author of nine books, including the best-selling Let Your Life Speak, The Courage to Teach, *and* Healing the Heart of Democracy.

Introduction

Every one that is proud in heart is an abomination to the LORD.

—Proverbs 16:5

*E*ver since I was little, I wanted to be big. Not just big as in tall, but big as in important, successful, influential. I wanted to be seen and listened to. I wanted to make a splash in the world.

Admitting this desire still feels like a huge risk. It contradicts much of what my church and my home taught me about the importance of humility. My Mennonite culture permeated my childhood, surrounding me twenty-four hours a day, seven days a week.

I've wrestled with the desire for greatness all my life, unable to give it up and yet unable to proclaim it boldly, afraid that I might be committing the worst sin of all—the sin of pride.

If ambition is a bad thing, and thrice bad for a woman and a Mennonite, I could take the easy way out and blame mine on Mother. She had her secret yearnings, her deep griefs, her desire to be what Mennonites call "fancy" barely hidden under her prayer covering and "plain" cape dress.

Or perhaps I could place the guilt for my aspirations on Daddy's broad shoulders. Daddy developed his strength through hard work on the farm, straining in vain to please his father. A friend once told me that hurt and anger like my father's should be enough to fuel overachievement in his offspring for at least two generations. Perhaps it has.

Whatever the cause, I was fated to enter the world at a particular time and place that would make my desires complicated. It all started with my name.

If you were called Shirley, you were probably born after 1938 and before 1955. Seventeen years is a relatively short shelf life for a name, even if Shirley was a wildly popular one for that brief shining era.

If you arrived into a plain-dressing, plain-speaking Mennonite farm family and were named for Shirley Temple—a movie star you would then be forbidden to watch—you might have been confused and perhaps embarrassed at times. As you grew up, old enough to sense the contradiction, you might have blushed.

Very young children seldom suffer from blushing, which can't happen without self-consciousness. In early life, rosy cheeks mean just the opposite of embarrassment. They are external emblems of invisible graces: health, innocence, exuberance, abundance—signs of exertion in both work and play. Before blushing is possible, a rosy-cheeked child lives in a place in which the inner world and the outer world are not separate. We see ourselves in nature and in those we love.

When I was baptized and joined the church at the age of twelve, I began to wear my faith on my head in the form of a prayer covering. Though it was a small symbol, it loomed large in my life. Every morning I pulled my long hair into a bun, stuck three straight pins in my mouth, and then, one by one, I attached the covering to the top of my head while knowing that all day, every day, other people would spot my religion before they saw me.

Nicknamed Rosy Cheeks by a seventh grade teacher, I became conscious of incongruities between Mennonite plainness and the glittering things of the world. I struggled to find a place where my inner and outer worlds could align, as they had in early childhood. I broke some rules and bent other ones. I blushed whenever I tried to be someone I was not.

I have lived a much bigger life than I ever could have imagined as a child and have traveled far beyond the small town of Lititz, Pennsylvania. Yet the farther I roamed, the more I began to feel a gentle tug on my sleeve in the other direction—home. I became curious about the rosy child and blushing girl I used to be. I wanted to see and hear her again, from a loving and unblushing distance, with new eyes and ears. She has become more than my past self. She is my touchstone for questing youth. In that way, she is a part of everyone. And everyone has some version of her inside.

In my life, winter beckons just ahead, and youth lies far behind. I think of the way my mother and grandmothers and their mothers before them prepared for winter, by "putting up" the fruits of their labors into glass jars and storing them in the arch cellar,[1] that part of the house sunk deepest into the earth.

I'm heading down into the arch cellar of memory now. Come along. The roots of who I am are stored here. I expect a little girl with big dreams will make her appearance soon.

Sitting on the sandstone steps on the way down to the arch cellar, April 8, 2013. Today, the Home Place of my childhood is known as Forgotten Seasons Bed & Breakfast.

---

1. A cellar used to store vegetables. This term, along with other words and phrases used commonly among rural Mennonites, is explained further in the glossary, 255.

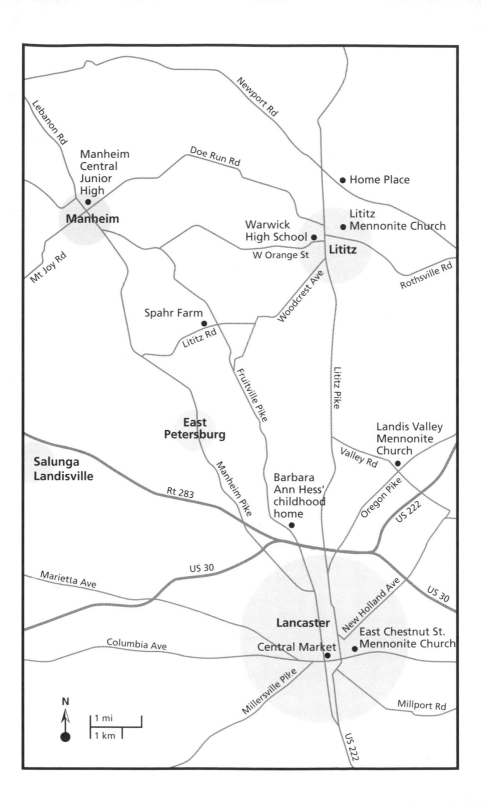

Newport Rd

Lebanon Rd

Manheim
Central
Junior
High

Doe Run Rd

● Home Place

Manheim ●

Warwick
High School ●

Lititz
Mennonite Church ●

Lititz

W Orange St

Mt Joy Rd

Rothsville Rd

Woodcrest Ave

Spahr Farm ●

Lititz Rd

Lititz Pike

Fruitville Pike

Landis Valley
Mennonite
Church

**East
Petersburg**

Valley Rd ●

**Salunga
Landisville**

Manheim Pike

Oregon Pike

Rt 283

Barbara
Ann Hess'
childhood
home
●

US 222

US 30

Marietta Ave

New Holland Ave

US 30

Lancaster

East Chestnut St.
Mennonite Church

Columbia Ave

Central Market ●

Millersville Pike

Millport Rd

N

1 mi
1 km

US 222

Family Tree

Hershey side	Hess side
Henry Huber Hershey	**John Buckwalter Hess**
March 9, 1872 – January 13, 1960	June 4, 1865 – March 27, 1953
m. May 19, 1891	m. October 28, 1886
Ella Anna Hostetter Hershey	**Barbara Lindemuth Garber Hess**
May 20, 1870 – November 21, 1944	March 3, 1866 – April 5, 1941

Hershey side	Hess side
David Paul Hershey	**John Garber Hess**
March 6, 1900 – February 14, 1985	January 14, 1895 – May 19, 1989
m. December 25, 1922	m. December 10, 1918
Susan Brubaker Snyder Hershey	**Anna Mary Herr Hess**
October 21, 1902 – April 4, 1985	November 30, 1895 – June 25, 1951
children in order:	*children in order:*
H. Richard	John Henry
Jane	Christian
Lois	Lloyd
Paul	Barbara Ann
Mildred	Allen
Ann	
Mark	

H. Richard Hershey	**Barbara Ann Hess Hershey**
May 2, 1925 – May 3, 1980	February 27, 1927 –

m. May 17, 1947

children in order: Shirley, Henry, Mary Louise, Sue, Doris, Linda

Shirley Ann Hershey, July 30, 1948 –
m. August 2, 1969
Stuart Wesley Showalter, January 11, 1946 –

One

Mother's Dream

Reach high, for stars lie hidden in your soul.
Dream deep, for every dream precedes the goal.

—Mother Teresa

My mother's name, Barbara, means "stranger." Growing up, she felt both strange and special because she was an only daughter. Most Mennonite farm families in the 1920s were large, so most little girls shared bedrooms, time on the lap, shopping, and instruction with a host of sisters and brothers. But Mother had no competition from other girls.

Even more unusual, her own mother was also an only daughter. Named Barbara for *both* her grandmothers, Barbara Ann Hess soaked up attention from the women of her family. As the oldest daughter myself, I would later benefit from generations of parents, especially mothers, devoted to daughters.

The concentration of love energy made Mother vulnerable, of course. It meant that the deaths of her two grandmothers and then of her mother, Anna Mary, left her desolate. Both grandmothers died in Mother's high school years, and she was only twenty-four when her mother lurched onto the daybed and died of a heart attack. The dynamo of her life suddenly quit running. It's a wonder Mother could go on, but somehow she did.

Mother grew up at her own mother's side, learning to perform all kinds of homemaking and marketing skills. She was the fourth of five children. She wanted a sister all her life but never got one. She loved her brothers, looking up to the three older ones (John Henry, Christian, and Lloyd) and looking out for one younger (Allen). Yet wonderful as these boys were, they could not satisfy her yearning for a sister.

The farm on which Mother grew up, like almost all farms close to Lancaster, Pennsylvania, has long since been developed into suburbs and commercial property. But in the 1930s and '40s, it offered a backdrop for her active imagination and was her teacher in the school of hard work. With the encouragement of my Grandma Anna Mary, she would often walk alone, out the back door, down the steps, through the garden to whole worlds she created in her imagination. She made mud pies, let them dry, and then sold them as though she were a vendor. She remembers her mother buying twenty pies for a nickel.

Anna Mary Herr Hess holds her only daughter, Barbara Ann, spring 1927, in the front yard of the Hess farm. Her husband, John Garber Hess, and three sons complete the family photo. Boys, left to right: Christian, Lloyd, and John Henry.

She also walked farther out into the meadow, where she created her own house out of stones and rocks she found on a pile. Using them to delineate rooms, she could imagine her dream house. She also imagined a sister, who sat with her on a stone chair and drank invisible tea from stone teacups. Out of love and necessity, she would become a storyteller and, eventually, my first teacher.

As Mother got a little older, she accompanied her mother to the Central Market[2] "stand" they kept on Tuesdays and Fridays near the square in downtown Lancaster, less than five miles from her home. It was the middle of the Depression, but people still needed to eat. The weekly butchering and dressing of chickens, baking of cookies, and gathering of eggs or anything else the farm had produced allowed the Hess family to survive relatively unscathed.

They were not wealthy, but they always enjoyed excellent food, adequate shelter, and a few fine objects of beauty—an organ, a violin, and nice clothing. Grandpa Hess splurged on a creamy white Cadillac in 1947. Though he lived forty-two more years, he never purchased another car. Since he drove until the age of ninety, Grandpa joked that his dollar costs had averaged out pretty well. "Choose a few fine things and make them last" was the maxim that came down to me.

Grandma sometimes took her only daughter shopping at one of the three department stores in downtown Lancaster—Hager's, Watt and Shand, and Garvin's. Hager's, in fact, provided a near-constant allure, since it was located directly across the street from Central Market. Mother and daughter gazed together at the store displays, fingered the fabrics, made friends with the clerks. Anna Mary understood how to take advantage of the clerks' knowledge about such topics as styles, fabrics, or body types. In those days, you could have a personal shopper by entering a good department store, but you had to know how to turn down

---

2. The Lancaster Central Market, the country's oldest continuously operated farmers' market, has been attracting visitors from around the world for many years. CNN named it one of the ten best in the world in July 2012 (www.cnn .com/2012/07/17/travel/worlds-best-fresh-markets).

the sales pitch and turn up the quality information. Anna Mary was a pro shopper because she made friends easily. Mother took note and benefited all of her life from an ability to make friends.

Getting ready for market twice a week and feeding the strapping young brothers who were working the land was a full-time job. It was, in fact, the only job Mother held until her wedding. "We had loads of stuff for market," she confided to her diary on Tuesday, August 25, 1942: "We had about 50 chickens, 60 dozen ears of corn, 2 bushel beans, 75 pints of [shelled] lima beans, onions, a big dishpan of cooked red beets (it's fun to peel them), sweet potatoes, potatoes, carrots, eggs, honey, noodles etc."[3] The chickens were all freshly butchered. When I look at that list, I have to give Mother credit. She earned the right to expect hard work from her children.

Most vendors in the market were current or former Mennonites and Amish. Their last names—Eby, Herr, Brubaker, Groff, Hess, Houser, Landis, Roth, Hertzler—belonged to old families. Like the Hersheys and Snyders, they had immigrated to America before the Revolutionary War and lived on farms within a twenty-mile radius of the original land purchased by their ancestors.[4] Most of the customers were not Mennonites. They were city dwellers who liked fresh produce at modest prices.

Without the market stand, the Depression would have been much worse for the Hess family. Farm prices for all commodities such as hay, corn, wheat, and tobacco were depressed, as much as 60 percent lower than in the good old days of the Roaring Twenties. Farmers with debt struggled and sometimes lost their farms. Farmers with cash could buy them at low prices. The rich got richer. The poor got poorer.

How did farmers get cash? The best way was to cut out the dreaded "middle man." Sell directly to customers. During the Depression, customers who were willing and able to pay a premium for fresh-picked, -baked, or -cooked farm food became

3. Barbara Ann Hess Diary #1, 1941–43, 30.
4. Joanne Hess Siegrist has identified seventy family names from original Mennonite immigrants. From handout prepared for her heritage classes, 2012.

more rare, but they still existed. Some of them pinched the tomatoes and selected the plumpest hens while wearing fur coats, well-coiffed hair, dark lipstick, and bright red fingernails.

Two days a week the Hess family flung all its energy into the literal marketplace, and one day a week they listened submissively in church to warnings about the world's vanity, especially temptations like the love of money or artificial stimulation or synthetic beauty.

As little Barbara Ann grew older and more able to navigate Lancaster traffic on her own, she was allowed to visit the stores during lulls in action at the market stand. She loved the basement level of Hager's store—the toy department. She would visit the doll section as often as possible to gaze with tender longing upon the object of her affections: a Shirley Temple doll.

Shirley Temple was everywhere in the 1930s. She was to girls what Flash Gordon and later Superman were to boys. The sixteen-inch doll Barbara Ann coveted had rosy cheeks, curly hair, eyes that could blink and wink, a short dancing skirt, and black patent-leather shoes. The only problem was that Shirley Temple was out there in "the world," and Barbara Ann was not.

One day after market, Barbara Ann convinced her mother, Anna Mary, to come with her to see The Doll. While my mother and grandmother were looking over the merchandise, one of Anna Mary's regular customers, Sally, entered the toy aisle and began a conversation.

"Hello, Anna Mary. This is your little girl, isn't it?" asked Sally.

"Hello, Sally. Yes, this is Barbara Ann."

"Are you ready for Christmas?"

"Well, Barbara Ann wants to show me something . . ."

"And what do you want for Christmas, Barbara Ann?"

"A Shirley Temple doll!!!!"

"Do you give your daughter everything she wants, Anna Mary?"

Mother never got the Shirley Temple doll she wanted so badly at age ten. Anna Mary Hess seldom denied her daughter her heart's desire, so it seems strange that she wilted under the gaze of a customer. My guess is that the question "Do you give your daughter everything she wants?" resonated with her fear that she might be spoiling her daughter.

The Shirley Temple dolls made in the 1930s came in sizes from sixteen to twenty-seven inches. They were large enough that my mother, had she owned one, could have pretended to have a sister. If she'd gotten the doll, my mother might have named me Anna Mary or some other good Mennonite name instead of Shirley. Yet, that Sally's one needling question stood in the way of the purchase.

Mother never understood her mother's decision, but she didn't brood over it, either. She found creative ways to convert obstacles into new dreams. Consequently, when I was born, I became both the doll and the sister she never had.

When Mother was in her teens, she kept two diaries of life as she experienced it on the Hess homestead during the war years of 1941–43. She started the first when she was fourteen. The second began two years, eight months, and fourteen days later, on her sixteenth birthday, February 27, 1943. She hid these diaries from her children until we were well into parenthood ourselves. I find them amazing documents; they illustrate how close Mother came to never becoming Mennonite and how different she was from most other girls of her time and place who grew up in Mennonite homes.

The diaries were written without thought of an audience—strictly forbidden by a warning on the cover—but with the need to record dramatic events and sort out jumbled feelings. The glittering world lay all around her. She describes her own good looks often. She knew what she wanted and she knew how to get it. In July 1941, as she anticipated ninth grade, she informed her diary:

> Very, very hot today. Planting flowers this morning. This afternoon did quite a few things, although I did not work very hard. Mother and Aunt Mary went to visit Aunt Ruth to see if they could do anything for her. She was very glad to talk. Tonight

Mother and Aunt Mary went to a sale at the Lancaster Storage. I am very glad when school starts. I have several goals right now. They are:

1. to be popular
2. to be slender
3. to get a speech for the ninth grade promotion
4. to win the American Legion Award next year
5. to be pretty

Such bald ambition in a Mennonite, focused on temporal matters, seems surprising when you discover it in the person who later became your mother and raised you in the church. But she was only writing in her private diary what many girls her age wanted—both then and now. She would not have been encouraged at Landis Valley Mennonite, the church she attended every Sunday, to have such vain desires. They smelled like the dread sin of pride.

The plan to "get a speech" and "win the American Legion Award" shows that Mother cared about excelling in school, and the route she chose involved speaking and writing. She placed them higher on the list than "to be pretty."

Even in her relationships, Mother set goals. On March 6, 1942, she declares, "Rhoda Esbenshade . . . is a very nice girl and I mean to have her for my best friend."[5]

Occasionally dreams, both literal and metaphorical, spill onto the page. One of the strongest ones occurs as Mother welcomed Betty, her brother John Henry's fiancé, into her life:

(June 25, 1941): I have longed and longed for a sister, oh so much, now at last I shall have one. I have four brothers of course and they are very dear to me but they can never be like a sister. I have often pretended I had a sister. She was tender and loving and she and I confided in each other about everything. We would each have a room of our own but if I were lonesome or afraid she would come over in my bed and she and I snuggled

---

5. Barbara Ann Hess Diary #1, 1941–43, 18.

together and fell to sleep in each other's arms. Vice Versa, also. That sister is still alive to me and always shall be, but she is only imagination and Betty is real.[6]

At the age of fifteen, Mother played the role of the Major-General's daughter in *The Pirates of Penzance*. In the diary she lingers long over the description of her dress, her hair, and the attention she received:

[My dress] fell to my ankles and was made of white organdy. It had a low square neck trimmed with lace. I had a satin sash looped around me and tied at the side. I wore my cameo golden necklace and silk stockings and high-heeled brown and white pumps. I had washed my hair and set it. I had the sides and top up and a big pink ribbon on the top. The back was in little ringlets. It was very attractive and looked rather old-fashioned. I was powdered, rouged and my lips and eyebrows were painted. I received a lot of compliments, but the highest one came from Uncle Christ [rhymes with wrist] who told Mother that I looked like a "beautiful innocent doll."[7]

Since this was a wartime diary, I was surprised to discover very little concerning Mennonite teachings about nonresistance to the enemy.[8] Mother laments the war, of course, but not in a theological way. She offers tidbits of war news when they are relevant. She and all the family wanted her brothers to get deferments—not as conscientious objectors but as farmers who were needed to keep the production of food and grain high enough to sustain the domestic population. At school, she sold war bonds. She reports going with her brothers John Henry and Allen to see the movie *Eagle Squadron,* a war propaganda film she enjoyed heartily. "It was excellent!" she reports, adding that it was about "our boys over in England and I'm telling you that movie made you think."[9]

6. Ibid., 5.
7. Ibid., March 30, 1942, 20.
8. See glossary, 255.
9. Barbara Ann Hess Diary #1, 1941–43, 41.

Mother's Manheim Township High School 1945 graduation photo shows why her classmates chose the word *thespian* to describe her. She was very comfortable on the stage.

Occasionally, the young diarist moves into spiritual territory. One of her most rhapsodic passages occurs after walking the trap lines late at night with her younger brother Allen who, like many farm boys during the war, set muskrat traps to eliminate pesky rodents and make a little cash from selling furs. The date of the entry is January 1, 1943, a day she notes that Russia regained Stalingrad and that food rationing would soon begin. She describes the scene:

> I put on a pair of trousers that were Dad's when he was young, a hood on my head, scarf, jacket, raincoat, gloves and galoshes. We had to walk far, cross a creek, walk in mud, and climb over a fence. But, honestly I *liked* that. The wind was eerie and howled as it rushed around the trees, as though driven by some hidden force. The cold, beating rain sent a tingling sensation through me.
> The cold wind and fresh air left my cheeks rosy, glowing red. . . . There was nothing in the traps. But that didn't matter. I shivered as I looked at the dark angry sky sending forth its fury in the stinging rain and moaning wind. My brother noticed it. "What's the matter, Barby, scared?" No, Allen. No—only this sort of makes me feel queer and so small.

"Yeah, it does," he agreed and then looked at me and said, "And it makes you think of God too." I nodded in silent agreement, and hand in hand we walked slowly toward the house.[10]

Carried away by her experience and the joy of finding words for it, Mother confesses next, only to her "dear diary," that she has always had a secret yearning to become a writer "because writing affords an outlet for those deep, emotional turbulent feelings that are somewhere in me."

She concludes that she is waiting for "an indefinable something. . . . Perhaps I shall never find it. If not I shall never write."[11] The "deep, emotional turbulent feelings" my mother felt would resonate inside all her children. In me, they would incubate a yearning that would require me to leave home. Her conclusion that "if not I shall never write" was not an outcome I was prepared to accept for myself.

Mother never seriously considered the usual precursor to a writing life—college. Despite this one and only musing on becoming a writer, Mother had no intention of leaving: "I think farm life is wonderful and would not exchange the freedom, fresh air, good water, trees, fields, meadows for city life no how. I shall always live on a farm. . . ."[12]

Mother's dream of becoming a writer did not disappear, nor did her attraction to the glittery worlds of pretty clothes and acting on stage and being popular. She would eventually follow her longing for God into the church. She would become plain, wearing both a prayer covering and the cape dress, but only as long as the church commanded it. I would inherit Mother's desires and try to ease her pains, even the ones too deep for words.

Her children would become the books my mother never wrote, and I would become the first of these.

---

10. Ibid., 44.
11. Ibid.
12. Ibid., June 16, 1941, 3.

This photo, taken in 1948, only three years after the graduation photo, shows how drastically Mother's look changed after she joined the Mennonite Church, donned plain clothing, married, and became a mother. I am the baby in her arms. On the left: My Aunt Jane and cousin Mary Ann.

Daddy's Dream

A good name is rather to be chosen than great riches.

—Proverbs 22:1

*I*t's hard for me to think about my father, Henry Richard Hershey, without seeing him through my mother's eyes. When she spoke about him to us, it was clear that she adored him. She called him "talldarkandhandsome," as though flirting with the leading man of her life. When I was young, she would sing to him the Rosemary Clooney song "Beautiful, beautiful brown eyes, I'll never love blue eyes again."

In most of the early pictures taken of Daddy, he towers over everyone—his parents, his four sisters, and his little brother.

Daddy told me once that his serious trouble with his own father, Paul, started in puberty when he shot up to six feet tall, too big to punish physically and handsome enough to attract girls. Apparently Grandpa resented height in his son. He himself was about the same height as Grandma, five feet, seven inches, and her Snyder genes were credited with Daddy's height.

I imagine his father called him Henry after Great-Grandpa Henry Huber Hershey, and his mother called him Richard for the pretty sound of the name. Richard was the firstborn of seven children and the ninth generation from his original Hershey ancestor, Bishop Christian Hershey, who immigrated to America in 1717, long before the Revolutionary War.

The name Hershey originated in Switzerland and derives from the German word for deer: *Hirsch*. The last name Hershey may refer to the "hart" of Psalm 42. All the Hersheys in America have

Richard (18); his father, Paul (43); grandfather, Henry (71); brother, Mark (3); ca. 1943.

the same ethnic origin: Swiss roots, a short sojourn in Southern Germany, and immigration to Pennsylvania in 1717. For the first decades of the eighteenth century, most of them lived within the boundaries of Lancaster County, but many later dispersed to all parts of the country.

In America, only one Hershey became a household name: Milton Snavely Hershey (1857–1945), the founder of the Hershey Chocolate Company. Daddy's grandpa, Henry Hershey, was a third cousin to Milton, whose mother was Mennonite. With that connection and a two-dollar bill, I can buy any Hershey bar I want.

The Hersheys were yeoman farmers of the type Thomas Jefferson extolled as the backbone of the country—he who designed his own house built with slave labor and probably never plowed a furrow in his life. To my knowledge, no one in my genealogy owned slaves, but, like all European immigrants, they benefited from the increase in national wealth made possible by slavery—and from the removal of Native Americans from their lands.

The Hershey lineage of my father's family also included a long line of minister-farmers that ended when my great-great-grandfather continued farming without assuming the additional role of minister. Compared to the Hess family, the Hersheys were more serious. They were also more rural. They did not engage the world twice a week at a market stand. They stayed home, labored to pay off the farm, and followed the church's guidelines in matters of dress and comportment. They didn't go to war, movies, or dances, let alone buy war bonds or sit on the school board like Grandpa Hess and Great-Grandfather Herr did. They didn't wear jewelry or makeup— not even in youth, before joining the church. Even as a child I sensed differences between the two families although I could not have explained them.

Daddy's family included an eminent forebear, Benjamin Hershey, who immigrated in 1717 and died July 7, 1789.[13] As a moderator of the Lancaster Mennonite Conference, he worked closely with the Quakers in Philadelphia and steered the church through three schisms. In 1775, he wrote a letter to the Pennsylvania Assembly, the colonial authority for the region, requesting release for Mennonites from military service: "A Short and Sincere Declaration." With humble tone, the petition offered to help all those in need and distress but requested permission not to assist in war efforts: "we find no freedom in giving, or doing, or assisting in anything by which men's lives art destroyed or hurt."[14]

Benjamin Hershey's leadership in helping to create a space for pacifism in the colonies makes him a Mennonite hero today. Founded squarely on the precepts of Jesus, the letter expresses gratitude for the assembly and its power, but reminds those in

---

13. Ira D. Landis, "Hershey, Benjamin (1697–1789)." *Global Anabaptist Mennonite Encyclopedia Online*. 1956. Web. 24 March 2013.
14. Guy F. Hershberger, Ernst Crous, and John R. Burkholder, "Nonresistance." *Global Anabaptist Mennonite Encyclopedia Online*. 1989. Web. 24 March 2013.

authority that they will someday come under the authority of an even greater Just Judge themselves. Hershey was standing squarely in the tradition of the sixteenth-century Anabaptists who called for Christians to take literally the hard demands of Jesus, such as loving the enemy and taking no thought for tomorrow.

I doubt that my father ever heard of this letter, now taught in Mennonite history classes. Nevertheless, he was influenced by his progenitor, at least in one way. The Hershey family piety, the long tradition of ministers in the family line, and the serious devotion to the church still echoed strongly in his generation and continue to this day.

At the time Daddy was born, May 2, 1925, his parents worked for Emma Brubaker Snyder, my grandmother's mother, who was a recent widow. On March 31, 1930, Grandpa Hershey bought the Snyder home place from my great-grandmother Emma. When Daddy was four years old, his mother delivered a second son, named for his father, D. Paul Hershey. Baby Paul lived little more than a year and died December 9, 1930.

None of Daddy's siblings recall hearing Paul's name referred to as they were growing up. They were not even certain about the cause of his death. Was it pneumonia? Diphtheria? This silent way of dealing with death was common, but it must have been traumatic. To lose a child is tragedy. To give up a little boy named for you must have been especially difficult for D. Paul Hershey. He had lost part of his own identity.

I've often wondered if the fact that Grandpa's namesake son died in infancy contributed to the later alienation he experienced from his strapping six-foot son, the one who became my father, and the one who would eventually own his farm.

Young Richard went to the one-room John Beck School and then to local Rothsville High School. The lone report card salvaged from his school days, seventh grade, would not have made his parents proud if they had highly valued academic achievement. He got Bs and Cs for effort, with a few As here and there—mostly in Arithmetic—and frequent citations for whispering too much. His teacher marked "wastes time" six out of the nine school months.

In church, he apparently did better. On Friday, November 6, 1936, Richard "stood for Christ," according to his mother's diary. Richard Danner from Hanover was the evangelist, and his sermon that night was from Genesis 12:1, the call of Abraham. My father told my mother several times in his life how wonderful that night was. I suspect that he wanted her to know he too was capable of feeling movement in his soul, even if it didn't happen as often or profoundly to him as it did to her.

In contrast to Mother, Daddy told very few stories about his childhood. I knew that he had but one toy all his young life—a red truck, possibly a fire truck. I heard that Grandpa Hershey was a hard driver and expected a lot of work from his children. One time, after Richard had made an error in his chores, his father said to him, "Ach, you're not worth the salt in your soup." Daddy never forgot those words, and they poured salt into all the wounds he would feel over the years as conflict with Grandpa mounted.

Since his father paid him very little to work on the farm, Daddy looked for other ways to make money. Like Mother's brothers Allen and Lloyd, Daddy bought metal muskrat traps and set them along the creek during the winter. He would then "walk the trap lines" early in the morning. In 1942–43, his frozen walks yielded twenty-three muskrats, for which he received thirty-five dollars. He carefully recorded every payment.

Daddy had no greater goal, after years of dating and driving eye-catching cars, than to become as successful a farmer as his father had been. There was a little spite, a little competition, and a lot of neediness in his yearning. He also wanted to hold his place in the unbroken Mennonite line of Hersheys who had always served the church.

I am the heir of all these desires.

Dapper Daddy and Plain Mother on their honeymoon in Kansas, 1947.

A Twinkle in Their Eyes

*The greatest force in the life of any child is the
unlived lives of their parents.*

—Carl Jung

He was tall. She was short.

He kept a ledger. She kept a diary.

He loved his two-tone green 1939 Buick 40 Super. She loved compliments and pretty clothes.

He wanted a farm and hoped his father would buy or give him one. She loved the arts, especially music, writing, and acting.

He was dyslexic before that diagnosis existed, and he struggled in school. She loved to read and played first violin in the orchestra and the organ in the parlor.

He focused on the task. She dreamed while she worked.

He leaned on his mother's love, which was a shield against his father's criticism. She grew up in a family of boys, craving a sister.

He arranged numbers in rows, recording income and expenses. She wrote a story at age seventeen that would shape all her children's lives to come.

He joined the church effortlessly at age eleven when God called. She resisted joining the church until a 1945 auto accident brought her to her knees.

He was tone deaf, growling like a wounded tiger when trying to sing the bass line. She had a lovely, clear soprano voice.

He slept in church. She heard God's voice in her ears.

They were my parents, both Mennonite farm kids growing up in Lancaster County, Pennsylvania, following the path laid out for them by their ancestors. They were children of the Depression and a world war. They were virgins only because, as Mother once confided, "I held the line, but it wasn't easy, especially that weekend at the shore."

My father had just turned twenty-two and my mother twenty when they stood in front of the bishop in her living room to exchange their vows.

Marriage was one of the seven ordinances of the Lancaster Conference Mennonite Church.[15] Divorce was nearly nonexistent. Making vows to each other for life was second only to taking vows to God and the church. My parents, although young, knew that they would be together forever until death, and they considered their vows sacred.

Richard Hershey and Barbara Ann Hess at the shore, probably 1946.

---

15. The other six ordinances were baptism, communion, footwashing, the prayer covering (veiling), the holy kiss as a greeting among believers, and anointing with oil for the healing of the sick. *Statement of Christian Doctrine and Rules and Discipline of the Lancaster Conference of the Mennonite Church.* Adopted at a special session at the Mellinger Mennonite Church, July 17, 1968.

As seriously as young people took marriage, weddings often tested the limits, the boundary between church and "the world"— the name for everything that wasn't Mennonite. Engaged couples liked to have fun, and they knew that "in the world" expensive and beautiful wedding veils and long trains and tuxedos made weddings special events. Partly to enforce discipline, bishops rather than ministers presided over the wedding service. One of a bishop's assignments was to keep worldliness from creeping into the church, using any means necessary. One of those means was to preach often on the text "Be not conformed to the world."[16]

Some weddings took place in church and consisted of vows made by the couple on a Sunday morning as just another part of the service. No fancy dress, music, decorations, or confetti. Nothing celebratory. Other weddings took place in homes, where control over permitted finery was a little harder for the bishop to establish and where all attention could be focused on the bride and groom. My mother's mother, Anna Mary Herr Hess, wanted Barbara Ann to have a lovely wedding at home because

Anna Mary Herr, fashion plate, ca. 1916.

16. Romans 12:2. For summaries of some key beliefs and practices, especially nonconformity, see glossary, 255.

she was her only daughter and because Anna Mary herself had enjoyed fashion and abundant hospitality in her youth. She had only adopted the plain dress and simple lifestyle required by the church *after* her marriage. She would have been happier to have her daughter follow her own model of wedding first, plainness later (after joining the church). The fact that most other Lancaster Conference Mennonites were now joining the church in their teen years did not influence Grandma Anna Mary. She liked the older, freer way.

The wedding pictures of both sets of grandparents hang on the walls now in my mother's apartment at Landis Homes, a Mennonite retirement community. Mother has often pointed out to her children her own parents' good looks and quality clothes in their pictures. "That wedding dress was gray silk with hand-sewn beading," she says when she shows me her mother's picture. Now that the two photos hang side by side, the contrast in styles is obvious. My father's parents were products of the first evangelical era, sometimes called the Great Awakening, among Lancaster Conference Mennonites.[17] The picture of my father's parents' wedding (December 25, 1922) illustrates the more conservative pattern. Grandpa Hershey wears the "regulation" plain coat (no lapels) with a small bow tie underneath, showing that he was not totally conservative. My grandmother's long dark hair is pulled back tightly under her large prayer covering, and she wears a dress she probably made herself. She looks much older than her twenty-one years.

My own parents' wedding included a drama that would have a lifelong impact on my mother. Even though Mother had not been plain when she and Daddy started dating, she was a church member by the time they were engaged in 1946. After being struck by a car in 1945, while waiting for a school bus to take her to play practice in her senior year of high school, she had promised God that she would join the church if she lived.

17. For a vivid description of how the change from adult baptism to adulthood baptism came about, read the historical novel *I Hear the Reaper's Song* by Sara Stambaugh (Intercourse, PA: Good Books), 1984.

Two wedding pictures: (left) Anna Mary Herr and John G. Hess, December 10, 1918; (right) David Paul Hershey and Susan Snyder Hershey, December 25, 1922.

A year later, Mother joined East Chestnut Street Mennonite Church because it was not as conservative as her home congregation of Landis Valley. Mother (and Daddy) needed to see the bishop of this church before making plans for their wedding.

They set up a meeting with the bishop one night, the only formal spiritual guidance the young couple had before marriage. It included no sex education, no communication or personality inventories, no assessing the needs of each partner. No, all these things were assumed secondary to commitment. Their promises to one another, along with the strong norms of the community, were expected to take care of any tendency in a marriage to drift. Unhappiness might happen. Divorce would not. So the bishop didn't need to linger on the latter subject as he faced the glowing young couple.

Instead, he laid out the rules for weddings in the home.

The bride could not flaunt a floor-length gown, a worldly train, or a wedding veil (the usual prayer covering was deemed to be enough). She must instead make a "cape" dress that gave her an extra measure of modesty over the bodice. Interestingly, there were no rules dictating the groom's attire. This inequality persisted through the 1960s, creating much covert feminist feeling. There were no restrictions on the material itself for the bride's dress. Shoes were to be black. Flowers were frowned upon.

My mother had a pair of white leather pumps she had worn at her high school graduation before she joined the church. She respectfully asked the bishop if she could wear them at the wedding. He hesitated. He was caught between two Mennonite values: frugality and plainness. It would be less expensive and simpler to wear shoes already in the closet. What to do?

I'm sure the bishop thought he had found the best, most generous solution when he said, "Since you already have white shoes for your wedding, you may wear them. But will you promise never to buy another pair of white shoes?"

Since there seemed no other choice, Mother said yes. She ended up getting another concession, however. She told the bishop there would be flowers at the wedding. He might not have liked it, but he did not object. He had, after all, extracted quite a promise from her.

So the boundaries were set. My creative grandmother and her eager accomplice, my mother, conspired to squeeze every inch of celebration and beauty they could out of the guidelines Barbara Ann and Richard agreed to at the meeting with the bishop.

Lancaster, the closest city, would not be the place to buy material for the dress. The 1947 postwar offerings there were scant. Philadelphia was the place to go if you wanted variety and quality, so off to the Lancaster train station and on to Philadelphia went mother and daughter.

They came back with their arms piled high with material in pastel pink and blue for the bridesmaid's dresses and white for the bride. The fabric was a new promotion—some type of nylon that didn't wrinkle but also didn't breathe. Upon further inspection, the cloth was deemed good for the maids but not good for the bride. So back on the train to Philadelphia went mother and daughter.

Where did my Mennonite grandmother, wearing black

bonnet, cape dress, and dark hose, find the drive, the chutzpah, to go by train to places she had never been before to find dress material she had never seen before? The bishop would have worried that the answer was love of the world. But I think of it as a strong longing for beauty, an ability to manage, and a devotion to her only daughter. Grandma Hess had given up luxury goods for herself for the sake of the church. She was probably also doing a little vicarious living.

When they arrived back in the fabric stores, they were once again awed by the bolts of material in every color and style stacked high to the ceiling. With the help of the Jewish proprietor, they selected his best creamy satin for the slip and first layer of the dress. Then they found a lovely lace material imported from France for the top layer and the cape. Satin-covered buttons completed the ensemble now ready for the dressmaker. Happy and tired, they made their way back home.

When the big day came, May 17, 1947, the house was ready. To prepare for the wedding, my muscular farmer uncles, directed by my grandmother, created a space for the wedding party and set up chairs for the guests. A Wissler's flower truck pulled up in the driveway. The delivery man opened the back door and brought forth a tropical jungle of ferns and flowers to place against the far wall, transforming a farm house into a bridal bower. If it was daring for the women to carry their bouquets, it was even more daring to fill the house with ferns and palms. Grandma Hess made it happen. Mother only remembers, "It was unheard of."

Imagine the surprise of the bishop as he walked through the doorway of my mother's childhood home. The musky smell of roses, gladiolas, and stargazers tickled his nose. Then a lush wall of ferns and flowers sprang in front of him. And then there was the matter of the bride in those white shoes. They didn't even have toes! And that layered dress with French silk lace over satin, that sweetheart neckline. O my!

The adrenalin must have been pumping before he ever greeted a single person. Was he angry, scared, or bewildered by the scene in front of him?

Since guests were arriving, the bishop felt obligated to go through with the ceremony, but he paused a long, long time, or so it seemed to the nervous young bride. For the bishop, however, the annoying thing was that this bride and her mother had broken none of the strictures he had laid out in advance. These innovations might seem harmless enough on their own, but where would it all end? Before you knew it, Mennonite brides would be dancing down the aisle to organ music and smashing wine glasses in the church!

Sixty-four years later, however, Mother has kept her promise not to wear white shoes. Close inspection of her closet might reveal some very light beige shoes though.

Once when visiting Mother as an adult, having heard this story often, I feigned shock when I pointed out that she was wearing white sandals.

"Sandals aren't shoes," she told me with a wink.

The wedding party: (left to right) Christian Hess, Lois Hershey, Ken Noll, Richard Hershey, Barbara Ann Hess Hershey, Evelyn Harnish, Marian Root, John Henry Hess.

Four

A Magical Childhood

Thou hast set my feet in a large room.

—Psalm 31:8

*M*y parents, while still newlyweds, conceived me either on Halloween or All Saints Day 1947. Even they didn't know for sure. How fitting, then, that I should spend my life on the edge between the secular and sacred, between the church and the glittering world.

Like every other baby, I had already overcome enormous odds. My mother had had an early miscarriage. Had she not lost that child, I would not exist. Nature is profligate, spreading seeds everywhere, most of which never find their match to grow and mature. So the fact that any of us exist is a miracle in itself. As the poet John O'Donohue says, "It's strange to be here." Young children carry around that sense of strangeness. Another name for it is *wonder.*

"You knit me together in my mother's womb," writes the psalmist, and that is the feeling I had growing up—that babies in general were a gift from God, and that I was a product of pure desire. My twenty-one-year-old mother and twenty-three-year-old father were young and inexperienced, but they both wanted children. "First comes love. Then comes marriage. Then comes Barbara Ann with a baby carriage." It was the assumed next step.

Memory begins for me at the age of three. Confident, I march down the open wooden staircase in the living room of the

My parents took pictures of each other holding me. Note my father's shadow on the left-hand picture and the very different way each parent holds me. Taken at the Home Place front porch, 1948. We moved to the Spahr farm soon after this picture was taken.

colonial-era farm house our family called the Home Place, wearing a pink dress, feeling the smoothness of the painted baluster in my left hand and gazing down at the landing below where my whole family awaits my entrance. My mother is holding my new baby brother.

"Come meet Henry!" she says.

I have been separated from my parents for several weeks, quarantined with measles and living with my Hershey grandparents on the farm that has been in their family for generations. My mother and father are finally collecting me to return home with them.

My mother's parents, the Hesses, are standing in the living room also. They have bought me a new tricycle. I hug my parents, pat the baby's fuzzy head, and stare at his tiny hand. Then I head to the real treat—the shiny red trike! I have no memory of having been separated from my parents for nearly a month prior to this day. The fact that I remembered no loneliness at almost age three means that my grandparents, all four of them, were totally integrated into my concept of family.

That glittering red trike would carry me all around the driveway, the sidewalk, and even under the "forebay" of the barn. Like other gifts from Grandma Hess, this one came direct from a store. Likely it came from Hager's, the same store where Mother's dream of owning a Shirley Temple doll had been dashed.

Back home with my parents, at the farm we named after its owners, Bertha and Leroy Spahr, I now recall only freedom and joy. Technically, we were sharecroppers, but that mattered not a whit to me. If I close my eyes today, I can still see the Spahr farm—the beautiful decorative grasses, irises, lilacs, lilies of the valley, daffodils, and peonies. I remember space—sky above, fields all around, a huge front yard where we could roll down the hill toward the road.

After my baby brother with the almost white-blond, peach fuzz hair started walking and talking, he and I did almost everything together. We made dandelion chains by hooking the skinny end of the stalk into the fat end. We blew hard on the white wispy seeds, watching them rise, separate, and fall like fireworks. No one cared. No one used pesticides to create the perfect green carpet. A lawn was equal parts grass and weeds. All you had to do was mow it. Dandelions were for color, play, and delicious salad with bacon, hot sweet-sour dressing, and hard-boiled eggs. In the evenings, after the cows were milked and before bedtime, Henry and I begged for our favorite Daddy activities. He tossed us in the air and turned us into wheelbarrows by holding our feet as we walked with our hands. Later, he played board games like Candy Land and Sorry with us. We combed his hair and begged to feel the stubble of his beard graze our faces.

Daddy had unruly dark hair. Every morning he parted his hair carefully on the left side and put oil on it from Gladfelter's Barbershop in East Petersburg (another place where I sometimes tagged along with him). Daddy would close his eyes when I combed his hair. He made me feel as though I had magical powers of relaxation flowing through my fingers, straight through the comb onto his head. I can still smell the aromatic mixture that accumulated in hair washed once a week—traces of tractor oil, fresh hay, the strong scent of cows—along with the faint, lingering scent of Sunday morning's Old Spice . . .

One Sunday afternoon, Daddy got out a kite he had picked up somewhere. He and Mother connected the dazzling new kite and the string, took us to the field next to the house, and worked hard to catch the breeze with it. I remember Daddy turning to offer me the chance to hold the kite string as the pale blue paper fluttered against the bright blue sky. It was so rare to have Daddy's full attention focused on us and on playing during daylight hours. I felt safe and loved, connected at once to the earth we sat on and imaginatively soaring into the vast heavens above. The pleasure of opposite emotions experienced simultaneously pierced me.

To a child on a farm, everything seems useful, perhaps in multiple ways, like George Washington Carver's three hundred uses for the ordinary peanut. After I read that story, I set up my own laboratory and collected kitchen tools and flora and fauna to conduct my own experiments.

Everything seemed to be connected to something bigger. As a free-range girl, I didn't distinguish between play and work for a long time. My brother and I explored the whole farm as though we owned it. Eighty acres was an ocean to us, and we rode waves of adventure together in all four seasons, feeling tiny but also huge. Gazing at a broad horizon, we could easily imagine a God who made the world and yet could reach down and touch us. Our capacity for wonder knew no bounds.

Yet there was sometimes trouble in Eden. All firstborns have the opportunity to be tyrants. They must be taught to be gentle to younger brothers and sisters and to share parental and social attention. Sooner or later, often shockingly, they must give up their heliocentric worldview that they are the sun around which the planets revolve.

Some firstborns have more desire for mastery, and some have less. I had a lot. In one conscious act of cruelty, I took advantage of my superior size to inflict pain. One day, as Henry and I played in the chicken house behind Daddy's workshop next to the milk house, a little demon whispered in my mind to shut the door and then run away before Henry could get out. Since there was no way to open the door from the inside, Henry began to cry.

Did I keep him in there five minutes or fifty? Was I punished? Did I apologize? All I remember is the momentary struggle between the angel and the devil on my shoulders—and that the devil won. And I know that every time I think of the little boy trapped with the chickens, my stomach tightens. It's always been a bit hard to discount Calvinist ideas of innate sinfulness, knowing that I am capable of unprovoked cruelty, without mercy.

The chicken house lock-in, fortunately, was not the way I usually treated my brother. I loved having my own little shadow. Henry and I played together as preschoolers endlessly, roaming the farm on our own. Mother even packed snack lunches for us. The very best season to play in the creek on the Spahr farm was springtime. On the first warm day, we would clamor to walk to the edge of the property, about a quarter of a mile from the house! I remember going barefoot, taking Mason jars in which to capture our tadpoles and snails and guppies. The banks of bluebells along the creek seemed like our own floral shop. We took them back by the bedraggled handful to Mother, who exclaimed over their beauty and our thoughtfulness before she put them in a little green vase with fluted edges.

At night, Mother always read to us. My favorite series was *Bunny Brown and His Sister Sue*. I identified with the boy, Bunny (the oldest), but not with Sister Sue (the follower) in their adventures. Chapters in those books would always have cliffhanger endings, for the author was sure to leave the two siblings hanging there at the end of the chapter, one hand dangling in space and the other attached to the rock. Mother noticed how clever the author was at making us, the listeners, beg, "Just one more chapter, Mother. Please!!!" Of course, when she relented, we begged again, for another cliff would make its appearance, and we would simply have to know whether Bunny and Sue would escape. Mother always assured us they would, as she led us in our prayers before bed.

Mother didn't like the standard children's tuck-in prayer with the terrible image of death: "If I should die before I wake / I pray thee Lord my soul to take." So when she found this one instead, she taught it to us:

> Now I lay me down to sleep
> I pray thee Lord my soul to keep.
> Guide me through the starry night
> And waken me at morning's light.

Mother's theology, as taught from the pulpits of the Mennonite Church in those days, was that children's souls were safe in God's hands until they reached "the age of accountability." If they died before that age, they were taken to heaven to be with Jesus. So the request that God take our souls if we died was superfluous. Better to have God as a guide to the starry universe at night.

Simple prayers were always the best. At mealtimes we had many ways of praying, but this verse was one of Mother's favorites. We liked it because it was short!

> Dear God, we thank you for this food,
> And other blessings, too.
> And as you give, so may we share,
> The good things sent by you.

It's hard to improve on a prayer like that. Sweet and to the point. And when a child witnesses sharing enacted, the concept becomes a reality. In some ways, my Mennonite farm community was teaching me this prayer by example every day.

In the 1950s, a few hobos still traveled the countryside, although most of them had disappeared after the Depression and World War II. I remember Mother making a delectable meal for one man who knocked on our door. She cooked up fried chicken, mashed potatoes, gravy, green beans, bread and butter, and home-canned peaches, along with chocolate cake for dessert. I could tell she was also a little afraid. As she confided afterward, she had heard that sometimes hobos set fire to barns, but she swallowed her fear after looking at the hungry man in front of her. She wanted to make him a meal he would enjoy, one that would stay with him until he met another generous farm wife down the road. The man ate the meal on the porch, sitting on a rocking chair. Henry and I played in the yard, watching him from the corner of our eyes. When he had eaten every morsel, the man returned the plate to Mother and thanked her.

"You're a good cook, Ma'am," he said.

We children were always given change to put in the offering plate during Sunday school, and Daddy would let us place greenbacks in the wooden offering plate when it came down our row during the service. In church, we learned about faraway places with exotic names—like Imokolee, Florida, where missionaries from our own congregation were helping migrant workers, and Addis Ababa, Ethiopia, where they were teaching blind boys how to survive.

Kindness and empathy were other highly valued traits in our family and community. When babies were small, they were major celebrities at church, family reunions, and other social events. Young children were taught to pat the baby and to be gentle. "Ah-ah" was one of the first words most babies spoke as they patted a soft toy or another little body. In church especially, everyone was safe because a child in need was everyone's problem to solve, not only the parents' responsibility. If I encountered any type of difficulty, I could trust anyone in our church to help me. If I saw a "plain person" in a long dress or wearing a bonnet or a "plain suit" on the street, I would never have hesitated to ask for a ride, for information, or even for money. All through my childhood, I was being trained to be that same kind of beacon of kindness for others.

Not all attempts to exemplify kindness worked as planned, however. Once my father was trying to babysit me. Mother was out with some of her friends for the first time in years. All Daddy was supposed to do was play with me, give me a bottle, and put me to bed. Mother came home to find Daddy asleep on the bed and me asleep on the floor beside him. The bottle he was supposed to give me was on the dresser where she left it.

Obviously, I survived, but there were a few other close calls.

The usual childhood diseases, particularly chicken pox, hit me hard. The doctor compared my case to smallpox. I ran a temperature of 104 degrees for two days straight. I remember being too weak to walk. Daddy carried me up the stairs to take a bath, in hopes of bringing down the fever, which it did.

Daddy and me at the Spahr farm.

Fortune granted me the same firstborn position that Daddy held in his family. As I grew older, he seemed to enjoy the fact that I preferred following him around the farm to staying indoors and playing with dolls. In some ways, he treated me like an "honorary boy." He showed me how to turn a blade of grass into a reed instrument by holding it just so between my palms and thumbs. He demonstrated how to aim a ball with my whole arm so that I'd never be accused of throwing "like a girl." And he explained how to catch minnows in the creek, just like he did when he was a boy.

He didn't talk a lot, but he was young and strong and enjoyed showing me his world. I was his tagalong. One of my favorite things to do as a youngster was to hop in the car and go with him to Eby Feed Mill, Leed's Meat Locker, Zartman's Garage, or various farm implement dealers. Often I would get a lollipop from the owner and attention from the workers. Daddy always seemed happy to show me off.

I laugh now, as I look at the photo at left. I am holding a kitty in my right hand just like Daddy held me when I was a baby— proudly, happily, but not cuddly. More like a sack of feed.

As a youngster, I trotted and skipped around the farm, following Daddy on his rounds of the cow stable, milk house, and fields. I also stuck my head into Mother's sphere, the kitchen, especially on rainy days. As I got older, I didn't just observe. I was expected to work, too, at first in the house and later in the barn.

Mother envisioned magic and merriment in work. Daddy saw the goal clearly and looked for the most direct path to achieve it. Mother was the half-time coach giving inspirational speeches in the locker room. She would wash the dishes at the red linoleum-topped kitchen sink and counter. I would dry while we listened to soap operas on the radio, totally absorbed in the dramas of *The Backstage Wife*, *Ma Perkins*, or *Young Doctor Malone*. Our hands would do the chores while our minds and imaginations traveled to New York City or wherever our favorite characters wandered. I was always disappointed when we had to work without the aid of soap operas.

Singing Sunday school and Bible school songs, with a few pop songs from the '40s mixed in, also helped make the time fly: "You Are My Sunshine," "Can She Bake a Cherry Pie?" "Beautiful, Beautiful Brown Eyes," "My Grandfather's Clock," "Climb, Climb Up Sunshine Mountain," "Jesus Loves Me," and "Peace Like a River." When WDAC, a Christian radio station, began broadcasting a dramatic program called *Unshackled*, I loved hearing about worldly people with worldly problems like alcoholism or jail or divorce, especially the climactic moment when they gave up the world to follow Jesus. But after that, I lost interest. I also much preferred the gory, messy Old Testament characters to the more pacific New Testament ones in Sunday school. My kind and graceful teacher, Anna Eby, smiled benignly when I told her my heretical preference.

Another way Mother beguiled us as we worked was to recite poems. She specialized in old-fashioned narrative poetry with regular rhythm and rhyme. Her favorite, which she can still recite to this day, is Mary Dow Brine's poem, "Somebody's Mother," about a boy who takes time to help an old woman cross the street. It ends this way:

> She's somebody's mother, boys, you know,
> For all she's aged and poor and slow,
>
> And I hope some fellow will lend a hand
> To help my mother, you understand,
>
> If ever she's poor and old and gray,
> When her own dear boy is far away.
>
> And "somebody's mother" bowed low her head
> In her home that night, and the prayer she said
>
> Was "God be kind to the noble boy,
> Who is somebody's son, and pride and joy!"

When Mother recited the poem in her thirties, she injected a theatrical tremor into her voice. Poems like these planted in us the desire to be heroic, humble helpers when she or others needed us some day. Mother sang two songs to us that were fun at first but later became a sure ticket to eye-rolling and groaning: "When We All Work Together" (sung when there were chores to do) and "When There's Love at Home" (sung when we were fighting).

Mother would have told stories and sung songs even if we didn't have so much work to do. As a reader, diarist, and aspiring writer in her youth, she poured into all her children the energy she might have spent on a career. She even made us into stars—the main characters in her very favorite story, "The Magic Elevator," one she herself wrote at the age of fifteen. She's kept that handwritten story for almost seventy years. All her children know it by heart, inserting their own names as characters.

Shirley and Henry Hershey, 1953, the first child heroes of "The Magic Elevator." With Daddy and Teddy, our collie, on the front porch of the Spahr house.

When Mother tells the story, all the characters speak in a different voice. Mother reads to her audience, gazing at the upturned faces of the children in front of her, inviting them to experience elation, fear, delight, disappointment, and wonder; her own face both guides and mirrors their reactions.

The Magic Elevator

Shirley and Henry were brother and sister who lived on a lovely farm. One warm, sunny day Shirley had an idea. Henry thought it would be fun, too, and so they asked Mother. Mother's eyes sparkled as she listened to this secret plan: they would pack a picnic and eat it in the woods all by themselves.

"All right," she said, smiling.

Shirley and Henry jumped up and down with joy. Mother packed a lunch for them and helped them cross the road.

"Have fun!" she called as she watched them walk through the meadow down by the creek. "I'll be waiting for you to come home."

Shirley and Henry enjoyed their lunch and had fun splashing in the creek. Then they decided to play hide-and-go-seek. Shirley walked deeper and deeper into the woods, looking for Henry. She hunted and called. Then she stopped.

"Henry," she screamed as loud as she could. "If you don't come, I'll have to go home without you and tell Moth . . ." Before she could finish the sentence, she heard Henry answering her.

"Shirley! I wanna show you something!"

Shirley forgot her anger and ran toward her little brother.

"See!" Henry exclaimed.

Shirley looked puzzled. "It's just a big tree in the woods."

"Yes, but . . . ," said Henry, "around on the other side, it's hollow, and there's something inside the tree. See this door?"

"Yes," said Shirley excitedly. "Look, Henry, here's a little gold key." She grabbed it off a hook in the tree trunk and stuck it inside the keyhole in the door.

Together they opened the lock, pushed the door open, crawled inside, and found themselves in a small room full of mirrors and panels.

"Oh, won't this make a neat playhouse!" said Shirley.

But Henry, who was looking at the row of buttons on the wall, said, "Do you think we would go up to the top of the tree, like an elevator in a store, if we pressed the button?"

Just like that, he pushed the blue button, and immediately they felt themselves moving up—right out of the treetop and into the sky.

"Oh!" said Henry. "Ohhhhhhhhh! I think we're on an elevator, and maybe we're going to the moon."

"I don't want to go to the moon," Shirley cried. "I want to go home to Moth . . ."

Before they could say anything else their speeding room landed.

Once again Shirley opened the door with the key. They both crawled out into a very strange place indeed, with white mountains and valleys that looked like puffy marshmallows. Through the middle of the white mounds was a path.

As they walked along, hand in hand, they saw a tiny little man not much bigger than a large raindrop. He had a smiling face with twinkling eyes, and his clothes were the colors of the rainbow. He sparkled all over like dew drops in the sunshine.

"Shirley and Henry," he said in a tiny, high-pitched voice (and how he knew their names, I'll never know). "You are the first children to discover the magic elevator in the hollow tree on your farm. We have it there for our rain elves to travel back and forth from the earth to the clouds. You are on a cloud, and we have a rain factory here. Come with me, and I will take you through the factory."

"But—but—but, we must hurry," Shirley said. "Mother is waiting for us."

"Okay," the rain elf said, and off they went down some steps into a factory where lots of little rain elves were busily mixing hydrogen and oxygen to make water and funneling it into a huge tank in the bottom of the cloud. The tank contained a huge sprinkling system.

Then the little rain elf turned to the children. "Come," he

said, "it's time for me to go home to my family. I'll take you to the path that will lead you to the magic elevator. When you get to the elevator, use your key to get inside. Henry, be sure to press the green button, and you will soon be at your mother's farm." With that the rain elf disappeared, and the children were all alone.

As they hurried to the elevator, Shirley asked Henry, "Do you have the little gold key?"

Henry looked at Shirley. "No! Don't you?"

"No," said Shirley. "I can't find it. Oh, whatever will we do?"

They both began to cry. "Stop crying, Henry. I'll think of something," Shirley promised, smiling through her tears. "Listen to me. Mother told me that it takes both the sun and rain to make a rainbow, and there's the sun. . . . Henry, you stay here. I'll be right back."

Shirley went running to the rain factory as fast as her legs would take her. Once inside the factory, she pressed the button that regulated the sprinkling system, asking the rain elf on duty to please stop the rain after a little while.

Then she dashed outside, hurrying along the path to Henry. Sure enough, when she got there, a gorgeous rainbow appeared, and the middle of the bow arched right over the cloud where they were standing. Without hesitation, Shirley and Henry jumped on the rainbow.

Angels must have been guarding them, for they had an absolutely fantastic ride, sliding down the rainbow, and when they got to the end of the rainbow, guess where they were?

In Mother's back yard! And there was Mother.

"Oh, my precious children," she cried. "Where were you?"

"Mother!" two voices cried at once. "We had a ride on a magic elevator, and we landed on a cloud, and we saw a rain factory and the little rain elves. Oh, Mother, they were so cute, and we slid down a rainbow because we couldn't find the little gold key.

"Mother, did you know the rainbow ended in our back yard?

"Mother, did you see the beautiful rainbow?

"Mother, did you see us?

"Mother, don't you believe us?"

Mother looked at them. She wanted to believe them. She really did.

"Tomorrow," Henry said, "we'll show you." So the next day Mother went with Henry and Shirley to the woods, but they weren't able to find the big hollow tree. And even if they could have found the tree, they could never have another ride on the magic elevator because, you see . . . the little gold key was lost forever!

Mother always half whispers these ambiguous last lines, her eyes wide open at the end. The listening children's eyes bug out also. They know the story is over, but how should they feel?

I never felt saddened by the loss of the little gold key, probably because Mother seemed to think everything was well. There could be many ways to interpret the loss though. One meaning cautions the listener not to go too far away from home, not to believe everything one sees, and not to expect miracles to happen twice. Another interpretation is that only children can see magic. Adults, no matter how loving and trusting, can't show their powers of imagination. Still another: Magic is real and you should always go when it beckons, but its power is limited. No place can be better than your own backyard, your own meadow. The brief shining moments of our lives can be reclaimed only by the telling of the story itself.

It's no accident that the young writer of the story, who would later become my mother, ventured further into "the world" in her teenage years compared to the other Mennonite girls around her. Acting in plays was her most transgressive behavior, but life itself was a drama to her, and she chose wardrobe, makeup, and attitude for her daily life as well as her brief "career" on the stage.

As a character in her own story, Mother could escape to an imaginary cloud above the farm. And, like the children, she would slide back home.

I must have heard "The Magic Elevator" fifty times: first in my own childhood, next as each grandchild became a featured actor, and then as nine great-grandchildren joined the family. When Mother visited our family in Goshen, Indiana, she told the story to our children's kindergarten classes. When my daughter was driving alone on a long trip, she once called to ask me to tell her the story as a way to build her courage.

As incredible as it seemed, given Mother's plain Mennonite dress when I was a child, I could easily imagine her as a teenage actress on the stage becoming the Major-General's daughter in *Pirates of Penzance*, Judy Abbott in *Daddy Long Legs,* and Miss Phoebe Titus in *A Letter to the General*. When she talked about those days and showed me pictures of herself in plays, I was totally captivated.

Not only did Mother carry her love of reading, writing, drama, and music into her adulthood as a farm wife, but she also implanted ideas in each of us with this one story. She taught us that the world around us is not ordinary. It's charged with the grandeur of God, as poet Gerard Manley Hopkins said. A walk in creation, especially a meadow, can lead to the heavens. A tree is not just a tree. It's a ticket to the world beyond this farm. Like Dorothy in *The Wizard of Oz*, Mother narrated an adventure that started on and returned to a farm. In our eyes, she made the black-and-white world of hum-drum chores spring into Technicolor.

The miracle of existence and the magic of those first six years were not conscious thoughts. They were vivid experiences with deep resonance in the soul, connecting me not only to the meadows and creek of the farm but also to an unusual great chain of being—ten generations of Mennonites in America. But even in the midst of that pastoral existence as a child, I was dreaming, like my parents before me had dreamed. I was waiting for something, maybe for someone, to burst into my life straight out of that glittering world.

Five

Fresh Air

The light of the eyes rejoiceth the heart.

—Proverbs 15:30

The year 1954 yanked me right out of the magic elevator of early childhood, leaving me in free fall, when a girl my age, our Fresh Air girl from a faraway place called New York City, came to live with us for two whole weeks.

Vicky Martinez and her suitcase.

Given the value my parents placed on service to others, she came as part of a program that my parents admired, The Fresh Air Fund, a venerable institution by the 1950s. At the time it began in 1877, the name had a literal meaning as tuberculosis epidemics swept through crowded New York City tenements and the preferred cure was "fresh air." A minister in a rural Pennsylvania parish asked for volunteers to give tenement children summer vacations away from the city. Later, the *New York Tribune* and then the *New York Times* helped sponsor thousands of country holidays. Lancaster County, less than three hours away, became one of the favorite destinations.

Mother and Daddy learned of the program by reading about it in the newspaper, the Lancaster *Intelligencer Journal,* which brought the world to our country mailbox every morning. Unlike other forms of mass media, the daily newspaper was not forbidden by the church. One could read it with discretion and in the privacy and sanctity of one's own home. The leaders of the church recognized that the paper contained information necessary for farmers.

Daddy scoured the farm news. Mother's interests were wider: local news, food, religion, culture. Mother was the one who found the story about the Fresh Air program, asked Daddy's permission, and then signed us up. She told Henry and me that we would have a new playmate fresh from the big city.

I had absolutely no concept of the city. My world was eighty acres of farmland, a church in the small town of Lititz, and occasional trips into Manheim, a town of about the same size. I had the vague concept of a playmate, having played with cousins, neighbors, and my Sunday school classmates. But I had never been to a sleepover nor had I invited anyone to stay over with me. I was excited to see what it would be like to have a playmate all the time. I imagined it would be like playing with Henry, only better.

Our Fresh Air girl was Vicky Martinez. When she arrived from New York City, Mother and Daddy said we would pick her up at the Lancaster train station. She was almost six years old, and, like me, she would be entering first grade in the fall.

The country families coming to pick up their Fresh Air children looked a little uneasy in the cavernous train station. You could tell the "plain" families because the mothers wore white prayer veilings (coverings) on their heads. Already I was trained to look for these mothers because they were like my own. They had familiar, comforting, kind faces. They did not wear makeup or jewelry. Many of their cotton or nylon dresses had been sewn by their own hands from Simplicity or Butterick patterns. Most plain Mennonites, like me, had never ridden on a train. They were not at home in this environment.

Waiting for our Fresh Air child to arrive reminded me of exchanging Christmas presents drawn by lot. If you picked the wrong package, you might get a crocheted hanky while someone next to you would get six kinds of Life Savers displayed under cellophane in their own fancy package. The luckiest kid of all would get a sweet-smelling box of sixty-four perfectly pointed Crayolas nested in descending rows. You picked either a winner or a loser.

My fear that we would get a loser disappeared the minute I saw Vicky. Her big dark eyes and abundant curly hair, her olive skin, and her pretty dress made an immediate positive impression. She was going to be fun! As we left the station, my mind was whirling with plans. We would give Vicky so much good country excitement that she would be filled with fresh air all year long.

As the elder child in our family, I was used to being in charge of things in the play department. Vicky was a few months younger than I was, and a guest, so I expected that she would appreciate my big sisterly guidance. She listened as I gave her a tour of the farm and showed her the room we would share. A curious child, she seemed to be impressed by all the right things: green grass; trees; flower and vegetable gardens; dogs and cats; long, wide fields of alternating green and brown; and especially cows.

We loved watching her eyes get even wider as she got close to a big black-and-white Holstein. Just presenting our everyday life and familiar animals to Vicky made them seem suddenly exotic. She wondered how milk came out of a cow, so my father knelt down, pulled on a teat, and sent a stream of milk that pooled right at Vicky's feet.

"Holy cow!" she exclaimed, much to our delight.

After a few hours of hitting the highlights of country life, we went back to my—now *our*—bedroom. When Vicky opened her suitcase, I smelled something pungent, sweet, and spicy—but not like any of the few spices in our cupboard. Was it garlic, cilantro, some perfume other than Evening in Paris, which my mother wore? Maybe it was all of the above, but my nose did not have many categories of experience for scents. So I just locked the aroma into my brain under the label of *New York City*.

Vicky's shorts and shirts and skirts came in a rainbow of colors. Her mother had very carefully placed enough little folded outfits with clean underwear and socks for each day of her journey to the country. I could tell just by looking at that suitcase that Vicky's mother loved her. Suddenly my own play clothes, a stained blouse over a plaid skirt with no shoes or socks, seemed drab and disheveled. I helped Vicky put her clothes into a drawer I had emptied by dumping the contents into the one below.

Back down in the kitchen, Vicky asked, "Where's your TV?" Mother explained to her that we were Mennonites and our church did not allow television because it was worldly. Mother wore a modest maternity smock, a sign that she was "expecting," as she and her friends always called this mysterious condition. Her hair was pulled back into a severe bun, and she wore a white prayer covering on her head, something a little girl from the Lower East Side surely had never seen before. I could see from Vicky's expression that she was beginning to wonder if *she* had pulled the wrong Christmas present out of the gift exchange. It had never occurred to me that our family might be judged as a set of losers by our own Fresh Air girl. I worried that Vicky might not like us.

That evening Vicky called her sister Annie, who was staying with the Snyders in a ranch house a few miles away. The Snyders were not farmers. They not only had a TV, but they also went to exciting places like Hershey Park, with its wonderful, scary roller coaster and other amusing rides. Vicky, while talking with her sister, made everything she did with us sound like a great adventure, but when she got off the phone, she was very quiet.

Soon, however, she was chattering again. She told us about her parents: her mother, Josephine, who was raising eight children, and her father, Joseph, a cook who worked in a hospital. She told us her full name was Carmen Victoria Martinez—lovely strange sounds that rolled around in the mouth. When I tried repeating them, the accent never seemed to fall on the right syllables. She lived at 178 Avenue D, Apt.11-B, New York, New York. I learned to chant her address, much easier to say than her name, along with her. It was much more fun to say than our own address: Rural Route #1, Manheim, Pennsylvania.

One of the most amazing things about Vicky was her ability to tease my father. I was used to his being quiet and serious. He made a few jokes and showed a playful side with us sometimes, but Vicky could get him to play much more than we could. I loved watching her make him laugh just by rolling her eyes or tossing her curls while, at the same time, I was a bit jealous.

Through Vicky, I began to imagine what it might be like to live in the city. She never talked about murders or muggings, or even sirens or gangs. Instead, she talked about a street full of kids trying to convince the police officer to turn on a fire hydrant— and how much fun it was when he did. She talked about buying Italian ices from a man with a little cart on the street. I couldn't quite understand what ices were. I assumed they were like crushed ice with syrup on it, something I had seen at a farm show once.

Her most lasting contribution to my vocabulary was a form of city pig Latin called "gibberish." The idea was to separate the consonants from the vowels and add some extra syllables starting with "itta" and beginning with the *g* sound. My name, Shirley, for example, became *Shirligirlittigee*. Vicky was *Vitigickittigee*. My brother Henry and I can still use it to talk to each other without anyone else being able to understand us. But we never got to be as proficient as Vicky and her sister, Annie.

Henry and I convinced Vicky to take her shoes off and join us in going barefoot, but only when we ran through the sprinklers in the front yard. The rest of the time she wanted shoes. Her tender feet weren't protected by callouses from stones, dirt, or the roughness of hard surfaces the way ours were. And she preferred to stay close to the house rather than wander into the fields and the creek.

Vicky had a city girl's preference for action, but she was a little afraid of the very thing I loved most about the farm—wide open spaces. For the two weeks she was with us, we went shopping in town more than usual, just so we wouldn't seem so boring in contrast to Annie's family.

Vicky, her sister Alicia (who stayed with my Uncle Levi and Aunt Mildred), and me at the Home Place while it still belonged to Grandma and Grandpa Hershey, probably 1955 or 1956.

Sunday presented a challenge for us, because Vicky was not sure she should go to our church with us, and no one ever considered taking her to the Catholic church just across the street from Lititz Mennonite Church. There was distrust on both sides of the denominational aisle in the 1950s. Catholics, Vicky told us, were forbidden to attend Protestant services. So she devoutly pinned a Kleenex on her head and stuffed her ears with cotton balls. This behavior came as a little shock, but we understood, seeing that we were never encouraged to attend services in any other church, Catholic or Protestant.

Bringing a Catholic to our church caused a little thrill on the women's side of the sex-segregated pews where we sat. Our service always included a time for the children to come forward. One of the adults would tell a story using a large piece of cardboard covered with flannel. Paper characters with pieces of flannel glued to their backs could travel anywhere on such a board.

Henry and me with Vicky at the helm, after a sprinkler "swim" at the Spahr farm.

Whoever invented Velcro must have watched flannel-board stories, because the principle of interlocking ridges was similar but not as effective. Flannel-backed characters from Bible stories could stop at a flannel-backed house, take a drink from a flannel-backed Samaritan, or sit in a flannel-backed tree as Zacchaeus did. Sometimes, however, when the flannel lost its stickiness and Zacchaeus fell out of his tree, we would snicker. Even through her cotton-stuffed ears, Vicky seemed to enjoy the stories. Everyone was especially kind to her, and I imagine there were some silent prayers that the little girl from the city would benefit from hearing about Jesus and then grow up to be saved.

I was less worried about Vicky's salvation than about whether she was going to be moody that day and want to stay in the house with Mother or be lively and want to come outside to play. But I also wanted to be a good friend and a good example, so I tried to go with Vicky's daily whim and not resent the usurpation of my role as leader of the children in our household. Vicky, not I, set the tone.

When it was finally time to take Vicky back to the train station, my mother hugged her and handed her a letter to take home to her own mother, Josephine. We waved goodbye, promising to see each other again next year. As Vicky packed up her little brown suitcase, almost as neatly as her mother had done, I again caught a whiff of the spicy city aroma inside that box.

"Goodigood bydiguy, Vitigickittigee," I said.

"Goodigood bydiguy, Shirligirlittigee," she said twice as fast, flashing me a smile as bright as Lady Liberty's torch.

On a recent Christmas visit to my family in Pennsylvania, I came across a stash of yellowed envelopes in Mother's basement. I noticed a familiar return address on one of them: 178 Avenue D, Apt. 11-B, New York, New York. This must be Josephine Martinez's letter, I thought. I examined the gracious flow of the handwriting. A woman who had carefully pressed fourteen outfits and placed them gently into a suitcase would have just this kind of penmanship, I imagined.

Sniffing the envelope—hoping for a faint hint of that New York City smell of garlic, cilantro, and perfume—I perceived only a whiff of aged paper. Inside were these words:

> We received your wonderful letter, yes so wonderful and special for both of us. We really enjoyed it and cried over it. It arrived a week before Vicky's birthday and her present too, of course. You did not have to send her a gift, that letter and the card you picked for her did it. You should have seen her, she was so proud and so small, too, drinking everything, every word from that very special card. I can never thank you enough for your thoughts for my daughter.

That letter brought Vicky back to me in a rush. I recognized her for what she was—my first window into the great world outside our small self-contained one.

Sixty years have passed since that plucky, lovely little girl entered my life. Without her in my childhood, I could not have known anyone who wasn't European-American. Neither school nor church brought me into contact with people whose skin color or language were different from my own. Vicky, in many ways, seemed more American than I was. I was just learning about how Mennonite life was similar to and different from other ways of being in the world. She helped me see myself from another point of view.[18]

For decades during my busy mothering and professional years, I seldom thought of Vicky. But while living in New York City myself, in 2012, I saw Vicky lurking everywhere like a vivid ghost. Finally, I took the subway to Union Square in lower Manhattan and retraced the steps to Avenue D that I imagined Vicky took in 1954. She had a long walk to the station, and she was carrying a suitcase, so she probably took the bus instead. I walked on for seven long avenues, at least a mile. Block after

---

18. This story has taken a surprising twist since I first published my memories of Vicky. Because the story was published online, Vicky's five surviving siblings have read it. I have been in touch with the youngest, Irma Weaver. She now lives in Lancaster County, the place she too encountered through the Fresh Air program.

block of brown, red, and orange brick apartments surrounded the streets. Much of the cityscape must have changed, but there was one place I had to see. I walked past a Catholic church, St. Emeric's, on 13th Street, between Avenues D and C, on my way to my destination. I could see Vicky in a white confirmation dress like the picture she sent us in 1960. Was this her church?

I kept walking. Finally, at the end of the street, there it was, 178 Avenue D. The public housing unit carries the name of Jacob Riis, a pioneering photographer I had studied in graduate school. No children were playing on the concrete jungle gym. I stood at the corner and looked up at apartment 11-B and remembered the phone call I got from my mother in 1985. "Vicky died," said Mother in a tender voice. "Multiple sclerosis."

There, on the street, twenty-seven years after the phone call, I grieved again for Vicky. I remembered the two of us as five-year-olds, together opening up for each other larger worlds inside small ones.

Those little-girl spirits, passionate and liberating, blew through me like a saving breath of fresh air.

Vicky was selected as the poster child for the Multiple Sclerosis Society and got to meet Mickey Mantle in 1970.

Six

From Magic to Mystery: Entering School

He that increaseth knowledge increaseth sorrow.

—Ecclesiastes 1:18

*I*t's late August and it's hot. I'm sitting in Joan Weidman's kitchen. There's no air conditioning, of course. Joan has washed my hair in the sink and put a towel around my shoulders. She parts my hair, placing only a few strands at a time into tiny curlers the color of Pepto-Bismol and Bazooka Bubble Gum. As she works, Joan talks with my mother. Stacks of neatly folded laundry Joan does for her family and a few customers (including my widower Grandpa Hess) are tucked neatly into baskets in the corner.

Joan warns me about what's in her bottle on the table, but the noxious fumes from the toner curl the hairs inside my nose before they curl anything else. Any time I've caught a whiff of that particular odor as an adult, my memory goes straight back to Joan's kitchen.

Why was I undergoing this torture? Because I was going to first grade! I was probably the only little Mennonite girl near Manheim getting a perm instead of wearing braids or a long ponytail down the back. I was getting a perm for the same reason that I was named Shirley, that Mother and I listened to soap operas on the radio, and that we subscribed to *McCall's* magazine. Mother had changed her own dress on the outside when she became plain, but on the inside she still had a touch of Shirley Temple doll syndrome, enough for both of us. Rosy cheeks, curly hair, and a stage all went together.

Her little girl was too young to be plain, and it was fun to dress her up for her first venture into the glittering world of public school. Young children were almost never censored by bishops. That would be interference in the sacred role of parents to "train up a child in the way he should go," a much quoted proverb. Perhaps Mother was willing to risk going to the Mennonite edge, as she had on her wedding day, to prepare me for my new role as a schoolgirl. I would have curls and new clothes.

Afterward, everyone seemed pleased and amazed by the miracle of curls all over my head. My first-day-of-school photo shows my beaming face above a sea of plaid—dress, book bag, and lunch box. If school was a stage, then I was ready with my costume, looking for all the world like little Shirley Temple on her way to see the Good Ship Lollipop.

My first day of school, 1954, school bell around my neck. Taken at the Spahr farm next to the picket fence.

I was so excited about starting school that on the first day I woke up at four o'clock in the morning, beginning a pattern I would follow for the rest of my life: waking up early to go where I had never gone before. Thrilled and terrified.

I got on the bus with our neighbor, Shirley Clark, a sixth grader and a foot taller than I, a giant in my eyes. But when I got to Fairland Elementary School, I was on my own, inside the first grade class along with about twenty other students.

We first graders all wore paper school bells bearing our names around our necks. At the front of the room was a bank of blackboards with alphabet cards: Aa, Bb, Cc. In the back was a long bulletin board featuring our new best friends: Dick and Jane; their dog, Spot; cat, Puff; and baby sister, Sally.

Soon it was apparent that a group of classmates, who lived in the town of Manheim, had already been going to school for a year. In kindergarten, they had learned things I didn't know, like how to write the letters of the alphabet. They were now the ones on stage, while I was in the seats watching them with awe.

Our teacher, Mrs. Gibble, was soon nicknamed "Gobble" behind her back. A short, spry, and nervous woman, she had guided many young charges from the darkness of illiteracy into the light of letters. She seemed old, but maybe that was because my own mother, my original teacher, was only twenty-seven years old when I entered first grade.

Mrs. Gibble seemed nervous about having all of us depending on her as our gateway to learning. Once she locked her keys in the closet and burst into tears. And once, under the pressure of those first days, one of the other Mennonite girls, whose hair clung to her head in tight plaits, was unable to contain her bowels. Mrs. Gibble sniffed the air and looked straight at the quaking girl, who was so uncertain of what to do that she moved to the next little chair in the circle. Before long, three or four chairs had been fouled, and Mrs. Gibble was in a dither. The poor girl survived, and the rattled teacher finally got things cleaned up, but in the meantime, all of us were suppressing all our own urges, including the desire to laugh.

After the final bell had rung that day, I stepped into the big yellow school bus with a lot of questions on my mind.

What if tomorrow I were the girl who didn't make it to the bathroom on time?

How would I be seen and heard among so many other students?

Could I sit still in a desk all day long when it was so nice outside?

And could I keep doing this for twelve more years?

Then the bus rounded the corner from Fruitville Pike, and I saw the familiar yellow house and barn of the Spahr farm begin to rise up out of the fields. The buzz in my head started to subside and so did the funny feeling in my stomach. I knew Mother would be in the kitchen with a snack. Would it be sugar cookies, a sweet bologna sandwich, or apple and pretzels?

The brakes screeched and Shirley Clark and I descended from the bus. She smiled at me and told me I looked very grown up with my plaid lunch box and book bag. Then she turned down her lane. I waved goodbye, turned, and started running.

Our dog, Teddy, ran to greet me, and beside him sprinted Henry. His teddy bear haircut caught the September sun and made him look like a little cherub. Peace settled into my heart. Mother emerged from the kitchen, wiping her hands on her apron, smiling.

Then I knew why Mother told us that magic elevator story so often. No matter where I went or how confusing that new place would be, I could remember that the rainbow's destination was home, Mother would always be there to greet me, and no matter what happened, we would make a story out of it.

Shirley Clark, sixth grader and safety patrol, and Shirley Hershey, first grader, at the bus stop in front of the Spahr farm, 1954.

Seven

A Scream in the Night

The heart of the wise is in the house of mourning.

—Ecclesiastes 7:4

*M*y mother is in the hospital, and I have a new baby sister!"
It was show-and-tell time in Mrs. Gibble's first grade
classroom. I was still new to school, but after three months, I had
selected show-and-tell as my opportunity to be seen and heard.
Show-and-tell transformed the classroom into a stage. Standing
there, each child in the first grade could become as big as the
story they had to tell. I was bursting with real news: I was the
first in our class to announce a new baby had been born in our
family.

"Do you think your mother could bring the baby to school so
we all can see her?" asked Mrs. Gibble.

"Oh, I'm sure she will," I replied. My teacher and classmates
clapped with glee.

Mary Louise Hershey was born on Armistice Day, November
11, 1954. Mother said the baby's round face and eyes reminded
her of me. Now we had the perfect 1950s family: Mother, Daddy,
me, Henry, and Mary Louise. Just like in our schoolbooks:
Mother, Father, Dick, Jane, and Sally. Mother said she would
bring Mary Louise to school after Christmas vacation when the
baby would be a little bigger. I couldn't wait to show off Mary
Louise to my classmates.

At home, Henry and I continued our own play together, but
we often checked in with Mother while she was breastfeeding
or standing watch over Mary Louise in her bassinet. At age six,

I was ready to understand the role of "big sister" now that I had had three years of experience guiding my brother into and out of adventures. We noticed that our sister sometimes had bluish fingernails and lips, but Mother said that Dr. Hess said babies usually grew out of this symptom.

Just before Christmas, after sundown on December 20, Henry and I were playing in the little stack of hay next to the cow stable, pulling kitties out of the feed storage bins, making tunnels out of bales, and talking about what we hoped for in our stockings. Down the row, cows chewed contentedly. The DeLaval milkers sounded almost like heartbeats—lub-dub, lub-dub, lub-dub—as they extracted warm milk from each udder.

And then we heard it: a horrible, penetrating, animal-like scream, piercing that night and my life to this day. Until Mary Louise died after only thirty-nine days on this earth, I didn't know one mother's voice could hold the sounds of all the weeping women of the world. The terrible sound grew louder as Mother came toward the barn. She ran to Daddy and, still screaming, started pounding him on his chest.

"My baby is dead. Our baby is dead. My baby is dead." That was all she could say, over and over again. Then she would throw back her head and wail like a wolf.

When a tiny white casket was wheeled into our living room, I touched the baby's cold skin and noticed that when I pressed, it didn't move. I marveled at the creamy tufted velvet lining all around the body. I looked once more at the face inside the white box. Then I said goodbye forever to my sister, Mary Louise.

The viewing was held in our home. The ferns and flowers behind the casket looked eerily similar to the bridal bower at Mother and Daddy's wedding. The two little children kneeling together in front of the casket stared death straight in the face at a very early age.

One whole page of the childhood scrapbook Mother made for me was a shrine to Mary Louise. Mother never attempted

Mary Louise, Henry, and me after the viewing held in the Spahr farm living room, December 23, 1954.

to hide her grief. Losing Mary Louise tore her scarred heart in two—again. She had lost two grandmothers when she was a teenager. Her first pregnancy ended in miscarriage. Her mother died suddenly just three years earlier when Henry was a baby and Mother was twenty-four. After that last traumatic loss, the abundant milk in Mother's breasts had dwindled to nothing, and Henry had to be weaned.

My mother already knew grief like a river. But this one threatened to engulf her and, with her, all of us. No other loss sears the soul like the loss of one's own child. I would not fully understand my mother's courage until I became a mother myself. But what I did understand was that my magical childhood had changed.

During the years that followed, our brief memories of Mary

Louise floated over my family like a letter that never made it to the mailbox, an empty canvas, a field of blossoms waiting to burst into bloom. My mother's grief magnified when she saw other mothers and their healthy, happy babies. She herself would have other babies, but none of them replaced Mary Louise. On every Armistice Day, November 11, we have remembered her. Only one picture remains of the tiny face that looked like mine.

Mother coped with this death by going back to her first dream of becoming a writer. With other Mennonite women, she started

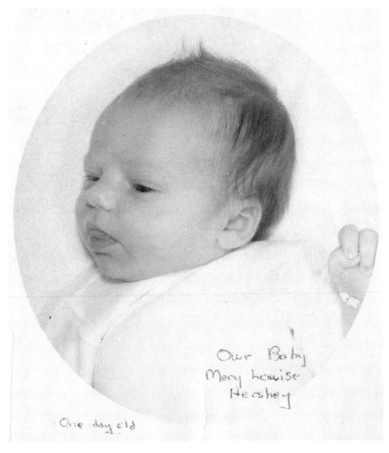

Mary Louise Hershey, soon after birth in the Lancaster General Hospital. All other pictures of her were taken later of her body in the little casket.

an organization called The Homebuilders. She and others sent packets of solace, letters of condolence, and poems to other grieving mothers when she found their names in the newspaper along with the notice that a young child had died. I didn't understand then how much work she was doing to transform trauma into growth. But that effort would teach me more than any words she could have spoken. For the next decade, Mother would help to lead the organization of other mothers by speaking, writing, and even acting in a play or two as a way to use her gifts for the church. Her healing happened best when she fulfilled her dream of expressing her deepest feelings in writing, the desire she confessed to her diary at the age of fourteen.[19]

The cause of Mary Louise's death was never very clear. Dr. Hess (not closely related to our Hess family, but a friend) said that he could find only two paragraphs on this condition in the medical books he consulted. There was no known cure.

If I ever want to know the limitation of words, all I have to do is hold the bronze-colored book provided by the funeral home for Mary Louise's viewing. Next to the guest register is a little sketch of a heart, drawn by Dr. Hess himself, and the words that took Mary Louise away from us: "subendocardial fibroelastosis."

One of the large bouquets of flowers delivered to our house in those sad and somber December days right before Christmas came from all the teachers and students at Fairland Elementary School. My parents read the card and wept again.

It would be a long time before I would stand up to make any new show-and-tell announcements in school. When I did, the words came from a new place in my heart, a place that had visited death.

---

19. Records of meetings of the Homebuilders 1955–70 and samples of the packets sent to grieving families have been given to the Lancaster Mennonite Historical Society.

Eight

Seven Sweets and Seven Sours

Like a doctor, I learned to create
from another's suffering my own usefulness, and once
you know how to do this, you can never refuse.
To every house you enter, you must offer
healing: a chocolate cake you baked yourself,
the blessing of your voice, your chaste touch.

—Julia Kasdorf, "What I Learned from My Mother"

*M*y sister Mary Louise's death brought the evanescent sweetness of life into my awareness. And so did the neighbors, the church, and the school in a most literal way. Everyone reached out to our family. The four of us—Daddy, Mother, Henry, and I—were alive, and we held each other up, sharing our grief. With wide open eyes and ears, Henry and I took in the memorial service held in our living room, growing up faster than anyone wanted us to. After the guests had left, we converged on the kitchen. Before us was a mountain of home-made food.

When someone dies in a Mennonite family, consolation will be carried to the mourners in baskets and Tupperware containers from all corners of the community. The bread will arrive still warm from the oven, and flowers or greens from gardens will appear on the table. Such tangible response to intangible suffering solidified grief and helped bring the mourners back into this world. This response is not unique to Mennonites, of course, but since Mennonites favored the Beatitudes, which link blessing for those who mourn with blessing for peacemakers, it's not too surprising that poet Julia Kasdorf, who grew up Mennonite, linked blessing and food together in her most famous poem.

Almost every culture and religion uses food to support its most cherished values. If it's true that we are what we eat, then I am a sweet-sour person. Like most people, I love the food of my childhood; it is my "comfort food" even after enjoying many other cuisines.

Pennsylvania Dutch[20] food, my childhood's staff of life, is famous for its "seven sweets and seven sours," a cuisine both bland and pungent. Above all, this style of cooking focuses on abundance (it got its name because all fourteen of these flavors were supposedly included in one true Pennsylvania Dutch meal). Without seven desserts or sweet condiments and seven vinegar-laden side dishes, you didn't have a feast. The label "seven sweets and seven sours" might well have been concocted by the tourist-restaurant industry, but it has stuck.

Lining the Lincoln Highway between Lancaster and Philadelphia are a host of places that compete to offer tourists the "real" Pennsylvania Dutch dining experience. No one seems to know why the number seven and why sweets and sours are singled out to the exclusion of the other taste buds found on the human tongue.[21] But my grandmother's spiral-bound cooking notebook and the *Mennonite Community Cookbook*, which was gleaned from many such notebooks, offer a clue. The "seven sweets and seven sours" are light on vegetables (no need for recipes for these) and heavy on desserts and pickles.

"Seven sweets and seven sours" also seems a perfect metaphor for my complex relationship with the Mennonite Church.

Any cultural group that carries on a tradition separate from the world, yet borrows selectively from other groups and traditions, will create a unique "taste culture." In the case of the Pennsylvania

---

20. This term, a misnomer, comes from the dialect word for German, *Deitsch*. See glossary, 255.
21. The best food historian of this ethnic cuisine is William Woys Weaver. His book *Sauerkraut Yankee: Pennsylvania Foods and Foodways* (Philadelphia: University of Pennsylvania Press, 1983) contains many fascinating facts and recipes from the nineteenth century.

Dutch, who had an abundance of pork and flour from the colonial era onward and who performed taxing physical labor all their lives, the emphasis was on dough, noodles, and dumplings as accompaniments to fatty meat. Since there was so much fat to absorb, vinegar and/or fruit juices became a way to "cut" the fat.

The love of food, prepared well in large quantities, was so great among my kin that we risked one of the classic deadly sins: gluttony. I heard a lot about sin as I was growing up. The seven classic or "deadly" ones included pride, envy, gluttony, lust, anger, greed, and sloth. The only one I never heard preached about was gluttony. If Mennonites needed a sinful outlet, a transgression they could overlook, perhaps gluttony was their safety valve. They could make up for the tolerance of one vice by denouncing the others more vigorously.

Seven Deadly Sins. Seven Sweets. Seven Sours. They all include the "perfect" number seven contained in biblical bookends: the seven days of creation in Genesis and the seven seals of Revelation. The Hebrew word for seven, *sheba*, is closely connected to *saba*, meaning fullness or plenty, so perhaps seven sweets and seven sours carries sacred meaning we didn't recognize. The feeling of physical, social, and spiritual well-being of eating a meal overflowing with every kind of food and extended family and friendship did, at least sometimes, seem holy.

Theological background aside, what would a seven sweets and seven sours menu actually look like? The seven sours are largely side dishes: pepper cabbage, pickled beets, red beet eggs, and chow chow (a beautiful combination of pickled corn, lima beans, green beans, cucumbers, green pepper, red pepper, and onions). The seven sweets tradition includes up to twenty kinds of pies. Most are fruit or custard, but the king of all pies is shoofly. Shoofly is simple and inexpensive to make from molasses, flour, brown sugar, eggs, butter, and water. It tastes best when served warm, with hand-whipped cream on top. What pecan pie is to the South, shoofly is to the Pennsylvania Dutch.[22]

---

22. Readers will find recipes of my favorite sweets and sours in the appendix, 261.

As in most cuisines, the traditions for banquets of plenty, such as the seven sweets and seven sours, differed greatly from "our daily bread." Summer meals are what I remember most about the food in our home. First, there were giant red beefsteak tomatoes. These dense crimson beauties weighed up to one pound each. They were so juicy that you could not eat a tomato-slab sandwich without red juice squirting everywhere. One of our favorite summer suppers was a plate of sliced tomatoes, a loaf of Roman Meal bread, and a platter of steaming Silver Queen sweet corn ears. After our prayer, we passed the two main dishes and added a few condiments—butter and salt to the corn and mayonnaise or vinegar and sugar to the tomatoes. The corn was so fresh that the slightest contact with a tooth would puncture the kernel, sending a stream of sweet hot liquid into the mouth.

Some Pennsylvania Dutch chewed "roastin' ears," our name for corn, by the row while others encircled the cob, which eventually emerged as a round rod from underneath the kernels. The first corn of the season was especially conducive to ecstasy. We seldom talked when we ate it. Instead, we listened to the sounds of satisfaction all around us, a veritable symphony of jaws, teeth, and mouth all moving in a kind of rhythm. The littlest children needed help, so Mother would take a sharp knife and slice off the kernels. Then, moving against the grain, she pressed the knife all the way down the shaft of the cob, leaving a little pool of sweet corn milk at the bottom of the plate. When we cleaned the table after a meal featuring corn, my mother would sometimes be amazed to find six large, cleanly denuded cobs on my plate.

My birthday is July 30, the very peak of Lancaster County garden season. The special meal I asked for every year came right off our land: a side dish of coleslaw (sour and crunchy, not creamy!) made with a new cabbage and accompanied by the entrée—a mélange of green beans cooked with huge chunks of ham and new potatoes in one large pot, or, to use Mother's word, kettle. I delighted in the way the crunchy, sour coleslaw contrasted with the salty ham, plump potatoes, and soft green beans soaked in the smoky ham juices. By the time I got to the freshly baked sour cherry pie and ice cream, I was sated but still eager for one more set of sweet-sour explosions in my mouth.

As a college student, I laughed when I read the scene in Henry Fielding's *Tom Jones,* in which food becomes seduction. I recognized that country living had prepared me for other kinds of pleasures. Later, when I read that food and sex are physically linked in the brain's limbic system, which controls emotional activity generally,[23] I smiled to think of how carnal knowledge grew right out of the earth onto our plates. One of my favorite wedding gifts was a handpainted pie plate in the manner of Pennsylvania Dutch *fraktur,*[24] full of bright primary colors, birds, and flowers. Punning on the name of my husband, Stuart, known to some of his friends as "Stu," and making up his own language, one of my professors had written *Guut Frau Guut Schtew* in beautiful calligraphy in the middle of the plate: "Good Wife, Good Stew." Passion flows where the channels are open, and for this farmer's daughter, the earliest and most open channels were the eyes, ears, nose, mouth, and throat.

Perhaps the test of any important cultural value is that it can be equally sacred and sensual. If so, food wins. It not only feeds the body, directly and simply, from the fruits of the earth, but it also feeds the soul the complex fruits of wisdom and holiness.

The notion of sweet and sour was so deeply engrained in my childhood that I can easily organize many of my life's memories in the same manner.

The sweet memory of my favorite sugar cookie, an old recipe passed down from three generations of mothers, was often combined with entrepreneurial stories and dreams. For my mother, the art of baking had been learned not only as a form of domestic skill and hospitality, but it also had a business history. Sugar cakes, hundreds of them spread out over every available flat surface and then bagged up one dozen at a time and sold at market, had helped to power the Hess family through the Depression years.

---

23. http://www.sirc.org/publik/food_and_eating_8.html.
24. See glossary, 255.

The dream of having our own "stand" was something our family talked about repeatedly over the years. Henry and I even tried it once. Mother, of course, directed the scene, and our little sister, Susie, born a year after Mary Louise's death, sat in her booster seat in the middle of all the activity, beaming.

We lived too far from Lancaster to set up a stand in the "real" market, but we could choose an alternative—a roadside stand. Our rural road had one location advantage: it was close to Roots Sale, a huge farmers' market. We referred to this market simply as "Roots" (rhymes with Toots). Operating only on Tuesdays from dawn to dusk, Roots brought vendors, farmers, and buyers together, transforming our little country road into a thoroughfare. People were going to buy farm produce at Roots, so why not buy from us and beat the crowds? We hoped they would think that way.

Sue, Henry, and me, about 1957, on a Tuesday at the Spahr farm. Fledgling entrepreneurs, joyous broadcasters.

Mother set us up with eggs and fresh sugar cakes. Henry and I could hardly contain our excitement. We yelled at every car. Some of them stopped and bought from us. Our neighbor, Mr. Clark, once drove by slowly. We jumped and shouted. He rolled down his window, a twinkle in his eye, and said, "Speak up. I can't hear you."

I loved selling things. If we had had our own stand in the Central Market the way Grandma and Grandpa Hess had, I might have become a Lancaster County entrepreneur instead of a college professor. It does not surprise me that both of my adult children are entrepreneurs.

Every summer, when we weren't yelling at cars, we made sweet meadow tea. We picked spearmint tea leaves growing wild by the creek in the meadow, washed them, poured boiling water over them, and then let the mixture steep. We added one cup of sugar per gallon before allowing the mixture to cool. Then we pulled all the metal ice cube trays out of the freezer, taking care not to touch the frozen handle while our fingers were wet. Sometimes we added lemonade concentrate to enhance the taste and fill up the container, eventually pouring some into a glass pitcher. On a really hot day, we could press our cheeks against the glass, letting the condensation on the outside cool us.

If the men were working in the fields, we took most of the cold tea in a "kettle" about the size of a stockpot, added a ladle, and placed the large covered container inside our red Radio Flyer wagon. One or two of us children would take off toward the end of the field where Daddy and his hired help would be baling hay, cutting tobacco, or harvesting corn or wheat. I loved watching their eyes light up and their hats come off, revealing their farmers' tans—red and grimy faces crowned by a white forehead where the hat had been. Although we took paper cups with us, sharing cups was common. No one was too concerned about germs in those days. The first gulps were slurped in thirsty desperation. The men reminded me of the cows at the creek after a hot day. And sometimes Mother tucked cookies into the wagon to go along with the tea. I noticed how pleasant it was to be a water carrier in a parched land. It was a role I would search for unconsciously from then on.

Sours never rated a course of their own the way sweets did. They were there to add balance and texture, primarily to the meats. Ham was salty and needed mounds of mashed potatoes to absorb the salt and some kind of pickle to complement both. Sausage and pork were fatty and somewhat bland, but became very lively in the mouth when cooked with sauerkraut.

Lively taste often came from some pretty pale food, so color in the form of sour side dishes served to balance the main course visually. Any vegetable can be pickled, with beets being a particularly vivid favorite. But watermelon rind can also be pickled, as well as lima beans, corn, green beans, and crabapples. Of all the places on the farm to look for color in any season, the arch cellar was the best, because that's where we stored our canned items, many of them pickled, all of them colorful. When sent to retrieve a jar of pickled beets or bright green sweet pickles, I willingly obeyed. A sandwich or meat dish without a pickle was like a horse without a carriage.

Everyone's childhood is some mixture of sweet and sour. My Mennonite childhood was sweetest when surrounded by family, including the forty families in our church who called me by name and knew where I lived, what grade I was in, and what part I sang when we opened the hymnals together. A phrase from a new hymn describes this kind of community perfectly: "We are each other's bread and wine."[25] It was easy to imagine Jesus eating with his disciples when we sat down to a meal. We knew that our job would be to care for the people cast out by the rest of society, the strangers, the way Jesus did.

It took years for me to notice some of the sour among the sweetness of our church. Now I see the irony that Mennonites thought it necessary, in order to follow Jesus as perfectly as possible, to exclude those who dressed or talked "loud," divorced, drank, or danced—unless they repented. If they were ever in a

---

25. "What Is This Place?" *Hymnal: A Worship Book* (Scottdale, PA: Herald Press, 1992), 1.

disaster, we could come to their aid, but if they wanted to join our church, they would have to adopt "plain" dress and a modest lifestyle, following the ordinances in the *Statement of Christian Doctrine and Rules and Discipline of the Lancaster Conference of the Mennonite Church*. After baptism, women would have to grow their hair long and put it under a covering and give up all vices except gluttony before we would let them in. I discovered along the way that most groups had some kind of sourness hidden in them. I began to see that identity formation always includes an "us" and a "them." It's easy to see all sweetness in "us" and all sour in "them."

Though my branch of the Mennonite Church has relaxed the rules requiring church members to be "plain," I admire many conservative Mennonites who continue to maintain boundaries between the plain church and the glittering world. We still get together for family reunions and in service activities like Mennonite Disaster Service and Relief Sales. What brings us together best? Food!

It may seem natural to prefer the taste of sweet over the taste of sour. Most people do. Yet I think I have learned more from the sour experiences in my life, my family, and my church than I have from the sweet. Whenever something or someone has died, whenever there has been anger or injustice, some new nourishment of body and spirit has appeared. The physical energy that food supplies has provided the basic metaphor of transformation. After lament, we the survivors can always agree on one thing: "Let's eat!"

Vinegar, the taste Jesus was given on the cross, does not satisfy on its own. All those sour dishes I grew up with included sugar. So not only do the sours balance the sweets in the cuisine, they also *contain* sweet within themselves. The purpose of sour is to point the way, to find the protest point, to reveal what needs attention. As I grew up, I would discover many such places, not only in my palate but also in my path.

Nine

Mennonite Cooking in the Betty Crocker Era

Then I commended mirth, because a man hath no better thing
under the sun, that to eat, and to drink, and to be merry.

—Ecclesiastes 8:15

y sister Sue's birth in 1955 restored joy to our family after a year of mourning Mary Louise's death. I was seven years old and excited and relieved to have a healthy new baby sister. She was so hardy and eager to arrive, in fact, that she was born in the car on the way to the hospital.

But about a year later, Mother experienced another loss. She had a miscarriage rather late in her pregnancy. Miscarriages, like pregnancy itself, weren't explained in great detail to children. After news of Mother's convalescence was carried by telephone to all the women of her Sunday school class, women swooped into our house, carrying buckets and mops, entering with an air of almost military precision. Their eyes were kind, their laps were warm, but their hands never stopped searching for work to be done. They had learned from their mothers how to express love by keeping busy, and they itched to perform a service.

They tackled every room, high and low. I could tell they disapproved of the cobwebs and disorderly closets they found at our house. I heard one whisper to another as they moved the refrigerator, "This place isn't very *redd up*.[26] I don't believe Barbara Ann ever cleaned under here." My ears burned as I listened,

---

26. A Pennsylvania Dutch expression meaning to clean up or put away.

unnoticed, in the next room. I heard not just the words themselves but also the superior tone. I wanted to tell the woman to
go back to her own house and clean under her own refrigerator.

In the not-so-subtle competition for Best Homemaker in
which women of the 1950s engaged, my mother never measured
up in the clean-and-organized house department. Mother's
good friend, Vera, called her to chat early Monday mornings,
usually announcing with satisfaction that her wash hung on the
line. Mother never could match her. Vera's reddish hair, pulled
back tightly from her face, still contained curly wisps. Like her
unruly curls, Vera was suited by nature to billow rather than lie
down. She followed the weekly schedule of other farm wives:
wringer washer laundering and hanging of clothes on Monday
(something to be dreaded in winter since we did this task in
the unheated "back kitchen"), ironing on Tuesday, followed by
cleaning and cooking and preserving and sewing the rest of the
days—but less on Sunday, of course. Mother admired Vera's
industry, but she couldn't win in her game.

Other women cleaned and sewed far more than my mother
did. She never developed a passion for either task. Instead, she
used the time other women spent on those activities for reading and writing. I shared her preference for artistic and spiritual
activities over domestic chores. We both loved the story of Mary
and Martha, because Jesus tells Martha that Mary has chosen
the good part, to sit at his feet, over the kind of kitchen work
Martha wanted her to do. Who's going to argue with Jesus? The
1950s were Martha's decade in America, but women like Mother
were sowing seeds of what would become Mary's platform in
later generations.

There was at least one domestic area, however, where Mother
excelled. In the baking department, Mother was a regular Betty
Crocker. Like other homemakers of the 1950s, Mother loved the
image of Betty, the modest woman (the earliest versions almost
looked like a Mennonite!) in the red dress used by General Mills
to sell products such as Bisquick and cake mixes. Mother's curiosity led her to try such newfangled shortcuts, advertised in

magazines and offered as samples in the brand new IGA super-market in Manheim.

All around us, motherhood was being packaged as a brand, guided by the benign hand of General Mills's Betty Crocker. Other companies too advertised enticing packaged foods like Spam, Velveeta, Jello, Twinkies, and Kool-Aid, all designed to provide instant energy and save time. On the farm we consumed our share of all of these prepared products, but they were the frills and fringes, not the staples, of our diet.

Mother enjoyed plying the old-fashioned crafts of cooking and baking. While she loved experimenting and being up on the latest food fads, she preferred making food "from scratch." At a very early age, she had learned to make pies, cakes, and cookies for four hungry brothers and many guests and, eventually, also to sell at the huge farmers' market, the Central Market, in down-town Lancaster.

Mother used to sing this song as she made pies. Singing and work went together.

> Can she make a cherry pie,
> Billy Boy, Billy Boy?
> Can she make a cherry pie,
> Charming Billy?
> She can make a cherry pie,
> Quick's a cat can wink an eye,
> She's a young thing
> And cannot leave her mother. . . .

As she sang, she might have been remembering days like this one recorded in her diary:

(July 25, 1941, age 14): I went along with Rhoda and her parents to the mountains to get huckleberries [native blueberries]. We went over the Blue Ridge Mts. Huckleberries are more expensive this year than last. 14 cents this year. Last year 10 cents. I baked 3 apple pies, 2 cherry pies, 5 custards, 4 shooflies, a pineapple upside down cake and a chocolate cake in one week and they were all very good.[27]

---

27. Barbara Ann Hess Diary #1, 5.

All this experience, including the confidence that the result was "very good," held Mother in good stead as she took on the tasks of wife and mother.

Throughout my early years, even though I preferred to play outdoors whenever possible, I spent more of my time in the kitchen because that's where Mother usually was. I especially wanted to be close when she made cookies and cakes. One day when I was about three years old, I was "helping" Mother whip up one of her famous chocolate cakes. She let me turn the sifter with the little red wooden peg at the end of the metal handle. She always sifted the dry ingredients twice and used cake flour, secrets to her high-rising masterpieces.

"See how the pan makes a perfect circle when you trace around the edge on the wax paper?" Mother noted. "And if you use a sharp knife, you may not even need to use a scissors. The circle will just pop out, like so!" We both laughed.

Mother talked me through the whole process, much like her mother had instructed her. She wanted to show me that work could be fun. I was being formed by my love of food the way a starry-eyed novitiate is prepared for the monastery.

Any work that involved licking the batter off the beaters was fun, without a doubt. While Mother slipped the two pans filled with batter into the oven, I eagerly grasped the beaters, the bowl, and the spatula and passed my tongue enthusiastically across the surfaces, making sure I didn't waste any of the dark, sweet goodness—which also meant that I paid no attention to my face, hair, or red corduroy jumper.

That day, just as Mother discovered what a mess I had made, there was a knock on the door. A well-dressed salesman[28] had arrived, asking to talk to Daddy. Mother pushed me behind her

---

28. Life on the farm was not totally isolated. We had regular visitors: a Fuller Brush man and a Watkins vanilla and cough syrup salesman. We bought quite a few products from such door-to-door salesmen: Lifetime cookware, religious books, and encyclopedias. We also had regular deliveries: Holsum bread, Kuntzleman ice cream, and Stehman potato chips. Before the IGA grocery store came to Manheim, we even had a grocery deliveryman. He had a black Ford coupe with the back end cut out to make space for bags and boxes of food.

as a sign I was supposed to stay hidden. Her wish was fulfilled for about thirty seconds. Then I darted right between her legs and rushed past the salesman out the door, prancing in delight, saying "Hi!" with a huge smile across my chocolate face. Mother remembers not only my exuberance but also her own chagrin. She blushed in embarrassment at her lack of control over her daughter so exposed.

My childhood kitchen contained two frequently used cookbooks. The first of these was *The Mennonite Community Cookbook,* a collection of favorite recipes from Mennonites who lived throughout North America. Published in 1950, it was the preferred cookbook among all the Mennonite cooks I knew. The second was an old spiral-bound notebook, brown and covered with coffee-cup stains. This book was filled with handwritten recipes that Grandma Hess had passed on to Mother.

Mary Emma Showalter, author of *The Mennonite Community Cookbook*, used old books like Mother's brown one as primary sources for the published cookbook. As one of the first Mennonite women to earn a PhD in home economics, Showalter[29] feared that the church was losing its heritage as more and more of these old books were destroyed in favor of *The Joy of Cooking* or some other modern cookbook. So she deliberately asked women from all over the Mennonite Church in the U.S. and Canada to send her their favorite recipes, hoping to preserve and unite family culinary traditions.

My own culinary heirloom, the brown spiral notebook now on my own shelf, contains "recipes" from my Grandma Hess— lists of ingredients without standardized measurements, instructions, or baking temperatures—written in her own hand, often in pencil. I still return to the brown notebook to make some of the recipes, trying to taste and see the goodness of my culinary tradition and to reach back to a grandmother who died before I knew her and long before my mother was ready to let her go.

---

29. Yes, she would become my Aunt Mary Emma in 1969 when I married Stuart Showalter.

The brown notebook also contains lists of customer orders for fresh-dressed poultry and two pages copied from some unknown source on the subject of "Mennonites." Among the recipes are twenty-six types of cakes and pies, three breads, one jam, three pickled items, one juice, and one dandelion wine. The wine recipe might seem surprising, given our church's witness against alcohol and the clear prohibition of its use in the Lancaster Conference *Rules and Discipline* book. But apparently, the Hess family connected with the more tolerant "old school" Mennonites who imbibed moderately of their own wine and sometimes even hard liquor before Prohibition changed their practice.

Holding Anna Mary's brown book is like holding an urn full of ashes. All those years of bustling and baking when Grandmother was queen of the kitchen and Mother was the princess exist only as residue—little carbon markings on the page. But the alchemy, the energy of earth converted to the energy of the body through the energy of love, remains.

The word *sage*, a synonym for wise person, was originally a verb meaning "to taste."[30] This connection between wisdom and food has a biblical tradition also: "O taste and see that the LORD is good"[31] might have been the mantra of many a Mennonite kitchen. We were taking in spiritual as well as physical sustenance, and our table graces tried to point us in the direction of wisdom through gratitude.

Simplicity was the theme of much of our cuisine. Pennsylvania Dutch cooking is not complex or highly nuanced, but it excels in abundance and variety. We didn't have any three-hour meals distributed over six courses at our house! We didn't entertain; we just shared. We opened up our home and our larder to friends and sometimes strangers.

We served what we called "company meals," not in the sense of company as business, but as the companions who were part of us. The signal to scurry was this: "Company's coming! Time to

---

30. Mark Nepo, *Seven Thousand Ways to Listen: Staying Close to What Is Sacred* (Free Press: New York, 2012), 52.
31. Psalm 34:8.

redd up!" But there was always food somewhere: the refrigerator, the cupboard, or the freezer. In the midst of the Cold War, when everyone in school was told to be prepared, I thought immediately of our arch cellar, buried deep under our house. We might have been able to survive a year, or at least six months, on the food we had stored there.

Sharing food and conversation was considered normal. Our family sat down together three times a day. We might move the time to adjust to baling, harvesting, calving, or other special farm tasks, but we seldom scattered to different places, at least not until I took a job away from home. If someone happened to stop by close to mealtime, the visitor became "company" by accepting the invitation to pull an additional chair up to the table. Such a spontaneous offer could be issued to any member of our large extended family living within ten miles of us, to visitors at church, to our neighbors, or to elderly single people whose families had left the area for a holiday. I remember being amused by one neighbor boy. He just loved our homemade bologna and would hang around the kitchen looking toward the Frigidaire until someone opened the door and produced a thick round slice. His delighted face was our reward.

Much of what the health food activists of our present day demand in the food supply was just normal everyday life on the Home Place when I was growing up. I drank raw milk from glass jars all during my childhood. No waste. No homogenization. The cream always rose to the top and tasted great over warm shortcake or cherry pudding. Our chickens had a little outdoor area outside the coop where they could roam freely. Nobody fed animals antibiotics or gave them growth hormones just to make them put on weight. Yes, there were fertilizers and pesticides and probably DDT, but there were no genetically modified seeds. The average cow produced about fifty pounds of milk per day. Our star milk producer, Jenny, was sired by Ivanhoe, a famous Holstein bull of the 1960s. She was awarded a lifetime achievement certificate for her average of eighty-five pounds of milk per day.

Our beef came from our low-producing heifers or bulls. We would sell these grass- and grain-fed animals to butcher shops and keep half a beef for our family in the home freezer or sometimes in a rented frozen locker in town. Out of this abundance, sharing food seemed natural and easy.

A company meal began with a simple appetizer such as a fresh fruit cup, crackers, and homemade grape juice, or a salad consisting of a leaf of lettuce, a circle of pineapple, and a dollop of mayonnaise. After that first course had been eaten, Mother moved into action, producing platter after platter, making sure they were hot and seasoned to her taste. The platters had to be ready all at once, with none of them under- or overcooked.[32] In rapid succession, each dish arrived piping hot: fresh bread, meat, potatoes, gravy, and then several vegetable dishes. Each person might have a "salt cellar" to the left of the plate for dipping celery or sprinkling on other foods. There might also be various kinds of pickles, butter, and jams. The dishes would be passed at least twice, along with encouragement to take additional helpings.

Though everyone was full, a meal was not complete without dessert: coffee or tea and some combination of pie, cake, cookies, ice cream, whipped cream, homemade applesauce or other canned fruit. Dessert was not just the *pièce de résistance* of company meals, but also accompanied everyday fare as well. The only things that were different about company meals and everyday fare were the location in the dining room instead of the kitchen, elegance of the linen tablecloth (rather than the usual oilcloth), silver and good china, and the number of dishes.

The high proportion of carbohydrates in our meals would appall a modern nutritionist, but we weren't sitting at desks behind computers then. Our family had a lot of work to do in the fields and barns and house, and it takes a lot of calories to stoke a human engine for five or six hours.

---

32. To my current tastes, all the vegetables were overcooked, especially the green ones, which usually had lost their bright green hue and had taken on a gray-green cast heightened by the addition, at the very end, of browned butter and sometimes hot milk.

Despite the fact that Mother's housewifery never measured up to her peers' extraordinary feats in all the fields of sewing, quilting, gardening, canning, and cleaning, she kept us all safe and clothed. When she did the wash, an enormous task she did well, she sometimes pinned one whole row of aprons, a clean one for every day.

As I grew older, watching Mother cook, then helping, and later producing whole meals by myself placed me in the tradition of all my mothers before me. Although I loved the outdoors more, I learned to enjoy the kitchen—its smells, its bustling activity, and delicious food.

In school, I took cooking lessons sponsored by the huge food brands emerging in corporate America. One recipe stands out, partly because it says so much about the direction our culture was already moving—toward fast food rather than slow, processed food rather than fresh, individual meals rather than communal, and gimmickry rather than wisdom.

Mother had a large collection of aprons. Here she pins up the weekly quota as a young woman at the Home Place.

Fast Pizza
Take a piece of white bread.
Spread a mixture of tomato paste and oregano over it.
Cover with a slice of American cheese and a slice of bacon.
Place under broiler until the cheese turns light brown on top.

After a demonstration in school, I couldn't wait to get home and try out this amazing new invention on my family. I placed enough fast pizzas on a cookie sheet for everyone to have at least two. Extras for Daddy. I broiled them with care, trying to get the bacon crisp without burning the cheese. I erred on the side of undercooking the bacon.

After the grace, I pulled my white bread pizzas out of the oven. Then I waited for the reaction.

My family seemed eager to find a way to compliment me, since I was obviously waiting for their approval. So they searched for positive things to say.

"Five minutes. Wow. That's fast," said Henry.

"I didn't know tomato paste and bacon went together," Mother said, her red mouth chewing vigorously. Was that a smile on her face?

"Could you finish my bacon in the frying pan?" asked Sue.

Daddy, of course, was the judge who counted most. All eyes were on him. "If this is what the Betty Crocker Homemakers of Tomorrow are cooking, what are the Future Husbands of America going to eat? Get me some real food. How about some of your mother's canned peaches?"

Feeling Small in School

Wisdom puts light in the eyes,
and gives gentleness to words.

—Ecclesiastes 8:1, *The Message*

I was standing next to the brick wall on the playground outside Fairland Elementary School during recess, still getting used to the idea of being a first grader and being away from my family all day long. The strangely dark October sky covered our heads like a pewter dome. The bricks had taken on a purple cast. Someone named Debbie sniffled and sobbed. The teachers were hovering over her. I heard snatches of their conversation.

"Hazel," said a teacher.

That's an interesting word, I thought. My mother says my eyes are hazel. So I crowded a little closer.

"I don't want my parents to die!" cried Debbie. Instantly, all the teachers reached out to her, cradling her in their arms, patting her hair and back. Just as quickly, I wanted to be Debbie.

As the teachers asked more questions, it became apparent that Debbie feared Hurricane Hazel, which had been barreling up the East Coast from the Caribbean and was predicted to hit Lancaster County the next day and also smash into Philadelphia where her parents had been visiting relatives. Debbie had seen pictures of the damage the storm had already done, and she looked terrified.

The word *Philadelphia* triggered memories of faraway places in my own life. My parents had mentioned that my aunt and uncle, who were missionaries in Puerto Rico, would be flying home sometime soon to LaGuardia airport in New York. Maybe that would be tomorrow! My sense of geography was very limited; I knew nothing about storms, weather forecasting, or locations of cities. But if Debbie's parents weren't safe, surely Uncle Paul and Aunt Ann weren't either. I began to feel tears well up, too. A small crowd of little girls now wailed around me. Suddenly, there weren't enough consoling teachers to go around.

My stomach began to tighten as I gasped little sobs. It was unclear who I felt sorriest for—Debbie or Aunt Ann and Uncle Paul. Maybe I was just catching "fear fever" from the other crying first graders surrounding me. I tried to tell my story about Aunt Ann and Uncle Paul, but no one was listening. There was too much hubbub.

No one consoled me. If I were at home, Mother would be there. If I were at church, my Sunday school teacher or some other kind lady would be there for me. But I was in an alien place—at school, a new place with new rules that weren't always clear to me.

I forgot to breathe. Then I started gulping air like a drowning fish. The only way to release it was to belch. Gulp. Gulp. Gulp. Belch. Gulp. Gulp. Gulp. Belch. I couldn't stop, the air built up in my chest until it exploded, and I wondered if I were dying. Panic brought on more gasping. It created a new pain in my throat connected to my lungs and my stomach.

The other first grade girls stopped crying and looked at me wide eyed. The teachers did the same. They asked me questions. I tried to answer. The teachers looked worried. They asked the name of my doctor.

"Dr. Hess in Lititz," I gasped. The teachers, after conferring with one another, elected Miss Frey, the third grade teacher, to drive me to Lititz to see Dr. Hess. I continued gulping air and "rifting," the Pennsylvania Dutch word we use at home for burping.

Miss Frey gathered her purse quickly and directed me to the last vehicle in the line of six teacher cars that spread out like a giant tentacle from the building. I opened the heavy door of a large green Hudson, still gasping and burping. Miss Frey was a young stylish woman with permed hair, red lipstick, and a long gray coat flowing in gored panels below her knees. She seemed more interesting and mysterious than Mrs. Gibble, my teacher. Sitting next to Miss Frey in the front seat, feeling noticed and cared for, I began to breathe normally again without thinking about it.

Miss Frey seemed relieved. So was I, as I began to notice the ways the bright chrome and dashboard lights of her car were different from our two-tone baby blue 1953 Dodge. I wasn't thinking about hurricanes or Hazel or dying any more. All of a sudden, I became aware that I had Miss Frey all to myself, driving along the narrow but paved back roads from Manheim to Lititz. And I was thrilled.

Dr. Hess, our family's source of all medical wisdom, asked a few questions, looked at the bright-eyed girl he had brought into the world six years earlier, and pronounced me fit as a fiddle. He may have called my condition "heartburn."

That kind of loneliness never erupted in a physical way again, but I did experience it intermittently all through the first three grades of school.

Another time, I noticed a large assortment of cars, trucks, and tractors on a mat at the back of a classroom. I had never seen so many shiny toy machines in any place other than a store. I wished three-year-old Henry could see them. We would have dived into that pile together if he were in school, too.

On top of the other cars was a particular red truck, a fire engine with miniature ladders and hoses on the sides. We didn't have a fire engine at home, but I remembered that Daddy said he had one long ago. I wanted to look hard at that toy and think about Daddy, who seemed far away in this big school. I waited until the other kids ran outdoors at recess and then indulged my desire to play with the truck. The other girls were playing hopscotch on the playground. Soon I would join them, but I always seemed a half-step off the beat.

First day, second grade, 1955. Plaid is the theme. Taken at the Spahr farm.

In second grade, I developed a puppy love crush on a boy named Ivan. He was taciturn and uninterested in me, but he seemed to have a fierce attraction to toy tractors and trucks. I devised the idea that if I were to open the wooden cupboard in our dining room at home, extract one of my brother Henry's lesser toy tractors, convince Henry that a boy at school needed the tractor more than we did, and then give Ivan the gift, a transformation would occur. Ivan would look right at me and really see me for the first time. He would smile!

I did somehow convince Henry to let me have the tractor. He really had no choice. I was a big-sister steamroller disguised as solicitor of good deeds, playing the role of little Lady Bountiful, offering him the role of Lord Bountiful. To this day, whenever I start justifying an action based solely on the good that I plan to do for someone else, I remember the beat-up red tractor I took to school in a book bag—and I blush.

Did the "gift" buy me my heart's desire? Ivan did look at me for a second, as if I were a creature from Mars. He took the tractor, but I never got to watch him play with it. He never looked at me again.

Grade school didn't produce the kinds of best friends forever that I craved, although it succeeded in teaching me the three Rs of readin', 'ritin', and 'rithmetic. School was a testing ground, the spot where church and world met each other, the place where I saw ways I fit and ways I did not. School, church, and home were the three legs of my childhood stool. Each carried both sweet and sour memories.

School, however, was the location where all three came together and sometimes clashed. The nexus of these forces shifted over the six years as I rode the big yellow bus to Fairland Elementary School in Manheim Central School District and then back home again to the mailbox at the end of the lane leading to the Spahr farm. My grade school memories follow the architecture of the school itself. A single hallway divided the school into the first three grades (one room for each) on the right and the next three on the left.

Above all, grade school was a stimulus to creativity. The most important lessons I took away were probably not in the teacher's lesson plan book. I learned to listen to my own feelings, search the environment for opportunities, and go out to meet them. This pattern took hold one day as second grade was just getting started.

"Today, Debbie, Kenneth, Bonnie, Betsy, Dale, Carl, Dottie, Judy, Carol, and Vernon, we will read our first story in the second grade reader. And you will be our Redbirds. Please come up to the front and sit on the chairs in this circle." Mrs. Rothenberger's voice was as sweet as butter and honey on toast.

I watched from my seat in the middle of the room as about

one-third of the class moved to the front of the room. Their books were red, just like their names, and most of my chosen classmates were smiling. They had just become Redbirds.

After they had read their story, Mrs. Rothenberger, a tall woman who favored flowing skirts and white blouses and liked to swish past her students as she patrolled each row, dismissed them back to their seats.

"And now, Betty, Carol, Dorothy, Marshall, Ivan, Shirley, Raymond, and Terry, please come forward to the circle. You are our Bluebirds." Her voice tone was still smooth, but it sounded less sweet to me. I took the blue reading book in my hands and looked at it with high hopes. When it was my turn, I was able to read about our friends Dick, Jane, Tom, and Sally. No problem— just a little boring. The red book reader sounded and looked like more fun.

I noticed other differences, too. At lunchtime, most of the Redbirds did not have plaid designs on their lunch boxes like I did. They had Roy Rogers and Dale Evans and Mickey Mouse and Donald Duck and the Lone Ranger and Tonto on theirs. Many of the Redbird girls wore bright red polish on their nails, glittering rhinestones around their necks, and rings on their fingers. How plain I suddenly felt. How unremarkable, dull, and invisible.

The books for each reading circle were located in the back of the room. At recess time, I went to the back and picked up one of the Redbird books that were stored on metal shelves under the windows. I handled it with care, a little awestruck by the heft of it. It smelled new. I felt like Annie Oakley, ready to do something dangerous. I took the book and slid it under my desk lid. When it was time for the Redbirds to read, I followed along in their book, with the lid up so that the teacher would not notice.

A few days later, I decided to go for it. When Mrs. Rothenberger called for the Redbirds, I pulled an extra chair inside the circle and sat down. I was trembling inside but tried to look matter-of-fact, like silk draped over a table. Mrs. Rothenberger looked at her circle of Redbirds, smiling. Then she noticed me.

"Why, Shirley, what are you doing here? You must be confused. Please return to your desk until it is the Bluebirds' turn."

"I would like to be a Redbird, Mrs. Rothenberger. I have the red book, and I like it. May I read it?"

"Well," she said, clearing her throat, "let's see how you do." Since I had followed along in the book, I could read most of the words. I scanned Mrs. Rothenberger's face, searching for signs of approval. She didn't blink. But she didn't send me back either. The next day I took the seat without asking, and she did not object.

Being a Redbird was thrilling, but it didn't solve all my problems. One day, for fun, Mrs. Rothenberger put a word on the board none of us had ever seen before: M A N U R E. Then she challenged us to figure out the word using its resemblance to other embedded words we knew or could detect. I desperately wanted to be the first person to figure out the puzzle. I remembered a word much like this one in the back of the room on the shelf in the same place I had found the Redbird reading books. I quickly went to the spot I remembered but was disappointed to see that the word was M A N U A L. Upon returning to my seat, I tried all the ways to sound out the word and finally stumbled upon sounding out the long U sound. I had been stumped by thinking that the emphasis of the word would be upon M A N, and I knew lots of words ended in R E. I was pronouncing the word "MAN ur." Until I tried the long U. In a split second, I knew the word, and in that same split second I found myself yelling, "MANURE, MANURE. The word's manure!"

This outburst did not bring me the glory and gold star from Mrs. Rothenberger for which I was hoping. Instead, I saw a stern look cross her visage. She beckoned for me to approach her desk. She reached in a drawer and extracted a roll of masking tape. Then she told me to sit in the desk next to the door where everyone who entered and exited the room would see me. She pulled off about three six-inch lengths and placed them over my mouth. Tears stung my eyes, and the time until recess seemed to drag on forever.

What did I think about? These were the messages my brain sent me: Don't try too hard. Don't want things too much. Control yourself. Get smaller! I was ashamed of my exuberance. I knew I had done the wrong thing, but I didn't understand that I had prevented other students from having the same eureka moment I had experienced. I just felt stupid in my hour of triumph. I knew that I had also felt pride, and I wondered what people at church would think if they could see the shameful tape over my mouth.

Once we started reading chapter books in school, I began to read on my own at home. My mother's bedtime and Bible story reading had planted a seed. Mrs. Rothenberger had allowed it to grow, and soon I discovered how exciting it was to read books like *Heroes and Heroines*, a collection of short biographies from early American history. Nancy Drew and the Hardy Boys started taking me into worlds undreamed of on the farm, while the Sugar Creek Gang and a writer with the strange and wonderful name of Christmas Carol Kauffman assured me that Mennonites had their own stories and their own adventures. I was indiscriminate

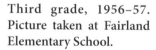

Third grade, 1956–57. Picture taken at Fairland Elementary School.

in my tastes. As long as there was a plot, I was ready to travel anywhere between the covers of a book.

Reading was my gateway drug into caring about academic success. By the time I left third grade, I had finally caught the rhythm of school content. It took a little while for the social side of the equation to catch up. I was a slow learner in both categories.

Fourth grade brought with it the most notorious teacher of them all, Miss Gibble, not to be confused with *Mrs.* Gibble, my first grade teacher. Rumored to have a Necessity Stick that was both thick and handy, with a hole in the middle of it so that the stick could travel more rapidly to a miscreant's backside, Miss Gibble ruled her classroom like Queen Victoria over Britannia.

The strange thing was that Miss Gibble was plain! She wore nondescript long dresses and pulled her hair back in a bun under a prayer covering. Just like my mother. There weren't very many plain teachers in the public schools of Lancaster County in 1957, but there she was, an anomaly, in front of my own classroom. Like everyone else who had heard the rumors, I was a little afraid of Miss Gibble. But I was secretly happy to have a teacher who was plain. I knew she would understand me in ways my first three teachers could not—even if she was Church of the Brethren and believed in baptism by dunking instead of the proper Mennonite way of pouring.[33]

One afternoon, seated in the last row near the closet full of coats and lunch buckets, I tackled an English assignment. We were to find the topic sentence in a paragraph, but I struggled to understand the concept. It seemed obvious that all sentences had topics! But as I searched over and over again, looking for the paragraph's theme sentence, I lit on one beginning with "Therefore," and my brain suddenly became incandescent. Some topics are bigger than others! All of a sudden, I was whizzing through the assignment, easily selecting the sentence that seemed to offer an umbrella to all the others.

---

33. Proper, that is, among our group of Mennonites. Globally, other Mennonite groups baptize by immersion or sprinkling.

Fourth grade was the time I turned the corner socially as well. I became part of an inner circle of friends in much the same way I had become a Redbird in second grade: by watching, learning, and creating my own alternative. The popular girls in our class developed little whispering campaigns on the playground and body signals inside the classroom like catchers and pitchers do on the baseball diamond. If you saw one of the cardigan girls making signs to another girl across the room, you knew that the other girl was *in* and you were *out*. I noticed that very few of the girls from plain families were *in*.

After one blatant display of in-group communication that excluded me, I decided to find a group of other rejects during recess. We looked across the way at the cardigan girls. They were laughing and talking in animated voices, their arms around each other.

"Does anyone have an idea for a name we could give our own club?" I asked. Lots of brainstorming resulted in a name that sounded perfect: The Hikta Stikta Club. And someone excitedly suggested a theme song modeled on something she had heard on television. We sang together with gusto:

It's Hikta Stikta time
It's Hikta Stikta time
We run around and laugh
And then we eat a calf!

Somehow this amalgam of Disney and the story of the prodigal son produced just the kind of gaiety—and notice—we were after. A few people asked to join. We weren't sure what to do about that.

"Passwords!" shouted one member. We went into a conclave to discuss. Applicants had to be able to tell us what *Electric City* stood for. This stumped all comers for quite a while, probably because they rejected the answer "electricity" as too obvious. Subtlety was not our specialty. It was hard to avoid being too obvious when you sang the Hikta Stikta theme song.

Meanwhile, the Hikta Stikta Club was the buzz of the playground. We were amazed at how easy it was to create the illusion of scarcity ("there are only a few places open in our club") and how effective that illusion was in transforming us from outsiders to insiders. We probably weren't any more inclusive than the original popular girls. In fact, when we returned to the classroom, we had devised our own set of secret signs and brandished them with hypervigilant gusto.

The funny thing about all these little clubs? Despite their lack of social prestige, the plain kids had lots of experience in exclusive environments. They attended churches that drew boundaries and defined identities very skillfully. On the playground, plain kids could borrow the tools not only of the country club but of the church.

Today, when I hear that schools are cutting recess, art, and music from their daily schedules, I shudder. I can't imagine what school would have been like without those highlights. We rushed outdoors for about twenty minutes at least twice a day. For a while, we hunted for gold—fool's gold or mica—in the blacktop we called macadam. With a bobby pin, we could extract nuggets of gold from tar and stones. What better way to symbolize the possibilities in all of life?

We also took the grass clippings left after the janitor had mowed and made "houses" of them with many rooms. Our first architecture was made with leaves of grass. I remembered those houses many years later when I read Whitman's advice to "look for me under your feet."

As long as we played games and explored the physical world outdoors, I loved recess. But often the conversations turned to television topics. There were impromptu imitations of commercials for Camel cigarettes, Alpo dog food, or last night's episode of *The Honeymooners* or *The Lone Ranger*. At such times I watched my most popular classmates' animated conversations from the sidelines, trying to imagine, from their reconstructions, what it must be like to sit in front of a television screen in your living room every night instead of reading books or doing chores or going to church.

Our school was located next to the old one-room structure it had replaced. Consolidation was happening to all rural schools in the 1950s. Instead of walking to a small place of learning within two miles of home, students climbed on school buses and rode for ten or more miles, picking up their peers in a wider swath and creating larger classrooms. When we played on the playground, we could still see the outhouse used by the students at the now outmoded one-room school. A story circulated on the schoolyard that if you sat on the wooden seat of the outhouse, a snake would come up from the pit below and bite you on your bottom. Henceforth, every time in my life I have needed to use an outhouse, I've cringed at the powerful image I still carry from that casual conversation long ago.

But of all the recess activities, softball was the one I enjoyed most. From third grade on, I played every day. When I went home, I begged for—and eventually got—my own ball, bat, and glove. I recruited Henry to throw the ball so I could learn to bat. I oiled my new glove every night and slipped the white ball with red stitching into the glove pocket, fastening big rubber bands around the outside as my teammates had advised. I coveted the well-broken glove of the best outfielder, Kenny. When he caught a fly and hurled it into the infield, all in one fluid motion, no ballet could have been prettier.

Girls and boys played together at school. And we picked up teams. Everyone wanted Ben, a roly-poly Mennonite boy who had two amazing talents. He could draw with accuracy and detail—cars, tractors, trucks—and he could hit the ball over the head of an outfielder. Being overweight might have made Ben the target of bullies, but softball was his ticket to glory. He also could play without any fear of church sanction because this was school. He didn't wear a uniform, and he didn't form any affiliations that might compete with work at home or devotion at church.

I wanted softball to be my ticket to glory also. I wanted it so much that once when I swung my hardest, I forgot to drop the bat at the plate. It went flying out to the field, hitting the pitcher, Terry, on the forehead. I was sent inside as punishment. And then, after supper that night, Mother and Daddy took me to Terry's house so that I could apologize to him in front of his parents. The goose egg on his forehead didn't disappear for a week. I was left with another lesson about desire and the need for discipline: Don't just think about how much you want something; think about the whole field and all the other players, too.

Despite the fact that fields surrounded our school and about half the class came from farm families, most of whom were Mennonite or Church of the Brethren, we were connected to the world outside our rural area there. I saw my first Elvis and "I like Ike" buttons at school. My tastes continued to tilt toward the tomboy. I remember trading baseball cards on the playground and listening in 1960 to the Yankees versus Pirates World Series on the classroom radio. There also some of the boys played with battleships, soldiers, tanks, and submarines as they studied World War II battles from a war that had ended just a decade earlier.

What hung over everyone was the invisible mushroom cloud of the Cold War. And what brought it home to all of us were the "duck-and-cover" drills used to prepare us for a nuclear bomb that could strike at any time. If there was a siren or an amazing flash of light in the sky, the first thing we should do was drop and find a desk. Curling up into the smallest amount of space possible, we were instructed to cover our skin. Using a turtle as our totem, we should think of ourselves as moving under a shell of protection. Of course, instead of making us feel safe, these drills only served as reminders that disaster could strike at any time.

Beyond the first grade scare of Hurricane Hazel, I had other opportunities to imagine analogies to nuclear disaster. First, there were the annual revival meetings in our church with their emphasis on being saved before you die. And then there were the radio preachers with their dispensationalist theology. I remember listening to *God's News Behind the News* on Saturday mornings when the preacher would parse the current headlines, looking for signs of the end times. Amazingly, they were ever present! He always began with an ominous reading of Matthew 24:44: "Be ye also ready: for in such an hour as ye think not the Son of man cometh." I remember being glad when the broadcast ended, leaving us still intact, but being drawn back to it again the next week as a moth to the flame.

So, there were definite places where church and school messages seemed to come together. Perhaps I was living in the end times—the last year, month, week, day, minute. If that thought pierced me with fear, the antidote was to hang on for another minute and pinch myself. Then I could run out to play or return to my chores or studies. I had survived one more scare! Looking back, however, I wonder about the effect those drills might have had on the millions of baby boomer children and their teachers who were watching daily for the imminent destruction of the world and trying to convince themselves of safety underneath an imaginary turtle shell.

Sixth grade was the very pinnacle of grade school, just as it had promised to be when I first entered that long hallway at Fairland Elementary. Having admired sixth-grader Shirley Clark's stature, safety patrol belt, and jewelry collection when I began school, I was now able to stand tall, too. By age twelve, I had grown to my full adult height of five feet five-and-a-half inches. I had become a member of the safety patrol a year earlier. Each school day, I carefully washed the belt and shoulder strap in Clorox water at home so that it would continue to signal bright-white safety when smaller children looked up to me.

By far, the most important event of sixth grade was my good fortune of being in Mrs. Lochner's class the last year she taught. My mother had noticed Mrs. Lochner's school leadership at the PTA meetings she and Daddy attended faithfully, since Mrs. Lochner was both the principal and the sixth grade teacher. Mother had a way of guiding me to people she admired or enjoyed herself, both at church and at school. Mrs. Lochner outshone all the others even before I moved into the best room in the school, the class that was across from the entrance, the first classroom visible from the door.

If Shakespeare had observed Mrs. Lochner, he would have said she "bestrode our narrow world like a Colossus."[34] A tall woman, she wore her gray haired pulled back in an attractive bun, which on her looked regal rather than plain. She was neither Mennonite nor Brethren, something obvious to my radar because she did not wear a hair covering. She reminded me of another woman I had met, again due to Mother's influence: Ruth Brunk Stoltzfus, a Mennonite from Virginia with her own radio broadcast who once stayed in our home after speaking at our church. The resemblance to Mrs. Lochner was her carriage, first of all. It was not haughty, but it was not humble either. I sensed a way of being in the world that rooted down deep and then spread out wide, an embracing stance that would not bend with the wind, but merely sway gracefully and rhythmically.

As soon as school started, I was all eyes and ears for Mrs. Lochner. If she threw out a challenge like "here's a photograph, write a story," I was all over it. Given a picture of an old barn, I told my story from the perspective of a mouse complaining about lack of food when the farmer no longer brought in the crops. Mrs. Lochner chose my story to be read aloud in class. Presto, a writer was born. After lunch, Mrs. Lochner thought it wise to settle our minds along with our stomachs, so she picked students to read classic tales to the whole class. I was selected to read *The Wind in the Willows*. Bingo, a public speaker was born.

Sometimes my admiration for my teacher was too hard to contain. Once, as she was walking down the aisles of our room, I looked up at her with unabashed adoration. Gently, she touched me on the shoulder and directed my gaze to the page lying open on my desk. I admired her all the more for not seeking or basking in my love.

As I watched the woman who became my first mentor and role model in the world outside my family, I developed the idea

34. Cassius' speech (Act I, Scene 2) in *Julius Caesar, The Complete Works of William Shakespeare* (London: Spring Books, 1958), 721.

that I, too, might become a teacher. I learned that I would have to go to college to reach that goal. So I began to pay attention when people talked about college. I even brought up the subject at home, where it was met with a tepid response. College cost money at a time when a wise young woman should be saving money—for her highest callings of marriage and childrearing, which would come soon after high school. College also took people out of the community, literally in many cases, and threatened their faith. The old joke was that you could send a Mennonite boy to Harvard, but you could not get him back again. Send a Mennonite girl to Harvard? Unimaginable.

The more conservative a church was, the more higher education was actively discouraged. Our church was middle-left on the Mennonite spectrum in Lancaster County, 1960. The fact that our beloved minister served on the Mennonite Board of Education that oversaw three Mennonite colleges was probably more significant than I could have known.

To skeptical people like my parents, who worried that their children would lose their faith if they went to college, my minister could point to institutions he admired, especially to Hesston College in Kansas, a two-year school with a focus on teaching practical skills. The other two schools, Eastern Mennonite in Virginia and Goshen in Indiana, appealed even more to me because they offered four-year degrees that would equip me for the highest goal I could imagine—becoming a teacher.

Though only one man and one woman in our congregation had college degrees, and most young adults were expected to end their schooling and get to "real" work (farming, business, or homemaking) as soon as possible, there was some openness to the idea of higher education. For a young woman, at least, it was an "insurance policy" in the case she might be forced by singleness or the death of her husband to earn her own living.

At eleven years old, I had glimpsed the barely opened doorway to the dazzling world of college. If I had to call it an insurance policy, so be it. The will was there. I would find a way.

Eleven

Getting Saved

Thick fingers twisting around perfumed hankies
Rough hands comforting a child

Furtive glances, whispers among the back-pew young
Pictures of Jesus on unfurled fans
filling the air with silent symphony

Sonorous singing of the shaped notes
Bobwhites chanting in the bush outside

Candies for the children in grandpa's pockets
The beef roast, basking in juices, waiting . . .
Remembrances of sermons past.[35]

—Shirley Hershey Showalter

*A*t the close of sixth grade, I had been fighting two inner
battles. The closer I came to adolescence, the harder it
got to understand my own desires. In sixth grade, I would have
blushed to admit it, but, like my mother before me, I wanted to
be both popular and smart. Though I never felt I achieved star
status socially or academically, I loved school and grew increasingly more comfortable in that environment.

At church, however, I was experiencing the opposite trajectory, moving from comfort to discomfort, while often feeling both. As early as third grade the light began to dawn about

---

35. Shirley Hershey Showalter, "Sunday Morning," in *The Gospel Herald*,
November 4, 1980.

Mother's changing expectations. Instead of the curly perms of first and second grade, when I was being sent to school as a Mennonite Shirley Temple, I began to look more like other Mennonite girls. Mother had decided it was time for longer hair and braids.

One Sunday morning Mother was combing my hair, getting me ready to go to church. She tugged hard to make the braids look smooth and straight, which hurt a little, but I stood patiently waiting for her to finish. I was either eight or nine years old.

"Last week at church Daddy noticed someone who looked proud," she said softly, as though confiding in me.

Wow. That was a terrible thing to say about someone. One of the first verses I learned was this: "Pride goeth before a fall."[36] I knew the Lord hated a proud look and a haughty spirit, and that the day would come when the proud would be destroyed. Pride, after all, was the devil's own downfall.

So my mind roamed over the congregation. Who could be the terrible proud person in our church? The rows of women around Mother and me in church seemed so sedate that my imagination ran dry. I couldn't figure out whom Daddy might have had in mind. It never occurred to me that the person could have been a man, despite having the devil as a male role model.

Mother twisted the rubber band at the end of my braid and then said in a near whisper, "That person was you."

If she had popped me with that rubber band, the sting would have hurt much less than the pain in my heart. Daddy was the godlike figure of both our lives. His approval or disapproval spelled the difference between a good day and a bad one. This was going to be one horrible day.

I was confused by mixed signals. Here was Mother, carefully braiding my hair as she had washed and ironed my Sunday dress, trying to make me look not only presentable but pretty. I knew that she enjoyed dressing me up, just as I knew she had wanted that out-of-reach Shirley Temple doll when she was little. Around the farm, I was a tomboy. Going to church, I was a

---

36. A conflation of words in Proverbs 16:18.

princess. Like Mother when she was a girl, I loved pretty dresses, jewelry, hats, and fancy hairstyles. When Mother's eyes smiled after she checked me out before church, I felt great.

So feeling great and looking like you enjoy yourself must be called "pride." What I felt inside myself the previous Sunday must have made its way outside for Daddy to see and disapprove of.

Suddenly, I could see the road ahead for my life. When I joined the church in a few years, I would be expected to give up love of the world. I would need to fit in—first within the youth group and then with my husband, some young farmer who was a younger version of Daddy. What was next? Why, producing a brood of children and grandchildren, while perhaps making quilts or afghans for each of them like Grandma Hershey did. Would I also learn to lower my eyes and my voice and walk as though gravity was not only the force that held me to the ground but also the name of my spirit? Unconsciously, I wanted to scream, "I'm not made to be like this. You aren't either, Mother. And I know it!"

Mother's own teenage ambitions to be pretty, popular, an actress, a writer, a violinist were gone now. She was a loyal Mennonite farm wife who would bring up her children in the way they should go under the leadership of God, the church, and her husband, in that divine order. Her creativity was not crushed, and she didn't want mine to suffer either, but she was showing me boundaries I had not been aware of. I had a sense, as she twisted my hair into its proper place, that she knew what was happening to me on the inside—and that she cared deeply.

My first spiritual impressions were formed in nature, and they had no names like Mennonite, Catholic, Hindu, or Jew. I didn't even call them God. On the farm I was surrounded by the sensuality of living things—lilies of the valley whose smell made me dizzy with delight, lilacs, peonies, roses, irises, blue bells. I loved finding honeysuckle along the creek banks and could be entranced by pulling off petals and sucking nectar out of the blossoms. Henry and I would play for hours at a time along the two creeks of our childhood, fishing for minnows, making dams, holding back the water until it couldn't be contained any longer and overflowed its banks.

Nature surrounded us even inside buildings. In the 1950s, before air conditioning became commonplace, windows were flung open and stayed open as soon and long as possible. On spring and summer Sunday mornings, the windows of the church sanctuary stood wide open. Trained by Daddy to listen, we children could hear the distinctive whistling call of bobwhite quail from the backyard of the house across the street during the service.

On especially beautiful mornings, Roy Brubaker, our chorister, would stand before the congregation and invite us to sing "I owe the Lord a morning song / of gratitude and praise / for the kind mercies He has shown / in lengthening out my days."[37]

Gratitude and praise on such a morning was so palpable that I could feel my nerve endings.

The pleasures of a cappella four-part harmony, when experienced first in childhood sitting on the lap of one's mother, can hardly be explained. The closest word for me is *wholeness*.

While Phil Specter was perfecting his Wall of Sound and the Beatles were still a few years away from "Let It Be," I was singing first soprano and then alto in church. Sometimes a tear would form as I let myself float out beyond my body while my voice trembled. The first time it happened, I was singing these words from the hymn "The Love of God":

---

37. Though Mennonites have a great singing tradition, few of the hymns of my childhood were written by Mennonites. Two exceptions are Lancaster Conference minister Amos Herr's "I Owe the Lord a Morning Song," 1890, quoted above. Another favorite was "Teach Me Thy Truth," lyrics by Edith Witmer, a member of Lititz Mennonite Church. This hymn would later become even more important to me because it is known as the "Goshen" hymn (music by Walter E. Yoder and sung often at Goshen College, where I would later become professor and president). Both are still sung often in Mennonite churches. Nos. 651 and 548, respectively in *Hymnal: A Worship Book* (Scottdale, PA: Herald Press, 1992).

Could we with ink the ocean fill,
And were the skies of parchment made,
Were every stalk on earth a quill,
And every man a scribe by trade,
To write the love of God above,
Would drain the ocean dry.
Nor could the scroll contain the whole,
Though stretched from sky to sky.[38]

The lush imagery pierced me inside a plain Mennonite church, and, for a moment at least, I floated right out of the building, over the bobwhites, and became part of the ink in God's quill. I was to experience myself getting larger by submersion several times in church. These moments sustained me when later I would experience conflict within the same walls.

For a child whose very nature was adventurous, mystical connections to God were thrilling. The church's rules, less so. I spent my early years ricocheting between two poles: one of simplicity, humility, and obedience and another of complexity, ambition, and rebellion.

School became the place where the contrast between early inclusive, mystical, and communal experiences of God's love got confusing. School reminded me that my family was Mennonite. From third to sixth grade, I was engaged in an internal battle that sometimes felt like life or death. I was trying to find my place in the world, and I wasn't sure what it was—or even if there was one. My teachers in the early grades had taught me kindly and well, but they had not seen in me what I believed I was capable of, even though I didn't know what that was.

About half the class at Fairland Elementary had connections to plain backgrounds, either Mennonite or Church of the

---

38. "The Love of God," Frederick M. Lehman, 1917. This third verse comes from a Jewish poem *Haddamut*, written in Aramaic in 1050 by Meir Ben Isaac Nehorai, a cantor in Worms, Germany. http://www.cyberhymnal.org/htm/l/o/loveofgo.htm.

Brethren. Unlike the Lutherans and Methodists in the class, we Mennonites and Brethren had not been baptized as babies. Carol Miller was a precocious plain girl. She had stood or raised her hand in a revival meeting at her church at age eight. As a result, she had already been dunked in the baptismal method her church required. Perhaps that was when I learned that Church of the Brethren members, such as Carol, had strong objections to the usual Mennonite practice of baptism by pouring or sprinkling. They explained the error of Mennonite ways to me quite clearly.[39]

Most importantly, Carol now came to school with her hair pulled straight back from her face, fixed into a bun at the base of her neck, wearing the symbol of her submission to the church and to God: a white prayer covering smaller than an Amish cap with strings but large enough to cover the bun and half her head. Carol's soul had been saved. Now she was protected by God, Jesus, her church, and the angels to lead a holy life of separation from the world. Her long hair, bun, and covering reminded her and the rest of us that she was, by her early declaration, a follower of Jesus, saved by his blood on the cross. But the covering on her small head just reminded me that all the Mennonites in my life wanted to see one of those coverings on my own head. It was not a comfortable thought.

The accompanying photo shows that by fifth grade, when I had three siblings at home instead of one, my mother was no longer curling my hair, braiding it, or adding bows and ribbons. I had a homemade haircut and was starting to let my hair grow long. I was not aware of the subtle signs, but I was being prepared to become plain—and soon.

Mother's own confused feelings about the church and baptism foreshadowed a similar mixture in my life long before age fourteen. During the years between Mother's youth and mine, the average age of Mennonite baptism had come down to as low as ten or eleven. Something called "child evangelism" had

39. Later, when I encountered Mennonites from the General Conference and the Mennonite Brethren Church, I learned that pouring and dunking were Mennonite practices in other places also.

Me on the left. Carol on the right. Fifth grade, 1958–59. From the collected school photo taken at Fairland Elementary.

influenced the church, and children were led to feel the weight of their sins earlier than their parents and grandparents had. Could I have waited until age nineteen as Mother had? Not without gravely disappointing every member of the church and not without feeling like the chief of all sinners, the one who defied the age of accountability and risked hell in order to live a selfish, proud life on earth.

I remember a homework assignment I had in elementary school: Ask your parents to tell you about a decision they made that they now regret. My mother's answer was that she regretted not joining the church at an earlier age. I knew that answer came from her interest in my soul's salvation and that it was intended to influence me, yet I also knew that I did not completely believe the answer. Why? For all her deep love of Jesus, something I never questioned, my mother still loved the things of the world, the things she left behind in her youth: her violin; her rouge; her jewelry; her curls and bows; and low cut, form-fitting dresses. It was because she loved these things so much that she wanted me to get saved from them before I experienced them. Or else I might be lost forever.

Well, it was too late for that. I already loved the things of the world. I craved the pretty things that other girls wore, but, more than that, I craved their ability to make choices.

Third grade was the year I began to feel the struggle most acutely between the church and the world. I loved my Fairland Elementary School teacher, Miss Frey, but I felt invisible to her at some level. I had a gut feeling that part of my invisibility to Miss Frey was that I was plain.

True, I did not yet wear my hair under a covering like Carol Miller, but I did wear pigtails. I did not have red nail polish and perfect crinolines and cardigan sweater sets like Beverly. I thought she and Bonnie were the teacher's pets. I was especially indignant when we did a unit in class on Native Americans. Beverly, Bonnie, and Betsy painted red nail polish on the life-sized Indians we were making down on our hands and knees on butcher paper in the back of the classroom. I said to the teacher that Indians did not have nail polish, hoping to be rewarded for my scholarship and affirmed in the aesthetic of plainness. Instead, Miss Frey said, "Well, maybe they used berry juice to make their nails pretty," and she then smiled at Beverly, Bonnie, and Betsy as though they all had a secret.

I could tell, even in grade three, that joining the church would lead to a life of either invisibility to, or else outright rejection from, a large part of the world I had already come to care about. So when revival ministers arrived in the spring for the annual series of sermons and altar calls, I gripped the edge of my seat during the "invitation" so that I would not go forward and fall into Carol Miller's territory, that of a ten-year-old who looked like she had stepped out of the last century.

I was affected, however, by the ministers' sermons. One preacher in particular was known for making the devil and all his legions very real and for winning souls by showing them graphic descriptions of hell. When he called the devil "the Prince of Lies," I went home and pondered. I reviewed my life for all the lying I had done in service to the devil. It was a sizable list. I had lied about getting permission to wear Shirley Clark's ring. I had lied about being a Brownie, something all the teacher's pets were and something I longed to be. I lied about my mother's ability to make butter (I know, it's crazy, but it was on the list). I raised my hand to claim a lovely pen that was in the Lost and Found. I found it all right, but I had never lost it. This list of sins was not exhaustive, but as I lay under my coverlet late at night, it was surely exhausting. I decided, however, that if I confessed these lies to God and to the people I had told them to, I would not have to join the church. I could seek God's salvation on my own.

I came clean while trembling inside. I told Miss Frey that I had lied about being a Brownie and about my mother being a butter maker. I don't remember her response. But I did feel relief. It got me to fourth grade without a covering on my head.

By the time I was in sixth grade, however, quite a number of the other girls from Mennonite and Church of the Brethren homes had gotten plainer after joining the church. Both at church and at school, most of the girls had raised their hands during revivals, gone through instruction, started wearing their hair up and under a covering, and had gotten baptized.

During the 1960 revival meetings at our church, my mother decided to talk to me at home about the state of my soul. She told me that I was facing the most important decision in my life. Would I give up my own will and all my other loves and be willing to follow Jesus? My mother's voice was soft, her eyes were brimming with tears as she explained how much God loved me. Did I not want to give my heart to him?

Of course I did. I didn't want either Mother or Jesus to be disappointed in me. So I knelt beside my mother next to a navy blue overstuffed velvet chair and gave my heart to the Lord of heaven and earth. I was hoping I would hear trumpets. But, instead, Mother and I hugged each other through our tears, and I knew that when the revival took place, I would need to accept the call to Christ publicly.

Fortunately, the revivalist that year was not a hellfire-and-brimstone preacher. His voice was warm, and the picture he painted was of a shepherd searching for lost sheep. I was a little lamb on the edge of a cliff. Jesus was reaching his crook toward me. All I had to do was grasp it.

I know the exact place where I was seated on the right rear side of Lititz Mennonite Church when I raised my eleven-year-old hand, grasping the lifeline Jesus extended to me. Afterward, I felt a warm glow as I was enfolded into the faith by the ministers and by the older women, who had made a point to tell me that they hoped I would respond to God's call in the revival.

I could not tell if my tears were as joyful as theirs, but I did know this: I was visible to these people, all the way to my soul. And through them, I could see myself visible to God. I had caught a glimpse of the paradox I would ponder all my life. The times when we feel smallest, in the presence of grace and mystery, that's when our souls expand. Instead of becoming big in the way the ego drove us initially, we submit to a loving God and become large beyond measure. Our acceptance of finitude sweeps us into infinity.

I had resisted the pressure to join the church mostly because I didn't want to become plain like Mother and stick out like a sore thumb at school. I had also resisted the word *saved*. I didn't like the smugness of the word, and I didn't like the thought that those who weren't like us were damned. But, like my father and mother before me, when the right preacher preached and the pain of resisting became greater than the freedom of letting go, I said yes.

When my little sister Sue, age four, asked me what had happened that night, there was a thick tenderness in my voice. "I got saved, honey," I said. "I got saved."

When I returned to sixth grade at Fairland, I was wearing my hair in a bun with a covering on top. The war in my soul had ended for all external appearances. I was Mennonite inside and out now. Over the next six years, from my baptism until leaving home for college, I would experience a whole range of emotions ranging from shame to pride. The prayer veiling, as it was called in church, could be called a "crash helmet," "a sin strainer," or just plain "lid" out in the world. Once a boy with cigarettes rolled up in his white t-shirt sleeve sneered at me as I entered the school bus. "You can take your helmet off. The war's over." Then he laughed hard at his own joke.

When one dresses plain, one is always signaling to the world a willingness to take a stand for belief. We members-in-training were actually reminded of this as we were instructed in the faith. People will observe you carefully when you wear a covering, we were told. Your actions, attitudes, and tone all leave an impression on others. They will either be attracted to godly living or repelled by your lack of it. You will add to the evidence of either religious hypocrisy or authenticity with every action.

Of course, I wanted very much to be authentic. As much as I had struggled before I joined the church, once I submitted my little life, I wanted it to count. I hadn't yet given up the dream of becoming big.

Magic in Manheim

He brought me to the banqueting house,
and his banner over me was love.

—Solomon's Song 2:4

The familiar yellow school bus, the one I rode every day for six years to Fairland School, pulled up to the playground one beautiful spring morning in 1960. Only the sixth graders piled into the bus, leaving all the other students gaping. The destination? The town of Manheim and the huge school we would be attending in the fall—Manheim Central Junior High. We were going to do a trial run through the maze of hallways and classrooms. That fall, we sixth graders who knew each other so well at Fairland would become strangers again. We would meet scores of other strangers from other schools. And each classroom would feature a different teacher teaching a different subject.

Junior high started for real in the fall. As usual in a new environment, I was both excited and scared. I was told to report to 7-B, a college-bound track. Seven B was a laid-back group, moderately interested in the school curriculum, but far more interested in sports—and for a while—politics. We didn't know it then, but we would observe a turning point election in American history. This was a coming-of-age election for our age group, since we were only eight years old during the last campaign.

Mennonites of my time and place took two paths in politics: abstention or straight-ticket Republican. The more conservative groups, the ones who wanted the thickest walls between church and world, abstained from voting, as did the Amish. Not surprisingly, Daddy's side of the family, the Hersheys, abstained. The Hesses participated eagerly and talked about politics nearly every time they met.

My parents followed the Hess family pattern, participating in presidential elections and voting Republican. They liked the emphasis on small government and moral living in Republican platforms. And they loved Dwight and Mamie Eisenhower, whose pictures presided over the bulletin board in our kitchen for almost a decade.

So it was surprising in 1960 when their first-born, twelve-year-old daughter, Shirley, didn't follow their lead on what they thought was the most important election in the history of the United States.

That fall, my social studies teacher did what every other social studies teacher in the country was doing. He set up a class debate between the supporters of Richard Nixon and John F. Kennedy. In our classroom, influenced by the politics of our homes, almost everyone wanted to defend Richard Nixon.

Our class included one Catholic student, Tom Caskey, who sat on my left. As I looked at him out of the corner of my eye, I empathized with him for being a member of a misunderstood religious minority group. Although Catholicism was the largest Christian denomination in the world, in Protestant-dominated Manheim, Catholics were exotic. And although the sixteenth-century Catholic Church had persecuted my ancestors, it never occurred to me to hold that old history against Tom. I liked him.

I also liked JFK, the handsome, young presidential candidate. So I volunteered to join Tom in the debate defending John F. Kennedy as the stronger of the two contenders. I had read a few political articles in our daily newspaper, the Lancaster *Intelligencer Journal*. It was our one source of news besides CBS and Paul Harvey on the radio.

I might have been the only Mennonite at Manheim Central Junior High willing to stand up for JFK. Every adult conversation I had heard about the election started with the danger of having a president who would be taking orders from Rome, like all Catholics do. That assertion, always spoken with the authoritative intonation of Paul Harvey reading the news on the radio, made no sense to me. I just didn't believe it. Vicky Martinez had already proved to me that Catholics were people, too, and not monsters. Rome would have had a hard time controlling Vicky, so I couldn't imagine the Pope telling the president what to do. Tom benefited from Vicky's unconscious presence in my life.

Without knowing any other Mennonite Kennedy supporters, I felt I was going out on a limb to join Tom Caskey on the JFK side of the debate. But a *little* danger was beginning to be my specialty. I enjoyed skating close to thin ice while wearing a covering on my head.

Now it's true that Tom was cute. I liked looking at him. But neither one of us would have considered the other romantic material. Tom appealed to me in somewhat the same way as had Ivan, the boy with the tractor, in second grade. Tom was outside the mainstream, and I wanted to stand out there with him. I thought he might like company. I kept gravitating to situations that called for the outsider's perspective.

During the debate itself, I talked about the importance of separation between church and state. During my instruction class prior to baptism the previous summer, I had heard that my ancestors in Europe had died supporting that idea, among others. Whenever I could make a connection to my tradition, I got excited. I made the simple analogy between Anabaptists then and Catholics now.

My classmates did not look impressed, but Tom looked grateful. I was happy for his smile. I wish I could tell you that we won the debate, but the score doesn't stick in my memory. It evidently didn't matter as much as Tom himself and the pride I took in my own tradition's contribution to one central idea of our democracy.

On election night my parents stayed up all night listening to the returns on the radio. In the morning, they were both tired and discouraged. I felt sorry for them when I heard Kennedy had won, but I didn't feel sorry for myself. I wasn't worried. I wanted this new young president to prove my parents wrong, and I thought he could do it.

On January 20, 1961, the torch was passed from the then oldest president (Eisenhower was seventy) to the youngest (Kennedy was forty-three). I listened to the inauguration on the kitchen radio, my back toward the window, Daddy on my left and Mother across from me. Though I had wanted Kennedy to win in 1960, I never felt comfortable being too oppositional to my parents. What I really wanted, and have wanted in every election since, was to help them see why I was attracted to the other party. I listened to the inauguration, hoping to hear something that would not only excite me but also comfort them.

When I heard the words "Ask not what your country can do for you . . . ," I looked up beaming. Kennedy was talking about humility and self-sacrifice and service! How many times had we heard sermons on these topics? Surely these words would touch and reassure my parents! Their faces seemed to relax a little.

The speech only lasted sixteen minutes, but the language sank into my spirit like footprints in soft clay. Kennedy's words—so carefully chosen for their rhythmic cadence, alliteration, parallelism, metaphor, and surprising yet satisfying juxtapositions—stirred me deeply. At the time I could not have named these signs of verbal artistry, but I could feel them in my heart. I heard the speech many times and decided to make Kennedy my hero. I wanted to be one of the "new generation" he spoke about. I also hoped to move people with words the way he did. I could see myself standing on a large stage some day.

In the months that followed, fear and elation gripped the country simultaneously. Multiple generations moved out of the stability of the '50s into the unknown future under an untested leader. A nuclear cloud was still hanging over the world.

But instead of dealing directly with the underlying fears, the country sought diversions. Like most Americans, I loved Jack and Jackie's glittering style. It was funny how nobody talked about the pope anymore as soon as Kennedy was elected.

Instead, we learned about Hyannis Port and French fashion and those darling children, Caroline and John-John.

Like other young people in the country, I devoured newspaper articles about the Kennedys and listened to them speak on the radio. I went around the house saying "Ahsk not, my fellow Americans, what your country chan do for you. Ahsk what you chan do for your country." I wondered what it felt like to glide through a room like Jackie Kennedy did, speaking in a near whisper and wearing a stunning bouffant hairdo atop lovely shift dresses in pastel colors.

That spring of 1961, the national political scene was exciting, but the real action in my life happened locally. My father had hatched the idea that I might join the 4-H Club and go into the capon business.

"What's a capon?" I had asked my father when he mentioned the plan.

"A desexed rooster," was his reply. I never asked what that meant, because I sensed that if the answer had the word *sex* in it, our conversation could turn into the same far more specific type my mother and I had had several years earlier while we sorted eggs in the basement. I simply memorized his answer and let the subject drop, but I agreed to my father's capon proposal for 4-H.

The birds arrived one day in cardboard containers shaped like elongated hatboxes. The little chicks were desperately scratching the cardboard, trying to stick their necks out of the air holes. The furry little fellows—or "used-to-be fellers"—jumped to freedom as soon as the lids were taken off the boxes.

Since the capons were my 4-H project, it was up to me to keep them fed, dry, aerated, and ambulatory; record their expenses; and eventually sell them. My father gave me a red hard-cover ledger just like the one he kept in the desk drawer and showed me how to make debit and credit entries. Going into the capon business didn't seem like hard work compared to milking cows or gathering and sorting eggs.

There was one task, however, that both fascinated and sickened me. Our capons arrived soon after their castrating surgery. Since the operation involved making an incision to extract the little testicle kernels, capons all suffered a bit of sensitivity in the belly region. Occasionally, some of them got completely bloated with air, a horror for which the antidote was a razor blade. After feeding my birds, I would look for suspicious obesity in my flock. If I saw a drunken trot, I would reach out and grab the furry belly. If it felt like a miniature beach ball, I took my razor to the tautly stretched skin and made a small puncture. After a little gasp, the belly would flatten against its backbone in my hands.

My parents were going through this capon business for the first time also. They were in their mid-thirties, much younger even than the youngest president of the United States. The advantage of our collective youth was that any adventure one of us had, all of us had. The project itself had been my father's idea. My mother liked it because she could use the poultry-dressing skills she had learned from her own mother during the hard years of the Great Depression and World War II.

The pinnacle of the year for 4-H Club capon kids came when our birds reached maturity and were ready to go to their reward. An event called a Round-Up allowed us to compete for prizes and to sell three of our best specimens. Other 4-H members talked about how much fun they had had at previous Round-Ups. We would butcher the capons the day before, carefully pick the best ones, chill them overnight, and take them to Lancaster the next morning.

Or so we thought. On Tuesday morning, just as I was preparing to leave the house for the school bus, we got a call from a neighbor, also a 4-H member, who offered to take me and my capons to the Round-Up, sparing my parents the need to drive. Had this call not tipped us off, we would have missed the Round-Up completely. Somehow, we all thought the date was Thursday.

I could tell by the horrified look on my mother's face and the way she raced to the refrigerator to check the date for Round-Up that something had gone terribly wrong with our plan. She thanked the neighbor and said I would be ready to go with them when they arrived at 11:30—four hours from now! She hung up.

Then my usually genial, often submissive mother drew herself up to her full five feet three inches of height and began belting out orders like a major general: "Richard, get the axe. Then go find the fattest birds with the straightest breastbones. I'll start boiling the water." Within a half hour, three unfortunate fowl had been selected and beheaded, flopping around the barnyard like, well . . . like chickens with their heads cut off.

Then came an unceremonial dunk in scalding water. The heat made the skin soft and the feathers easier to pluck. The downy ones on the belly and back peeled off like the skin of a ripe peach. The wing feathers were much tougher and had to be extracted one or two at a time. We "singed" the birds over a flame in a pie pan to take off remaining feathers, creating an acrid odor of slightly burned flesh. Mother searched for pinfeathers—the new little ones that remained behind if you did not get a clean pull—and pounced on them with a paring knife until the whole surface of the bird was smooth.

The feet were cut off at the joint, not the bone. Then came the amazing cut of the lower abdomen and the complete disembowelment, followed by one great sucking sound as my mother reached the whole way into the bird's body cavity and pulled out the steaming innards. Great care had to be taken to get the liver and not the bile duct. Mother knew exactly how to cut the gizzard open so that she could take out the grit with just one skillful tug of the lining. Then the clean liver, gizzard, and neck went back inside the bird. Most of the fat was removed, but not so much that the prized virtue of the capon, moistness in baking, would be lost.

By eleven o'clock, we had finished the job and now had to figure out how to cool down the still-warm birds. My mother did her best with an ice water bath for fifteen minutes but still had to dry them, put them in plastic bags, suck all the air out with her mouth, and put them in a cardboard box. The birds looked good to us, but we knew they were not chilled the way they should have been.

"Put your ear down low," my father teased. "You can still hear them squawk!"

My mother placed the box of birds in my hands.

"Well, Shirley," she said, "have a good time. But don't set your heart on winning anything!"

The Kiwanis Club met in a hotel that seemed very grand to me. The twenty-one 4-H members all looked a little nervous at the fancy luncheon. The food was good but different from both our farm fare and the school cafeteria. I inspected the first hard roll I'd ever encountered and considered putting the whole thing into my mouth before I saw the doctor sitting beside me break his open and spread butter on it.

While we were being royally entertained, a man in a black suit was busy judging our capons. I watched him furtively out of the corner of my eye. His method was to keep moving sets of three up and down the table. When I saw my three lonely birds at the end of the line, I felt disappointment. Then I remembered

Capons in the trunk, ready for delivery to customers. This photo was taken by my brother Henry later than this story occurred (about 1965), after many Hersheys had won 4-H championships.

my mother's warning, so I turned my attention to cherry pie, ice cream, and the treasurer's report.

Soon the time came to announce the winners. The man in the black suit came to the podium and congratulated all the 4-Hers on their excellent projects, declaring it a very difficult job to pick the winners. I tucked this speech away as something to tell my parents when I shared the news that we had come in last. Then the man strode to the end of the table and walked back to the podium—with my three capons! Until he spoke my name as recipient of the first prize, I still could not believe that the last had become first. I flushed bright red, walked up to the front, had my picture taken with the judge, and returned to my seat. I sat there dazed as other prizes were handed out. The neighbor who brought me, and who knew those birds had had their breakfast this morning just like the rest of us, winked at me.

It only got better from there. Round-Up included not only judging but also selling. The Kiwanians loved to outbid each other for the prizewinner, so by the time I left Lancaster, I had sold my three capons for sums I could hardly believe. The going rate for the best capons was 60 cents a pound, but the competition took the price to more than $1 a pound for these three. I

Lancaster *Intelligencer* newspaper photograph. 1960–61 school year. I'm a plain seventh grader witnessing the judge pointing out the straight breast and even skin tones of my plump, prizewinning capon.

opened my hand for the $32 given to me by the president of the club. I tried to repress my delight, but it must have oozed out around the edges of my smile.

"Enjoy," the man said, his eyes twinkling.

I could hardly wait to tell my parents the whole story in great detail. I knew their amazement would be even more pronounced than my own—and it was. I walked in the door waving the cash while they dropped everything to hear the whole story from beginning to end. I didn't feel "plain," and neither did they.

The next day I climbed on the school bus, headed to Manheim Central Junior High, spirit still soaring from one magical encounter with the glittering world. But when my math teacher asked me, newspaper clipping in hand, what a capon was, I said immediately "a de-sexed rooster."

And then, wouldn't you know, I blushed.

Thirteen

Rosy Cheeks

The race is not to the swift, nor the battle to the strong. . . .
but time and chance happeneth to them all.

—Ecclesiastes 9:11

*W*hat is more exciting and terrifying to a twelve-year-old than the move from elementary school to junior high? Moving from one home to another and to a second junior high school—all in the same year.

In the fall of 1960, Mother and Daddy announced to Henry, Sue, Doris (my newest sister, a toddler), and me that we were buying the farm where Daddy was born, the farm we had called "Grandpa's House." It would soon become known to us and the whole Hershey family as the Home Place.

Like the teenager I was fast becoming, I reacted to this news through one lens—the impact on me. The new friends I had made at Manheim Central Junior High wouldn't be able to come with me. I would have to start all over again. Not only that, I'd have to start at the end of the school year (we moved in March 1961) after all the other kids in the new school had found their friends.

Even though I knew my parents had been searching for a good farm to buy, I wasn't prepared for my first conscious experience of uprooting. There was a going-away party for me at school. A teacher, who had written a note on my report card saying "very careless work in English," attended the party and smiled forgivingly at me.

My classmates sang, "From this valley they say you are going.

Moving day, Spahr farm, 1961. Uncle Ken's truck was our moving van. Family and church members were our movers.

We will miss your bright eyes and sweet smile. . . ." Tears salted my eyes as I said goodbye. I knew then, rightly, that I would never see most of these people again.

When I got home, there were trucks in the front yard and people everywhere. The huge, rambling, yellow and brown house would be filled by some other family, and the barn would shelter their animals and equipment. Ours were going with us to Lititz! All of a sudden, the focus was on the future, not the past.

Lititz was only six miles away geographically, but emotionally it stretched me much farther. In a few days, I stood on the threshold of my new school at the end of West Orange Street. It was even bigger than the old high school at Manheim Central, and this school was truly new, not only for me. It had been built just a few years earlier and included both junior high and high school. Warwick was the name, after Warwick Township, which included the town of Lititz and several miles of farmland on either side. The name Warwick likely came from the original place name in England, as had Lancaster as well as nearby York and Chester Counties.

I walked half a mile each morning to the bus stop across from Spruce Villa Dairies on the Brunnerville Road. Everything seemed strange. New. Different. Most of the time that was a good thing. I liked adventure.

My homeroom and history teacher was Richard Pohner. The class was studying world history and used the same textbook we had at Manheim Central. On my first day in class, Mr. Pohner uttered the dreaded words "Take out a sheet of paper," a sure sign that an unannounced quiz was about to be popped.

I asked if I should take the quiz. Mr. Pohner said, "Sure. Let's see what you're made of." Now it just so happened that I had read that portion of the text already at Manheim Central. I scored very well, and Mr. Pohner made a big deal out of it.

From this single event, my new classmates began a rumor: "Did you hear? The new girl, the plain one, is a brain!"

Clearly, at Warwick, such a designation was a good thing. If you were a brain at Warwick, you were somebody, and it was okay to let your little light shine. When Bill Pezick in the class ahead of us became a National Merit Scholarship recipient, everyone walked a little taller, just as we did when his classmate Joe Carl led the school to basketball championships all the way to regional play-offs. People actually wanted to be on the honor roll and in the National Honor Society. And, thus, a new Shirley emerged.

From day one, I had a reputation to live up to, one I hoped to maintain. So I took stacks of books home with me every night. I kept little tallies in my notebook of my grade-point averages. I burned with a desire to be intellectual and cultured, even though I barely knew what either of those two words meant.

Having quickly enhanced my intellectual reputation with the quiz, I soon found myself facing a new test. This one was social. At Warwick, if a student had a birthday, someone in the cafeteria would start singing the birthday song and soon several hundred students would join in. One of the students in my class got it into her head to sing "Happy Birthday" to me, knowing it was not my birthday. As the room began to fill up with the sound of singing, I debated what to do. Was this an attempt to embarrass the new girl, confuse her, make fun of her? I had about ten seconds to figure out what to do. Hide? Cry? Try to ignore the incident? Smile weakly? Sing along as if to someone else? My cheeks started to burn.

On impulse, I sprang to my feet and took a deep bow. The girl who started the singing was surprised and cracked up. I laughed along with my new classmates. I had to do the bowing thing a few more times, as though I were the pet parrot of the school. After a while, the novelty wore off as I got past the initiation stage. I was soon a Warwick Warrior, an odd name for a pacifist Mennonite. By then, I was used to oddities.

Gym class in the new school was the surprising setting for my next turning point. Gym was always a bit problematic for junior high students in the early '60s, especially girls, what with cotton bloomers that had to be washed, ironed, and inspected every week. Group showers with a gaggle of other giggly girls whose bodies were in various stages of puberty made all of us nervous. Instead of playing sports, which I loved, we often did drills and calisthenics, which I hated, even when accompanied by the fun, silly "Go you chicken fat, go!"

Our teacher was Miss Joan Riehl. She had a very gruff, almost army-sergeant style. She loved to tell each of us to get up off the "gluteus maximus" and out onto the field. She confused me because to me she sounded Amish, as though English were her second language. She had a very heavy Pennsylvania Dutch accent, stronger than anyone I had ever known, with the exception of the radio announcer we listened to in the cow stable every morning on *The Jack Haines Show*.

But Miss Riehl was not Amish. She had short hair framing her perfectly round face. She was slim and fit. I wasn't used to someone who sounded "plain" but looked "fancy." She upset my categories, and that interested me.

I wasn't used to a woman who barked orders and who made up nicknames for her students. Before long, she had given me the moniker that stuck with me throughout high school whenever she was around, "Rosy Cheeks." Oh, how I hated it. Or at least I pretended to—as a plain girl infatuated with fancy. It reminded me of everything I was but wished I wasn't. Soon everyone in the school, even other teachers, picked up the nickname.

I was "pleasingly plump" with round cheeks that went with rounded hips and breasts and strong arms and calves from carrying milk and tossing hay bales. My feet were wide, my fingers thick. I wanted to be as thin as Jackie Kennedy, wear rings on my long fingers with painted nails, and dangle a slim ankle showing off Italian leather pumps.

"Rosy Cheeks" also made me even more self-conscious at a time when I was hoping to turn my attention elsewhere. My cheeks burned the moment I was embarrassed or uncertain or angry, all of which were feelings I wanted to hide. I wanted to control my body with my mind and deal with my emotions privately before they went public.

The fact that Miss Riehl had given me this name saved me. I took secret delight in being singled out by her. Despite her accent and her gruffness, I liked Miss Riehl a lot. And I really wanted her to like me. In fact, I sensed that she did. Though she didn't say so directly, I imagined a bubble above her head, like in the cartoons, that said: "That girl is going to go somewhere, and I am going to help her."

Whether or not Miss Riehl said those words or anything even similar, I began to look for reasons to hang around her. And when I was with her, I began to be very conscious of where her gaze was. Once, in the locker room, as the gaggle of girls was waiting for the bell to ring, I felt her watching me. I did not return her look but instead acted as though I were listening to the chatter of my classmates, smiling benignly but not engaging them.

"I wonder what she is thinking about me?" was the question in my mind. I wanted her attention to be a singular circle of light around me, and in that moment I felt it was.

That year, in phys ed, we ran the fifty-yard dash. Miss Riehl held a stopwatch in one hand and a grade book in the other. We would take turns running the race individually, starting at the sound of her whistle. When my turn arrived, I focused hard on listening for that whistle and took off the instant I heard it, running my heart out. Miss Riehl looked at the time of 6.5 seconds and then looked directly at me, her eyes smiling.

"You ate your Wheaties today, Rosy Cheeks," she said.

By June of 1961, I had made my first lap around the junior high track. I had returned to the place of my ancestors and staked a claim to a different identity with the help of new teachers and friends.

I was far from finished, but I had started the race.

The Home Place

We come and go, but the land is always here.
And the people who love it and understand it are
the people who own it—for a little while.

—Willa Cather, *O Pioneers!*

hat is it about land that evokes our greatest longings?
What does it know that we can only dream of?
My ancestors from the Palatinate in southwestern Germany
traveled across the Atlantic Ocean in tiny eighteenth-century
boats to Philadelphia. Upon their arrival and settlement, did
the land groan? Did it rejoice? Did it know that the compelling
dream of a Peaceable Kingdom in Pennsylvania would eventually lead to war, even if William Penn and other Quakers and
Mennonites did not participate?

Did this land grieve for its first peoples, who were known
variously as Susquehannocks, Lenape, Iroquois, and Conestogas
and who lived in longhouses built close to springs? Did the land
protest as these people gave up their hunting grounds to those
sturdy Swiss-Germans who cleared the trees to plow and plant?

These kinds of thoughts didn't occur to me until our family
actually owned the Home Place and until I was old enough to
hear Pete Seeger on the radio, singing "This land is your land,
this land is my land." Few others took his broad view of land
ownership. The 1950s were not years of reflection about possible
limitations to American culture and power. In fact, the myth of
Manifest Destiny that justified European dominance over all
the land was expanded to its cultural height in this period by

147

Hollywood and television. John Wayne movies on the big screen and the Lone Ranger on the small one filled Americans with dreams of rugged individualism that wiped out responsibility for many injustices committed by settlers against Native Americans.

In elementary school, we played Cowboys and Indians, never Indians and Cowboys. All things western glittered, and the new mass media found many ways to dangle western status symbols in front of children. I wanted all of it: fringed leather shirt, cowboy hat, six shooter, BB gun, boots. I got none of them. They were not appropriate toys for pacifist Mennonites. Except the hat. I did get a hat! And my brother did get a bow and a set of arrows, which we enjoyed shooting into straw bales. We could pretend to be Indians on our own land, the land that long ago was theirs.

Later, sitting in tree limbs or walking barefoot through the creek of the Home Place, I imagined the sighs of people of ages past, even long before my immigrant ancestors. I looked for their arrowheads in plowed rows but never found any. Something

Linda Weidman, Marshall Weidman, Henry, and me at Roadside America, a tourist attraction located an hour north of our home. Possibly because we were with our non-Mennonite neighbors, we all got western hats. Great day, about 1954!

about abundant space produces the sense that time, also, is infinite, long, and deep.

When I felt most connected to the land, I would feel both inarticulate and inspired. I sang "How Great Thou Art" to the trees, hoping they would carry my feelings up to God. I was grateful that, for a little while at least, our family would be the caretakers of this place.

My father once explained how the early Mennonite settlers had selected the land. "This is limestone soil," he said to me once, picking up a handful of dirt and letting it seep through his fingers. The stones lying in the fields told the first farmers that the soil would be good. Their practiced eyes, honed sharp by years of toil in Switzerland or Southern Germany, attracted them to fertility.

The walnut trees were another sign. So, too, the abundant creeks and springs. The land's relative flatness made it easy to till once the forests were cleared. The Swiss-Germans were reminded of home. Only the mountains were missing.

When our family arrived in 1961, the farm had been owned by three generations of Snyders and three generations of Hersheys. We children were fated to be the sixth generation to till the soil in this place.

The Home Place farmhouse. Now Forgotten Seasons Bed & Breakfast, www.forgottenseasons.com. Note open arch cellar door.

On the top of the hill stood gravestones so old that we could not read the lettering on them. The iron fence sagged in places, and tree roots upended some of the stones. The dead hardly ever entered our minds. What wisdom might they have whispered to the fathers? To the sons?

My grandfather D. Paul Hershey was born on Walnut Springs Farm, just a mile west from what would become his own farm, which we would later call the Home Place. When Grandpa and Daddy were negotiating over the sale of the Home Place in 1960, Grandpa was also carrying out his duties as the executor of his father Henry Hershey's estate. Great-Grandpa Henry had died on January 13 of that year. It's easy to imagine that Grandpa felt squeezed by Henry Huber Hershey (his father) on the one hand and Henry Richard Hershey (his son and my father) on the other. My grandfather was hoping for an inheritance, of course. That was how many farmers were able to continue through bad seasons as well as good ones. However, after his father died, he was not happy with the amount of inheritance he received nor with the unequal amount of support the ten children had received from their father.

At the age of twelve, I only picked up on the undertones of these feelings. I didn't know the details of the estate settlement disputes, but I understood that my grandfather was angry with several of his siblings, especially his two brothers. Unable to collect on his father's debts, my grandfather, Paul, felt bitter. He was so upset he wasn't able to take communion at church. Twice a year before the serious communion services all members had to peruse their hearts to see whether they were "at peace with God" and their "fellow men." If you denied your feelings, pretended to a peace you did not feel, you risked "drinking damnation" unto yourself. Better not to take communion at all than to lie about the state of your heart.

I remember Grandpa standing in front of the congregation on a Sunday morning, confessing that he harbored anger against his brother. The meetinghouse at Lititz was the only one he ever attended. His Uncle Jacob, brother of Henry Huber Hershey, had been the minister there in his youth. Grandpa deeply respected the teachings of the church, but he was also a proud and stubborn man, totally focused on his version of a story.

Seeing my own grandfather confess his sin of anger in church, yielding his pride and his will for the sake of peace, had a powerful effect on me. When I participated in my first preparatory service about the same time and was asked, "Are you at peace with God and your fellow men?" I felt the gravity of the question and scanned my own heart thoroughly.

Every agricultural society has tried to solve the dilemma of how to pass land from one generation to another and has done so imperfectly. *Primogeniture*, the passing of land from father to eldest son, was an old and powerful tradition brought over from feudal Europe. In fact, primogeniture was a major force in the settlement of the colonies, often by younger sons seeking opportunities to become landowners like their elder brothers. In the New World, it was more pronounced in the South, where the landholders had larger estates, made possible in part by the institution of slavery.

Mennonites, both in Europe and in early Lancaster County, were yeoman farmers. They had learned how to woo the land and make her happy to receive the plow, taking full advantage of all she could produce, husbanding and harvesting and passing their skills down from generation to generation. Becoming self-sufficient on several hundred acres of land, or even less, allowed Mennonites to remain relatively separated from the rest of the world. Their theology and their livelihoods found harmony with each other.

As the eldest son, Daddy would have been happy with the idea of primogeniture, and he overtly envied any of his friends who had their farms given to them.

While my grandfather struggled with feelings of injustice toward his brothers, my father was searching for land to call his own. During the years 1956 to 1960, Mother and Daddy combed the "For Sale" sections of *Lancaster Farming, Hoard's Dairymen,* and any other sources they could find. I remember trips to other places in Lebanon County and even more remote places in western Pennsylvania and New York. The search was on for one hundred acres that could produce enough to sustain twenty dairy cows and ten acres of tobacco, the two biggest sources of our income. Several times my parents thought they had purchased a property only to have someone else outbid them.

Finally, in a conversation shortly after Great-Grandpa Henry Hershey's death, my father told his father about a new farm he was considering in Lebanon County. Much to Daddy's surprise, Grandpa blurted out, "I know someone who has a farm you could rent."

"Who?" asked Daddy.

"Me," said Grandpa.

Daddy was surprised that Grandpa would even think about turning over his farm at age sixty. But at age thirty-five himself, Daddy didn't want to work for his father again. He wanted to be his own boss. He wanted to call the shots. He wanted the farmer's dream. And he said so. He didn't want to rent. He wanted to buy.

After thinking things over and talking with Grandma (after all, it had been her father's and then her mother's farm), Grandpa said he was willing to sell.

Daddy was immediately both surprised and thrilled. He knew how fertile the land was. He also suspected that the location so close to Lititz could some day make the land valuable, although back in 1960 no one could have predicted the land rush of the 1990s. In addition, Daddy felt the presence of his Snyder family ancestors buried in the hilltop graveyard. Yes! He wanted this land! All 103 acres of it.

The first price they talked about was somewhere around $65,000. The farms on which my parents had bid were more in the $40,000–$50,000 price range, so $65,000 seemed like a stretch. The average price of farms and all their buildings according to the USDA was $165 per acre in 1960.[40] The average

40. "U.S. Farm Real Estate Values, 1950–2011 USDA/NASS," included in Ron Plain, "Historic Land Values and the 1970s Land Price Bubble," Slideshow, University of Missouri Extension, Slide #3, 2012.

price per acre of farmland in Lancaster County was between $400 and $500. Grandpa's was a better-than-average farm, but how much better?

Now here's where things got sticky. Grandpa, fresh off his sense of inadequate inheritance, feeling like a cheated sibling, wanted to be fair to *all* six of his children. Since he was the fifth child and second son, he did not identify with the position of eldest son. He had been angry with his own elder brother. He also was more solicitous of his daughters than were many farm patriarchs. Grandpa wanted his girls to get an inheritance. And then there was his youngest child, Mark, also a son, fifteen years younger than Daddy and the apple of my grandfather's eye. How could he be fair to Mark?

Despite his expectations of hard work done well and despite his gruffness, Grandpa wanted to treat all his children better than he felt his father had taken care of him. Although my father failed to appreciate the effort, my grandfather succeeded in his goal of eventually giving every child some financial inheritance. In this regard, Grandpa was aided by the quiet peacemaking of my grandmother, Sue. Since she managed to convince *all* her children they were loved, Grandma Sue stood between Daddy and Grandpa as a buffer. Daddy adored her and Grandpa depended on her to never cross him.

Here's the story about the sale that Daddy told me many times. He thought he was going to get the chance to buy the farm at what he thought was the highest price he could afford, $65,000. One day soon after Daddy thought they had agreed on a price, Grandpa "roared up the driveway in his Oldsmobile," demanding that the price had to be $70,000 or no sale. He had talked to all the other children and they had agreed that Richard could buy the farm, but Grandpa had decided that in order to be fair to the others, the price had to be higher than the price the two had discussed earlier.

After Daddy agreed to the price (made possible by my Grandpa Hess who had given my mother a downpayment, a gift that caused Daddy to revere him thereafter), the mortgage terms presented a new arena for disagreement. Grandpa agreed to hold the mortgage at the going rate banks were charging. That way Daddy could avoid dealing with bankers, as he might not have had enough collateral for a loan of that size.

You would think Daddy might have been grateful for those terms, but, sure enough, every time Grandpa bought a new car or took a trip, Daddy's jaw tightened. Even if he controlled his words most of the time, you could almost hear him thinking, There goes my blood, sweat, and tears.

Moving back to the Home Place from our sharecropping arrangement on the Spahr farm replicated a pattern of previous family land transfers. We had left the Home Place in 1949 when I was nine months old. When we returned, I was thirteen. As we moved in, Grandma and Grandpa moved out, to a house on Second Avenue in Lititz. Great Grandma Snyder had also moved to town after Paul and Sue bought the farm. That transition seemed to have gone smoothly, but ours in 1961 hit some rough spots.

Throughout the years of my father's youth, and before his marriage in 1947, he and Grandpa had tussled emotionally and verbally many times. Because Daddy never felt that his hard work on the farm in his youth was appreciated, he bore the sting of many reproofs, especially this one: "You're not worth the salt in your soup!" The boy in the man would carry these words all his life.

Another grievance Daddy carried came from the time in his late teen years when he had an accident with his car on an icy road. He walked home in the bitter cold. The next morning, Grandpa refused to help him pull the car out of the ditch. "It's your car. It's your problem."

Land ownership has been the cause of war and heartache throughout the centuries. Some families pass land from generation to generation and handle disputes over inheritance well, but many do not now and did not in the past. The Mennonite

Church forbade lawsuits[41] because they were viewed as a form of coercion to be avoided by nonresistant Christians. The absence of lawsuits did not guarantee the presence of peace, however. Between my father and my grandfather, the fur sometimes flew furiously while at other times a chilly silence took the place vacated by trust.

As I got older, I observed conflict growing between Daddy and Grandpa. Their Oedipal struggle reached out like an octopus and wrapped its sticky tentacles around our whole family, especially Mother and Grandma Hershey.

From 1961 until 1975—when Daddy sold his cows, got out of the dairy business, and, most importantly, paid off the mortgage to Grandpa—they disagreed on almost every issue of the sale, whether the original price was high or low, and continued to include arguments over property boundary and interest rates.

When at Christmas time Grandpa was generous with us grandchildren, offering us peppermint gum from the fragrant drawer in his rolltop desk and silver dollars as gifts, Daddy had a hard time rejoicing along with us. We loved Grandpa Hershey! And the more we did, the more Daddy chafed. In his mind, he had paid dearly for his children's and siblings' inheritances.

In the end, of course, Daddy was wrong about the injustice. The farm would become valuable beyond his imagining. He would die in 1980, several years before his elderly parents, and thus was spared one more round of bitterness over the settling of his parents' estate.

In the six months that preceded Daddy's death from the rare disease scleroderma, he had time to reevaluate what was important in his life. He and Grandpa found peace with each other at the last. They didn't have the kind of verbal exchange

---

41. "Suing at law and taking the bankruptcy law for personal advantage or revenge are violations of Scripture and are not permitted." *Statement of Christian Doctrine and Rules and Discipline of the Lancaster Conference of the Mennonite Church,* adopted July 17, 1968.

of forgiveness the women in their lives hoped for, but they did let go of their mutual resentments. In his last months, Daddy stopped adding up debits and credits in the ledger of his relationships, even in his most troubled one, with his father.

Had this not happened, I might still be carrying Daddy's pain, his resentment against Grandpa, something I did unconsciously from adolescence until early adulthood. I was thirty-one when he died. Having been his confidante in life, I felt called to be a peacemaker as he lay dying, working along with other members of my family to locate the place where all of us could say that we are "at peace with God and our fellow men."

After Daddy's death, Mother managed the property, renting it to a fine young farmer. She struggled to pay taxes and maintain the many buildings and dairy according to the exacting standards of other Lancaster County farms. After eleven years, she decided to sell the Home Place. Thanks to cooperation between my mother, her children, Warwick Township, the Mennonite Foundation, and the developer Gerald Horst, the former farm also now includes a recreational park, a wetland, and a nature preserve. It was difficult to see the farm sell eleven years after Daddy's death. It was hard for all of us to say goodbye to the lush fields and beautiful barn that was the Home Place. With effort, however, we saved the house.

Now a new highway curls between Brunnerville Road and the Lititz Pike, and a housing development greets the traveler, spread out over the acres where corn and alfalfa used to grow.

The meadow across the road from the house, the setting in my mind for the magic elevator story, remains. The barn does not, but Amish workers pulled apart enough of the original limestone, gathered from the fields in the 1730s, to build a beautiful new home on the hill. While the land is no longer a farm, the barn stones are still in use in other buildings, and acres of woods, trails, meadow, and recreational area are now shared with the entire town of Lititz.

Now that the Home Place no longer exists as a farm, my lenses have taken on the same rosy nostalgic film of others whose farms are "lost" today. My mother gave the house to the Mennonite Foundation, which sold it to Dale Groff, a local self-taught historian who, along with his wife Suzanne, turned it into a bed and breakfast called Forgotten Seasons. In 2008 the Groffs sold the house to Jay and Kathy Wenger, conservative Mennonites, who look and sound much like the Lancaster Conference Mennonites of my childhood.

The history of the house has never been more alive. The Wengers are now restoring the original stone under a layer of 1940s Formstone. Members of our extended Hershey family have enjoyed a new kind of hospitality at the Home Place. And hundreds of tourists have learned some of the stories it holds.

The strivings of my father and grandfather have been laid to rest. Their graves are just a few feet apart from each other in the Hess Mennonite Church cemetery, located a few miles east of the Home Place. On top of the hill, Snyder bones are feeding the roots of the ancient tree in the family plot. Under all of them are the sighs and whispers of the Susquehannock Indians. And in my memory, the Home Place will always look like this.

The Home Place, ca. 1966. My youngest sister Linda is running down the hill on the right.

Dueling with Daddy

Family quarrels are bitter things. They don't accord by any rules. They're not like aches or wounds; they're more like splits in the skin that won't heal . . .

—F. Scott Fitzgerald, "Babylon Revisited"

One Sunday afternoon, very soon after we moved to the Home Place, I saw a new side of my father. We had invited the whole Hershey family over, and I was very excited. My cousin Mary Ann, nine months my senior, was also my best friend. She and I together were the two oldest cousins of what would later become a sea of twenty but was already a little pond of about ten.

Mary Ann and I had a great time exploring my new bedroom in the southwest corner of the house. I had a room to myself, as did Henry, and so did our parents. Sisters Sue and Doris had twin beds in the fourth bedroom. Sister Linda had not yet been born. Amazingly, even when we became a family of five, I never had to share a bedroom. By having a brother after me, and because of the death of Mary Louise, the siblings tended to fall into two groups: Shirley and Henry, and "the girls" who always shared their rooms. Therefore, Mary Ann and I could explore space together unhindered by younger children, which is exactly what teenage girls want.

We investigated the familiar, yet strangely new, house. Our eyes were opened because now, instead of being at Grandpa's house, we were at "my" house, and what a house it was! The walls of colonial-era houses, especially stone houses like ours, bore the weight of the whole structure. This meant that every window sill was two feet thick—a great place to curl up with a book and an amplifier of summer breezes.

The other notable features of the house were Dutch doors, which were hinged separately on top and bottom so that the bottom half could be closed and the top half open. The hinges on all the doors in the house were wrought iron curlicues artistically fashioned by a blacksmith. On the front porch was a bronze plaque from the Lancaster Historical Society honoring this place for its role in the establishment of the town of Lititz.

Mary Ann and I took the tour of the house that our family would give often, pointing out the original sheepskin deed, hanging on the wall, that had been signed by William Penn's three sons.

Outside, the four stately trees stood like sentries, two oaks in the back and two sycamores in the front. Not only did they provide a canopy of shade, the oaks also rained down acorns in the fall, and the sycamores gave up their bark. We grandchildren had always found the trees entertaining when we visited. Now I saw that all that exfoliation would turn out to be work also. Everything I looked at on this "new old" place brought up new questions, new possibilities.

Mary Ann loved to go for walks along the country roads where she lived, so she suggested the two of us explore the territory surrounding the farm that was now my home. Even though Mary Ann knew the Home Place almost as well as I did, my rediscovery of it with her led to a shivery sense of adventure. I now had a second pair of eyes, a new sensibility, to magnify the thrill of mutual reinvention of familiar places

We walked out the Dutch doors and past the sycamore trees, going by the horse heads made of lead and painted silver to match the fence, the very same horse heads used as hitching posts when the Home Place was Jacob Hoober's Tavern.

Both of us knew that Count Nikolaus Ludwig von Zinzendorf had preached in that tavern in 1742.[42] Both of us had heard sto-

---

42. More information about Zinzendorf, including the story of his missionary journey through the colonies and the wording on the historical marker, can be found at the Forgotten Seasons website: http://www.forgottenseasons.com/

ries about him. The Hershey family was proud of the fact that this house predated the Revolutionary War and was the site of a religious conversion that led to the establishment of the town of Lititz as a Moravian community. As Mary Ann and I headed across the porch to the road, we paused to read again the historical bronze plaque on the front of the house.

We started on Newport Road and then meandered up Snyder Hill Road, named for our Snyder ancestors, talking about our usual girl subjects: which boys were cute and what was happening in school.

We were on our way home when my father came roaring up the road in the car, slammed on the brakes, and shouted to us to get inside. Stunned and confused, heads bowed, we crawled in.

"I never want you to go out on these roads again without getting permission," he yelled. "You're lucky no one else tried to pick you up before I did." I was sorry Mary Ann had to witness his anger; I was sure that her own mild-mannered father would never talk the way mine just did.

Though I loved the farm itself, I didn't like the effect that buying the farm had on my parents, especially Daddy. At some preconscious, preverbal, level, I sensed that we were living the drama of Exodus 34:6-7: "The sins of the fathers will be visited unto the children into the third or fourth generation." Given this biblical promise, I wondered what effect Daddy's struggle with his daddy and his daddy with his daddy would have on the rest of us.

These are the kinds of things I noticed: When the larger Hershey family got together several times a year, my father didn't play the role many eldest sons might have played—that of convening and interacting with everyone, almost like a secondary host. He greeted everyone but seemed eager to take a back seat, remaining more introverted than usual. He also didn't engage much with his one and only, much younger, outgoing brother, Mark, whom my cousin Mary Ann and I idolized.

---

history.html. Many Mennonites recognize him as the author of several beloved hymns, such as "The Lord Is King, O Praise His Name" and "Heart with Loving Heart United."

In contrast, the "girls" in the family, my aunts, all acknowledged each other and their mother the way adults in the church performed the ritual, same-sex, "holy kiss."[43] I observed this custom often from a rocking chair on the porch, watching each aunt approach Grandma Hershey as she gathered them to herself, one at a time, like a hen with her chicks. In the gesture of those serious kisses was great love and respect quite different from the effusive hugs I later saw and envied in other families. It carried a tone of awe for the divine order of things and for the great commandment to love one another as God has loved us.

The Hershey family did everything with a kind of solemnity. They had a natural piety and precision that did not preclude laughter and games but certainly did not encourage frivolity or carelessness. If one of us children went up the staircase touching the wallpaper to the left instead of the handrail to the right, any one of the aunts might quickly help that careless individual reform the habit.

Grandpa, the patriarch, set the tone. Table grace with the Hershey family was different from saying grace in our own home. Grandpa would not pray out loud so that you could hear his words. Nor did he lead in a silent prayer. Instead, he bowed his head, and we all followed suit. Occasionally he picked someone to lead the prayer (never my father, as I recall), but whether words or silence prevailed at the other end of the table, he always did the same thing. He talked to God in a monotone just above a whisper, loud enough for everyone to hear but not clear enough so that we could understand, as though he and God were exchanging secrets. It was most evident at the end of a meal when Grandpa would say, "And now we will return thanks."

Those words were a signal to all the children, typically desperate to leave the table. With our heads bowed for the second

---

43. The "holy kiss" was one of the ordinances of the Lancaster Conference Mennonite Church. "The salutation of the holy kiss should be observed and practiced by the believers, brethren among brethren and sisters among sisters, as an expression of fervent love. It should be practiced when meeting for worship as well as when meeting for social fellowship." *Statement of Christian Doctrine and Rules and Discipline of the Lancaster Conference of the Mennonite Church,* 1968, 16–17.

prayer of the meal, our hands were on our chairs, prepared to push off in a fast getaway. Sometimes, when I sneaked a peak, I could see Grandpa moving his lips in a semi-audible prayer. The older I got, the more tension I felt from my father when he was forced to listen to his father intone gratitude so publicly and fervently.

As my mother and the aunts cleared the table—washing, drying, and putting away the dishes in a flurry of friendly efficiency—Daddy would seek out Uncle Ken. Together they would huddle in a corner, talking about farming: the weather, prices, land sales, Republican politics, and equipment. Grandpa was never in their circle. Neither were the two other uncles who weren't farmers. A third uncle, who might have been included in the farmer corner, lived far away in upper New York State. We didn't visit together very often as a result.

I noticed Daddy's distance from Grandpa not only at family gatherings but also in everyday conversations. One of Grandpa's favorite phrases was "thanks a million." My father recoiled from any expressions of exaggeration and outward excess. His

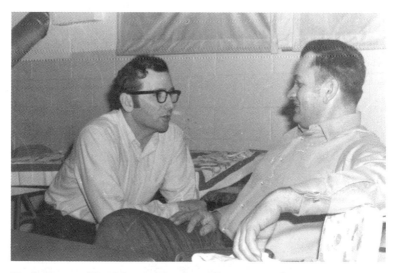

Uncle Ken and Daddy at a Hershey Christmas gathering, in the basement of the house Grandpa and Grandma moved into on Second Avenue in Lititz in 1961. Picture was probably taken in the mid-'60s.

scrupulosity was not just natural shyness. It was also a reaction to something essentially hypocritical he believed he saw in Grandpa. Grandpa's effusiveness with others rubbed salt in Daddy's childhood wound.

Grandpa seemed unable to show his elder son love in ways that Daddy could feel it, yet he always had so much of it to share with little children. In church and at home with grandchildren, Grandpa was the "candy man," distributing peppermint gum sticks, jellied orange slices, and round pink "horse pill" candies. That generosity seemed galling to Daddy. Where was all that abundant love when he had needed it as a child?

After Daddy bought the farm, things went from bad to worse, and they started to affect me. My father's needs and his ideas of what my emerging life should be conflicted with my own, especially with the yearning to control my own destiny. As opposed to many of my friends who struggled with their mothers, I had only minor skirmishes with mine. I wrestled with Mother over details like when to go to the barn for chores or how to fix my hair, but I always felt I could trust her and that in some secret place she wanted me to fly, perhaps even to fly away, for my own good.

I knew she enjoyed every new stage of my life as though she herself were doing these things. Such vicarious energy made me want to reach beyond, to sail for seas she had never explored. I wanted to bring trophies and lay them at her feet, like I did as a child when I offered her bluebells from along the creek banks at the Spahr farm. I even told her about some of my secret teenage crushes.

With my father, it was another story. It seemed as though I actually had two fathers and they split in half just as I was entering my teenage years. I was twelve going on thirteen when we moved from the Spahr farm to the Home Place. When my father perceived his mortgage obligation to be like indentured servitude to his father, little worry lines began to appear around his eyes and mouth, just at the time when my hips and breasts were becoming womanly. What a recipe for hormonally charged turpitude!

Fortunately I could still hear the notes of Daddy's love from my own carefree childhood. Those remembered notes brought me through adolescence when I might have revolted more overtly. Just a few memories from those days were enough to sustain a belief that I was loved, even when my authoritarian father was barking orders at me and my heart was bursting with resentment about my restricted life. I still remembered him as Young Daddy, the man who wanted to bless his children even though he himself was waiting for his own blessing. Daddy under the forebay, a twinkle in his eye, taking his hat off to wipe his brow, cigar smoldering on the windowsill, Chiclets to share in his pocket . . .

One Sunday afternoon, when I was nine and Henry was six, Daddy cleaned off his bedroom dresser top, and, in a spurt of generosity, he decided to give both of us presents. He handed me an old wristwatch. Henry got a round pocket watch. We both pounced eagerly on these gifts. Henry put his watch up to his ear and crowed with delight. It was ticking. After Daddy helped him set it, Henry started walking around, constantly taking the watch out of his pocket to ask everyone in sight if they wanted to know what time it was. I'm not even sure he was old enough to tell time.

I was old enough to be jealous though. My watch was a dud compared to his. All I could do was pretend to tell time, and that was no fun after five minutes. So I sat at the kitchen table and stared really hard at the object before me.

I wondered, What is wrong with you, watch? I decided to treat it like the "scientific" experiments I enjoyed performing in a pretend laboratory made of household items in one of the storage rooms at the back of the Spahr place.

Using a paring knife, I pried open the crystal and pulled the case away from the works inside, staring in amazement at the intricacy of cogs and wheels. I turned the watch over and gazed at the face without glass over it. The tiny brass hands were stuck on 6:30, as though the end had come and time was no more.

I looked closer and closer, trying to penetrate the mystery of the watch. My curiosity was not that of an engineer. I really didn't care *how* it worked, although I found all its parts beautiful and exciting. What I really wanted was to heal it, make it spring back to life again. I wanted a miracle with every fiber of my being.

My fine motor skills were developed well enough for me to touch the hands gently, knowing that it would be easy to break them. As I did, I held the face up to the light and could see the problem. One of the hands had been caught on the other while trying to round the bend past the six. By bending the hand ever so slightly, I was able to free the big hand from the little hand. I carefully replaced the face over the works, set it into the bezel, stopped breathing, and wound the stem. Lifting the watch to my ear, I was rewarded by the sweet music of regular ticking. Jumping up from the table, I ran to find Mother, Daddy, and Henry.

"I fixed it! I fixed it," I cried. Then I told them the story about the hands being stuck and just needing a little adjustment. They were all duly impressed.

"Now *both* our watches work," I declared triumphantly to Henry. His basic good nature made him happy for me.

The band, which was fitted to my father's huge hands, did not fit my smaller wrist. So I asked if we could go to the jewelry store in Lititz on the next trip to town. I wanted a new watchband. A creative jeweler found a way to help me, and for part of fourth grade, I wore a huge watch on my left wrist strapped on by a little mesh watchband.

That was the year I also fancied and then purchased white canvas high-top basketball shoes, cheap knockoffs of the Converse brand I admired. I had my own sense of style, and it had a definite masculine bent, despite the fact that I wasn't allowed to wear pants, jeans, or shorts. I knew some kids snickered at me, but I didn't care. I was willing to risk a little ridicule so that I could keep the gift from Daddy that I myself had fixed and shoes on my feet that made me feel like flying.

Fourth grader Shirley sporting Daddy's old watch with first grader Henry. Spahr farm, 1957.

A year later, 1958, Daddy gave Henry and me gifts again.

I had been riding a bike all over the Spahr farm since I was six years old. I owned a twenty-six-inch, used, two-wheeler, probably purchased at Roots Auction for a few dollars. Certainly no Schwinn Flyer, but it worked. I could pump up the hill to the barn, crank a few fast pedals, and then speed down the driveway with the wind in my hair. I could attach a worn out Old Maid playing card or a worthless baseball card to the fender frame with a clothespin and enjoy the flap-flap sound as it hit each spoke.

Every winter the bike would hibernate in the barn next to Daddy's workbench for protection from the weather. As soon as the sun rose high enough on a March afternoon, I would head to the barn, pulling my musty and slightly rusty bike out of the cobwebs. The smell of oil and chicken feathers and metal and dirt only heightened my sense of anticipation for the first ride of spring. My nostrils expanded along with my heart as I lifted the bike up over wire chicken baskets and random tobacco lathes. Daddy would use the portable air pump to fill up the tires, and off I'd go.

Henry wasn't able to ride my big bike very well, but he was ready to leave training wheels behind, so it was time to find him his own two-wheeler. I was all in favor of him having his own bike. That is, until the day I saw the gorgeous red and black beauty that popped out of the trunk of our car for him. His twenty-four-inch bike might have been a hand-me-down, but it had obviously been much nicer than mine to begin with. It gleamed in the sunshine, and so did my brother's face.

I, on the other hand, suddenly felt deprived. As he and I rode our bikes around the barnyard, I tried to participate in my brother's joy. When we took the bikes back into the barn for the night, however, I looked at them side by side for the first time. I felt almost sick with envy. My bike looked like winter, even without cobwebs. His looked like spring. Even to this day, whenever I smell the combination of new and old life—say, hyacinths and compost—that nauseating feeling of bike-envy pops up in my memory.

Among the treasures I had loved to explore in the area around Daddy's workbench was a collection of paint cans, brushes, and turpentine. So, one day, without asking permission from anyone, I pried open a can with a screwdriver, examined the light blue color, and, right there in the barn, began painting my bike. What happened next I don't recall clearly, except that I do know the bike was a mess. I knew nothing about preparing the bike for paint, how to prevent drips, what kind of paint I needed, or, perhaps most importantly, what to do about the old leaves and chicken feathers that seemed to gravitate toward the wet paint.

Halfway into the project, I began to get scared. My hard work was ruining the bike rather than fixing it. I tried getting rid of the paint with turpentine, but that only resulted in more streaks, drips, and feather attraction. Was I smart enough to go to Daddy and confess my sin? I think I must have, because, amazingly, I remember no wrath, only surprise—perhaps coupled with some hidden amusement. I told him that my bike looked ugly now that Henry had a pretty, newer one. And then I hit pay dirt with what turned out to be magic words: "I think you must love Henry more than me."

Boy, did that sentence hit a nerve. Daddy told Mother. Mother got out the big green book about raising Christian children that she had bought from a traveling salesman. There at the kitchen table, she looked up *envy* and had me read the section. I became contrite.

Daddy, however, did not try theology or psychology or moral stories. He just drove to the hardware store, bought two small cans of paint, one metallic red and the other metallic black. He bought two small brushes, paint remover, and a steel brush. He took the fenders off the bike. He spread newspapers on the ground in the driveway and painted each fender, using Henry's bike as a model. When all the metal was shiny bright and new looking, he compared the two bikes. And then he found a way to make a pinstripe with a pencil on each whitewall tire. Following the line, he painstakingly took a tiny brush dipped in red paint all the way around each whitewall on both sides. The whole process stretched out for several days as he waited for paint to dry. I watched in awe.

"There," he said, after he reassembled the bike and oiled all its parts. "Maybe you'll like this bike better now." He didn't lecture me about never opening up the paint cans without permission. He didn't tell me he loved me as much as he loved Henry. He didn't read the passage about envy in the book. He didn't need to.

In those comparatively relaxed years, Daddy sometimes enjoyed the role of teacher. He came up with creative solutions to his need for more labor as his dairy herd expanded, and he used his authority more like a teacher than a boss. The summer I turned ten was the time I first began "choring" in the cow stable. We had about fifteen Holstein cows that we milked twice daily and other heifers and calves that needed to be fed. Mother had helped Daddy when she wasn't too busy with babies, but after I grew to be five feet tall and weighed almost a hundred pounds, I was old enough to carry milk in buckets fifty yards from one end of the barn to the milk house at the other end.

Daddy wanted me to be motivated to help, rather than just working because I had to. So he bought me a little red journal. No, not the kind Mother used as a diary long ago. Nor the kind I occasionally used to record stories. I had a diary with its own little key and lock for that. This one was a ledger, a smaller version of a journal he kept himself. It was a place to record debits and credits and to see at a glance how the money was accumulating—or fleeing.

What money? Daddy had a plan for that, too. He explained to me that instead of an allowance he would give me 1/100th of each milk check to pay me for my work. If we had a good week, that amount might be as much as four dollars. More typically, it would be two to three dollars. I should save some, give some, and spend some, he advised. I think he suggested saving half and giving 10 percent.

I didn't keep the ledger very long. Nor, alas, did I ever persist in keeping a childhood diary. Still, I felt rich. None of my friends had allowances so large, not even the few farm kids who drove tractors and carried milk. I also felt rich in Daddy's attention and trust, which spelled love. He was treating me like a business partner. I understood at an early age that money doesn't come from trees. On our farm at least, it came from cows. And I wanted this dairy enterprise to succeed.

At age thirty-five, Daddy became Old Daddy to me. I seldom saw Young Daddy again after we moved to the Home Place. At the Spahr farm we were sharecroppers, but I felt abundantly blessed and secure. At the Home Place, we were always pinched, even though the farm was bigger and more productive, and we were landowners.

Whereas I had once been an adoring tagalong daughter in childhood, I now became a tug-of-war combatant at the Home Place. Daddy jerked back hard on my rope after we moved, but I didn't give up. I jerked back in the opposite direction

One place we dueled was in the cow stable. I carried milk morning and evening just like I had done at the Spahr farm. We had more stalls at the Home Place barn, and soon we were milking thirty to forty cows a day, which made our farm one of the larger ones on the Graybill Dairies milk route. That meant the milking process took three or four hours per day from me, not one or two—and much more from Daddy.

In addition to carrying the milk as Daddy poured it out from the stainless-steel milking machine, I had to feed each animal. I would take a book with me in hopes that I could read a few chapters between tasks. Daddy never told me I couldn't read, but he seemed to wait until I opened the book before barking the next order: "Give two scoops of dry feed to Elsie and one to Nancy." Cows in those days had names, not numbers. We all knew them by name and personality. I also knew them because I drew their black and white spots on a grid pedigree diagram, a requirement of the Dairy Herd Improvement Association. The diagrams had to be accurate enough for owners, veterinarians, and buyers to recognize the animal from the hand drawing.

Instead of continuing to issue orders for food all the way down the line of cows, Daddy would often make me wait. Probably he had weighty things on his mind. But I suspected he wanted to drag out the task so that I wouldn't go back to the stack of straw behind the homemade desk in the middle of the stalls and read a few pages of my book. To test my thesis, I started taking my book with me, placing it in the portable feed bin with the pages spread open. Sure enough, as soon as I reached for the book after a lull, a new order would come.

Generally speaking, I enjoyed the many outdoor tasks of farming better than the ones I performed inside the barn. The ones outside allowed me to work on my tan, and even though I didn't watch *American Bandstand* on television, I knew that the coolest teens found ways to acquire a lovely walnut color over as many square inches of their bodies as possible. My own inches were covered by blouses and skirts, but I hiked up the skirts and rolled up the sleeves whenever possible.

As I entered puberty, I began to recognize the double restrictions of both my religion and my gender. Secretly, I found ways to resist the traction that was tightening my choices. I saw clearly that boys could continue roving the world while girls were expected to stay at home, and that plain Mennonite clothing was intended to reinforce the differences even more.

I would sometimes stand in front of the mirror while wearing my white wool blazer and an oxford cloth shirt and one of my brother's ties. I would pull my hair back as tightly as possible, take my covering off, replace it with my father's gray Fedora, and pretend to smoke a cigarette. I imagined myself to be like one of my favorite teachers or one of the popular boys in school. I knew all along it was pretense. I never felt that I was a boy. I just wanted to imagine how boys and men walked in the world. So free and easy. So big. If anyone would have seen my little charade, I would have blushed deeply.

I also read somewhere that it was possible to lower your voice through practice. So I practiced. The song I sang to myself while I worked was this one:

> When Israel was in Egypt's land
> Let my people go!
> Oppressed so hard they could not stand
> Let my people go!
> Go down, Moses,
> Way down in Egypt's land
> Tell old Pharoah
> To let my people go!

When I got to the end of the song, I would switch to a lower key until I could no longer hold the lowest notes on the words "way down." I could get amazingly low. Sometimes I would sing this song for my younger sisters, Sue, Doris, and Linda, to watch their eyes get wide when I nailed a low E note. As for the words of the song, I loved what were then called Negro spirituals. They called to the subversive leader in me.

Then there was that day in July when Mother, Daddy, Henry, and I were hoeing. We grew about ten acres of tobacco as our only cash crop.[44] Since we had purchased the farm, cash was more important than ever. We were beginning the middle stage of the elaborate tobacco planting and harvesting process, whacking out weeds that might otherwise overtake a young tobacco plant or sap its growth. In addition to weeding, we loosened the soil around each plant, helping it to absorb whatever rainfall would come.

Now, however, the sun was frying all living things. I could actually see heat waves forming a mirage in front of me. I began to visualize a tall glass of sweetened tea, made with mint picked from the meadow by my little sisters. Ice cubes were clinking in my imagination. The glass was covered in the kind of cold sweat that was the perfect antidote to the hot sweat on my cheeks.

"Look at this big fella!" my father said. We all turned to see him take off his Eby's Feeds cap, exposing his white forehead in contrast to the dark red of his cheeks. Dangling from his other hand was the plumpest neon-green tobacco worm I had ever seen. It was about three inches long and half an inch wide. As it writhed in Daddy's hand, I felt the little hairs on the back of my neck stand up. We all made faces.

I could tell that Daddy was expecting more reaction, so I briefly considered letting out my best scream but instead decided to try another tack. I pretended to take a scientific interest in

---

44. Growing tobacco was both a tradition and a controversy among Lancaster Conference Mennonites in the 1950s and 1960s. My mother, especially, struggled with the increasing awareness that this crop was harmful to health. After George Brunk's tent revivals, many farmers plowed up or stopped planting tobacco. But not Daddy. He couldn't figure out how to pay off the mortgage without his only reliable cash crop. And he also smoked cigars, another habit Mother lamented. He kept his Muriel cigar boxes and his Chiclets chewing gum in the same spot. But he never smoked in the house.

the little black tentacles under the accordionlike sections of the bright green body. Daddy looked at me observing the worm, so cool and calm. Then he did something rare. He spoke spontaneously, recklessly.

"I'll give you five dollars if you bite this worm in two," he said.

The worm dangling from his outstretched hand that afternoon suddenly became as treacherous and tantalizing as a snake in the garden. Daddy did not go around doling out five dollar bills and seldom said anything without thinking about the consequences. He must have been pretty sure I would never bite a worm.

Why was he taking this risk? Daddy's motives confused me as I stared at the worm, but my decision came swiftly. My ten-year-old brother's mouth hung open and my mother clutched her hoe. Then I looked into the hazel eyes of my father, sustaining the tension as long as possible. It was time to be the eldest daughter of an eldest son. The hot earth below and the blazing sun overhead merged into one. Like Daddy when he was under pressure, I would not waste any words.

I took the worm from Daddy's hand. I held it up to the sun as if blessing it; then I took it into my mouth, biting down hard and fast, spitting almost before the green hit my teeth. I gagged and spit more than necessary, jumping all around my brother, trying to give everyone enough entertainment for such a high price of admission. Daddy's eyes twinkled and his smile was wide. He said nothing but reached in his pocket and pulled out his dilapidated wallet. He extracted his one and only five dollar bill and gave it to me. I discreetly tucked it into my bra.

I knew I had risen to the task. I knew I was worth the salt in my soup. The taste in my mouth was sour. The taste in my heart was sweet.

Mennonite in a Little Black Convertible

Do I contradict myself? Therefore I contradict myself.
I am large. I contain multitudes.

—Walt Whitman, "Song of Myself"

*M*ennonites like to show off their holiness with special plain dress," my friend Jeanette Engle said to me one day, "but look at their cars! And look at all those girls practically sitting on the laps of their boyfriends while they drive hot rods! Way over the speed limit, too!"

Jeanette, who was Presbyterian, went to Warwick High School with me. As she uttered those words, I remembered the Robert Burns poem "To a Louse" that we had just studied in English class: "O wad some Power the giftie gie us / to see oursels as ithers see us." Jeanette and I had loved to roll those dialect sounds around in our mouths when we first read it. Since the Burns poem was about a woman sitting in church, the comparison seemed apt.

From the moment Jeanette talked about the hot rod Mennonite boys and their conspicuously attached girlfriends, I suddenly felt that I was seeing my fellow Mennonites the way many people saw us, even those who lived right next to us. They saw the incongruities, the paradoxes. Where I saw kindly and helpful people, even saints, outsiders sniffed at us for our hypocrisy. I couldn't deny there were wild Mennonite young people. While I had criticized many aspects of Mennonite life myself,

I felt surprisingly protective of my faith when others did so. It dawned on me yet again that both things were true. Mennonites were indeed saints and sinners combined. Most of their cars hummed humbly down the highway, but some of them roared, preening and careening, looking for a race.

The glittering world had entered through an unsuspecting portal—the relationship to farming. The more a boy worked on his father's farm, the more likely he was to own a really racy automobile.

The system functioned like this: Almost as soon as they could walk, young people on farms worked from sunup to sundown alongside their parents. They may have received some form of pay, but few earned anything like the milk check profit-sharing plan my father had put in place on the Spahr farm. Parents varied in their philosophies about childrearing, but all farmers expected their children to become economic gains, not drains. That was how nature seemed to intend family farm life to operate.

Conversations among Mennonite farm teenagers often focused on how parents treated their children in regard to compensation for their labor. Some mothers and fathers encouraged children to work "out," not on their own farm but rather as hired help—clerks, factory workers, or secretaries. The rules for the family policy varied depending on age and gender of the child, whether the work was full time or part time, the type of farming (dairy being the most labor intensive), and the degree of economic security enjoyed by the family.

Working "out" brought in welcome cash to the family. Some children were allowed to keep everything. Others, especially after schooling had ended, were charged a bit for room and board. A few unfortunate souls had to give everything they earned back to their parents, due either to economic stress or multigenerational tradition. All farm children had to help with chores when they lived at home, even if they worked forty hours a week elsewhere.

"Forty hours a week, ha!" I remember my father saying. "If that's all I worked, this farm would go to ruin and we'd all starve."

Daddy worked eighty-hour weeks and never took a substantial vacation, from the time of his honeymoon in 1947 until he sold the cows and farm equipment in 1974. He kept his buildings and equipment in good repair, calling farms that were not well kept "Peter Tumble-Downs." He was elected to leadership positions in church and in farm organizations; he plowed a straight row and kept the road banks mowed. But he felt he had labored too hard for his father, so he wanted to be more generous with his children.

Girls were never in line for property transfer, nor could they take on farm financial obligations. They lived under their father's roof until they transferred to their husband's. Some, like my mother, worked only for their parents and no other employer.

So how did fathers keep young farm boys motivated? The answer for many families, especially in the 1940–70 era, was a car. Here again, both sides of my family and both genders provide interesting contrasts.

The Hess family rewarded all four sons with cars soon after each turned sixteen years old. Uncle John Henry, the oldest, got a 1936 Ford roadster convertible with rumble seat, Uncle Christian a 1941 Mercury convertible, and Uncle Lloyd a 1941 Ford convertible.

Uncle John Henry also bought an airplane, which he wrecked on September 28, 1941. He kept a promise to his fiancée and mother never to fly again after that.

The fact that every single Hess boy owned a convertible proved the Hess family flirted with Mennonite boundaries. Uncle Ken Noll, for example, growing up in Rohrerstown at the same time, also wanted a convertible, but his father would not buy one due to such a machine's worldliness and the fact that he might get a visit from a minister or bishop or, worse yet, be disciplined or asked by the church to sell it. I suppose my uncles escaped church reproof because most of them were not church members subject to discipline, just as mother was not a member at the time.

Uncle Lloyd's car became both a Hess household treasure and a grim reminder of his absence when he enlisted in the Army.

Several photos from that time period show other members of the Hess family standing guard next to the convertible. Grandma Anna Mary has a worried look on her face.

Mother's younger brother, Allen, promised his older brother Lloyd, in a letter that he wouldn't let their sister (my mother, Barbara Ann) drive the car, which was a joke. Mother got her license only after she graduated from high school, the war had ended, and she was dating Daddy. Here was another gender gap. Girls put their own savings into more domestic hope chests. Their job was to attract boys who drove hot cars, not to covet their own fancy wheels.

What, if anything, did the written rules and regulations of the Lancaster Conference Mennonite Church say about cars? Nothing! A gorgeous car could certainly be tempting, all shiny with chrome and sleek with aerodynamic perfection inside and out. It's amazing, actually, that the church advised boys against wearing neckties but usually said nothing about what kinds of cars they drove.

But one overarching statement by the Mennonite Church, under its Article of Separation and Nonconformity, no doubt

Grandma Anna Mary Hess stands beside the convertible her son Lloyd left behind when he joined the Army in 1944.

applied to the most outrageous cars. "Section 4. The Simple Life" admonished: "We believe that the spirit of materialism is not in harmony with the Christian life, and we urge our members to live the simple and unselfish life. Extravagance and intemperance in any form are not consistent with the teachings of the Scriptures."[45]

So ministers and bishops actually had something to guide them when they observed the various types of cars in their parking lots. And they did exercise both direct and indirect influence for simplicity. In the 1940s, in some congregations, that meant not buying a convertible.

There were ways to be cool that didn't require buying a convertible, though. My father found one when he bought his first car on April 27, 1943, in his senior year of high school: a two-tone green 1939 Buick 40 Super, the pride and joy of his young life. He loved that car. Coupled with his good looks, it meant that girls seldom, if ever, turned him down for dates.

As vigilant as the church leaders were about outlawing television, one would have thought they might have recognized the automobile as a threat to simplicity. In American culture, a youth with a car was viewed as a rebel without a cause long before the movie of that name made juvenile delinquency famous in 1955. A car created a portable private space that enabled other worldly customs to flourish, including listening to the radio, drinking, and sex. The car revolutionized youth culture. Mennonites were no exception, but they did it their way.

"Where were you in '62?" was the tagline for the 1973 film *American Graffiti*, which heightened nostalgia for the '60s custom of "cruising." Where was I in 1962? Right there in Mr. Sload's art class. The assignment was to draw a picture of your dream home. My dream house property began on a winding road leading up a steep hill to a modern house made of glass, wood, and steel. Its main features were a huge room walled with books on three sides and glass on the fourth, which looked out over a long

---

45. *Statement of Christian Doctrine and Rules and Discipline of the Lancaster Conference of the Mennonite Church*, 1968, 20.

cantilevered edge to the water below. I drew my own version of Frank Lloyd Wright's Fallingwater house.

Though it wasn't part of the assignment, I went one step further. I drew myself behind the wheel of a red Karmann Ghia convertible driving up the winding path to the dream house.

"Karmann Ghia" and "cantilevered edge" were phrases I loved to say, although I knew almost nothing about either of them. How I even found these words is a mystery to me. I don't remember ever seeing one of these cars on the streets or at school. I certainly never saw one at church. Even the hottest hot rods were all American-made cars. Going against the grain meant choosing a European-made car.

I loved low-slung lines and flirtatious headlights. What I really dreamed of in my drawing, however, was freedom, comfort, and risk all combined in one place. The books and the car were freedom and comfort. The cliff and the ocean below represented risk, living close to the edge. The fantasies for my adult life, when I could make my own decisions, were far edgier than my teenage home life.

I'm not sure if I ever showed my art project to my father. He would definitely have liked the car in the driveway better than the elements in the rest of the drawing, which would have seemed foreign to him. He liked to talk about cars, and he seemed to understand why all young people wanted one. He didn't consult me about what car I might want when I turned old enough to drive, but he probably asked the advice of the friendly car salesmen at Zartman Dodge, the dealership where he had purchased all his cars since the infamous Buick 40.

The first car Daddy bought for me (to drive, not to own) was intended to help me get to school and work while I lived at home. I still remember the day I got the '53 Pontiac he first chose for me. In its day, said Daddy, it was a great car. The color was what my friends and I loved to call "puke green," but it had other interesting features: leather seats, electric radio antenna, fancy hood ornament, visor—and a "straight eight" engine. Daddy paid $100 for it and knew that it would be a safe car for his first daughter. He seemed to get a kick out of watching me drive it. I decided that my unusual car was so old it was cool. I never asked for a different set of wheels.

One day, however, when I got home from school, a surprise awaited me. Sitting in the driveway was a shiny black car with a white "rag" top. I skipped up the front steps, wondering what kind of interesting visitor would be inside. I didn't know many people who drove convertibles, and I had never even ridden in one, so naturally I was curious.

I looked around the kitchen to find our visitor, but no one appeared. Instead Daddy asked, "Did you see the car in the driveway?"

"Yes," I nodded. "Who's here?"

"You are," he said. Did Daddy know about my dream house and my dream car? Was that the reason he was laughing now?

It took me more than a few more seconds to figure it out, but soon it was clear. Daddy had been to Zartman's Garage that day. Mr. Zartman, knowing Daddy had bought one car for his daughter, wanted to show him another car that had just arrived

On my high school graduation day, June 7, 1966, I could think of no better place to be photographed in cap and gown than next to my partner in teenage adventures, the 1960 Studebaker Lark.

on his lot—a 1960 Studebaker Lark convertible. Daddy, who had loved the Buick 40 he worked so hard to earn at age eighteen, wanted to give me something that he wished his own father had given him.[46]

"Want to take it for a spin?" Daddy handed me the keys.

In that moment, my "Young Daddy" was back again. He had done something reckless, despite the mortgage pressures. Maybe he had gotten more for milk or for selling corn or hay that week. Mother was right there with him. They both wanted me to know the joy they had shared while "running around" in Daddy's Buick. It didn't matter that I was a girl and hadn't asked for a new car. They wanted to see my face light up. Whatever happened to the father who wanted to teach his daughter humility? He cared about modesty in dress and deportment, but apparently he made an exception for cars. Anyway, it was a good Mennonite color— black! That was the kind of joke he liked.

Of course, I wanted to go for a spin! I raced outside, put the key in the ignition, and drove off with Daddy. Then we stopped so he could show me how to put the roof down, and we took off again. I could not believe my luck.

The 1960 Studebaker Lark was a little like the '53 Pontiac in one regard. It was an oddball car. The Studebaker company had already gone out of business in 1963, which is one reason why my father could buy a six-year-old car for a mere $600. My first car, the '53 Pontiac, had been a special edition. There were almost no duplicates of either car on Lancaster County highways. I liked that.

Driving a convertible while wearing a head covering takes a bit of forethought and a certain amount of rigging. Prayer coverings are attached to the hair with straight pins—one on each side of the head and sometimes one in the middle front if extra support is needed. In the case of a convertible ride, that anchor was essential.

---

46. Daddy meticulously recorded his earliest arrangements with Grandpa in his journal: "I got my car April 27, 1943, which cost $850. Of this, $500 was given to me from Daddy and Mother and $350 I had of my own. I got this from growing tobacco, raising pigs, and day laboring prior to this time."

Yet even a third straight pin nailing my covering to my hair was not enough to prevent my symbol of submission[47] from sailing off in 55–65 mph breezes. I took the wheel while wearing my head covering underneath a see-through scarf, just in case the pins didn't hold. I had read about how Isadora Duncan died, her signature scarf killing her instantly as its long tail twisted in the spokes of the racing car in which she was riding. My own scarf was much more modest and less lethal.

I liked to drive with the top down as fast as possible, skirting the speed limit the way I brushed against other rules—close to the edge but not close enough to fall off.

I drove the Lark during my last year of high school. I worked at Stauffer's Market part time and enjoyed being able to drive home sometimes with the top down. The very best time to drive a convertible is on a warm summer evening under the stars on a country road.

I remember great conversations during drives with my friends. I had my most philosophical conversations about being Mennonite with my Warwick High School friend Jeanette. Whereas she thought of herself as playing catch-up to her brilliant older brother and sister, I perceived her to be brilliant in her own right. After all, she played acoustic guitar, was on the tennis team, and (this mesmerized me) she wrote all of her small *e*'s as though they were shrunken capital *E*s. Soon I found myself writing *e*'s that way also.

She grew up in a much more "cultured" environment than I did. She didn't read Christian fiction or even popular fiction. She was reading Faulkner before I ever heard of him. Her brainy brother went to MIT, and she told me she wanted to go to Wellesley College. I drew a blank on the name, but I could tell from the way she talked about it that it must be like Harvard.

---

47. "According to 1 Corinthians 11:1-16, a woman's relationship is symbolized by her long hair and veiled head. The veiling shall be of sufficient size to adequately cover the head. It shall be worn at all times. This gives testimony to the Christian woman's privilege of unceasing prayer and constant witness and that the church accepts the order of headship and submission designated by God." *Statement of Christian Doctrine and Rules and Discipline of the Lancaster Conference of the Mennonite Church*, 1968, 17.

Jeanette told me, with one eyebrow cocked, that if *I* applied to Wellesley, being Mennonite might be an advantage. Even before the era of identity admissions began a few years later, Jeanette assumed that I might be a "first" Mennonite for Wellesley. I'd have an unusual story, something that might make my essay stand out. There was a new name for my kind of peculiar religion: "subculture."

I was intrigued by this idea. What if there were a way to be nonconformist that the world might reward rather than despise? Wouldn't that be a neat trick? God must have a sense of humor after all, I thought, but what an awful dilemma! It was just like humility. Once you were aware that you were humble, you became proud. Once your religious identity granted privilege, it lost its purity.

I never applied to Wellesley. Jeanette and I both ended up in church colleges. Hers was Florida Presbyterian and mine was Eastern Mennonite. Had Jeanette and I enrolled in Wellesley for the fall of 1966, we would have been classmates with Hillary Rodham, and life would have turned out differently for both of us.

Lives are like rivers, starting in springs and creeks, meandering along paths worn into the land, eventually meeting up again in the sea. I would separate from Jeanette, dream about her, and remember her especially when I had dinner fifty years later with Diana Chapman Walsh at the president's house of Wellesley College overlooking the Charles River. This place was not a Home Place for me, but I felt at home in it. There are many ways to arrive at a place, many of them unimaginable at the beginning of a journey.

The Studebaker Lark in many ways justified Jeanette's critique of Mennonite double standards. And it got me into a peck of trouble. The summer before my last year of high school, when the car was still a novelty, I was staying with my cousin Mary Ann. She and I and one or two other girls decided to skip church and go for a drive instead. We had a marvelous time in my convertible, talking, laughing, even singing. The buttery morning sunlight danced on our faces as we rode along country roads deserted by the more devout who were singing in church. All was fine until we decided to change direction, requiring a U-turn. No problem, I thought to myself. Just stop, turn, back up on the narrow road, and go again. What could be hard about this?

The weeds and tall grass along the side of the road obscured the fact that the shoulder dropped off steeply and concealed a fence next to the shoulder. Before I knew it, the end of the convertible had drifted under the fence. Fortunately, the fence was not broken, and a good pump on the accelerator got us out of the ditch, but the left rear was scratched and dented. Oh no!

They'll know I skipped church! was my first thought.

I'll have to pay to get this fixed! was my second thought.

What surprises me now about this memory is how little I suffered once I found the courage to blurt out to my parents what happened. I considered the option of not saying anything. Maybe no one would notice? The dent was minor, but my conscience pricked me. I had learned the "truth cleanse" from parents who seldom punished hard when they knew I had opted to be honest.

Mother and Daddy said little about my skipping church. They must have known the bubble would burst after one misadventure. Daddy suggested I take the car to Miller's Body Shop, owned by one of my classmates. I did so the next week, with trepidation.

Trying to hide my fear, I asked, "How much do you think it will cost?"

Mr. Miller looked over the dent, rubbed his chin, and said, "Well, I've seen worse." He smiled. "Maybe $60."

I sighed and thanked him.

Having had no dealings with body shop repair work before, I wasn't sure what to expect. The lesson had been an expensive one. I would have to work an extra ten days at Stauffer's Market to recoup that amount out of my checking account.

But I also knew Mr. Miller had cut me a break. His smile told me so. I was grateful—and ever so glad to have my car back.

When you want to be big, you sometimes drive too fast and too close to the edge of the glittering world. The role of mistakes is to teach you where that edge lies.

After wondering for many years what had happened to Jeanette, I found her online. Like me, she had spent most of her life in academe and was preparing to retire. Jeanette changed her name to Jean in her adulthood. I was able to visit her on a trip that took me past her home. I learned that she's an environmental activist, a lesbian with a long-term partner, and that she hasn't been to church for years. We reminisced about how she taught me her favorite chords on the guitar, the only ones I know to this day: A, E, and B7. I told her that I am capable of transposing almost any song into those three chords.

"You know," Jean said, with the knowing tongue-in-cheek moxie I remembered well, "those are blues chords. Did you realize you've been singing the Mennonite blues?"

Jean said one other thing in a later conversation that I have been thinking about since. "You might think that I would have trouble with Mennonites, especially the ones that still dress plain. But I don't. They are reputed to take good care of the land. I know they disapprove of lesbian lifestyles, and I wouldn't expect them to understand me. They have an attitude of kindness and simplicity that makes me feel safe—or at least safer than I do with the other kind of Christians who form their opinions before they know who you are."

The contradictions of Mennonite life continue, but the Lancaster County car culture I grew up with has changed a lot. Mennonite farm families still like big American cars and trucks, but most *American Graffiti*-era gathering spots, including Joe's Diner in our area, have closed, and Mennonite boys don't usually get hot rods for their sixteenth birthdays.

If you have a 1966 Karmann Ghia convertible you want to sell, however, give me a holler.

Seventeen

Standing Up to the Bishop

Obey them that have the rule over you, and submit yourselves:
for they watch for your souls, as they must give account.
—Hebrews 13:17

While I was driving the country roads of Lancaster County, with prayer covering on head and scarf making sure it stayed attached, I could take a breather from tensions that sometimes cropped up at home between Daddy and me and between Daddy and Grandpa.

Most of the time throughout the turbulent '60s, I loved going to church. After I raised my hand in a revival meeting, took instruction classes, and got baptized in 1960, most of the fear I had about God's judgment diminished. I had always felt loved by the forty families who made up Lititz Mennonite Church, along with a similar number of widows, bachelors, and "maiden ladies." These were people who had patted me on the head and commented on my rosy cheeks from the time I was a child. I knew any one of them would help me if I were ever in trouble—be it a flat tire or cancer.

The atmosphere in our church services was mostly harmonious. A touch of chaos due to the presence of babies and children was viewed as normal; children should participate, even if they couldn't understand completely what was going on around them. All adult women were prepared to help entertain children. Their commodious black bags were like doctors' medical kits, packed and ready for any emergency. Inside them, scores of tiny treasures resided: little tablets, cloth books, boxes of eight Crayolas, men's big white handkerchiefs, and small containers of Cheerios.

My favorite distraction came in the form of a tiny cardboard box with a picture of a black Scottie dog on one side and a white dog on the other. Inside rested little plastic dogs just like the ones on the box cover. They could do all manner of tricks, from attracting each other over and under the pages of a hymn book to repelling each other when facing the opposite direction. A skillful churchwoman could entertain a whole pew full of small children for ten to fifteen minutes at a time with creative adaptations of the Scottie dog powers.

A men's large white handkerchief usually came out of the bag after the Scotties lost their powers to magnetize and mesmerize little ones. My own mother knew a variety of things to "make" with a handkerchief: two pigs in a blanket or a mouse with a little tail. The beauty of this form of entertainment is that it was all done quietly on a lap or a bench.

Women helped other women. The children were in some ways community property. If a mother had several toddlers, and many did, another woman might offer to take one sleepyhead upstairs to the crib room where the service could be heard through the intercom speakers.

I see now that my parents, especially my mother, influenced my view of my home congregation. Mother saw saints everywhere and wanted me to see them, too. She also wanted to be a saint herself since the other options available for a woman of her talents, like being the wife of a minister or a full-time writer/speaker/actress/teacher, weren't available.

I sensed my mother's narrow range of options as a Mennonite woman. Consequently, as I entered puberty, started dating, and continued my education in the academic track of a public high school, I began thinking about my own options. At home, I was a leader in my role of "big sister." At school, I made the honor roll every semester and kept track of my grade-point average in each class, aiming for the top even though I fell short.

At church, leadership opportunities for girls were limited, but when available, I took them. Gender roles were quite segregated, and the most often quoted explanation, next to Saint Paul's admonition that women should keep silent in church, was 1 Corinthians 11:3: "But I would have you know, that the head of every man is Christ; and the head of the woman is the man; and the head of Christ is God."

Boys in our youth group led singing or read Scripture in the service. Girls weren't asked to do those things, but there were young people's meetings at Hess Church and at Mellingers and East Chestnut Street where young people of both genders were asked to give talks on "topics" such as the importance of daily devotions or on the two most important ideas Mennonites had about following Jesus: "nonresistance" (pacifism) and "non-conformity" (to the world). There was an unspoken "first tier" and "second tier" of meeting hierarchy, involving both time and place. Only men spoke from the raised pulpit during Sunday morning services. On Sunday evenings, and if they stood below the pulpit, women could speak.

One of my first talks was ghostwritten, or at least ghost edited, by my mother, eager to help me get over the stage fright that made my early teenage years difficult. Perhaps she was eager to relive her own moments of deep satisfaction on stage through me. When an older girl asked if my mother had written my talk, I blushed.

Only one time in my first eighteen years do I recall attending a non-Mennonite church on a Sunday morning. That was the time I accompanied Jeanette Engle to the stately First Presbyterian Church in Lancaster. Of all my school friends, Jeanette intrigued me the most. She could speak to me openly about our religions. When she invited me to go with her and her parents to their church, I was eager to go, though a little unsure of what to do.

I arrived on a Sunday morning attired in one of my three or four "good" dresses, probably my light blue "whipped cream" dress or the old-fashioned beige eyelet my mother admired but my college friends would later banish. My long hair under my covering may have been crowning my head with glory as the Bible promised, but it also made me self-conscious in a new setting. Jeanette's parents were much older than mine and rather quiet people, so the seven-mile ride in their sedan to worship in Lancaster was mostly silent. I lived only a mile from my church, which was in Lititz, a totally familiar town. Lancaster may have been only seven miles down the road, but it seemed alien to me as a place to go to church.

We parked along a narrow side street. I recall a cast-iron fence along a brick street. Lancaster was then the biggest metropolis in my known world. I seldom went into the city itself, except to shop. Being Mennonite *and* rural created both anxiety and attraction toward Lancaster in equal measure in me: The city was a dreamscape, a daguerreotype image now blurring around the edges in my memory.

A white spire crowned the large First Presbyterian Church on Orange Street. Compared to the flat, rectangular simplicity of our Mennonite meetinghouses, this edifice seemed like a mansion to me. One of the older churches of the region, it was built in what Jeanette explained was Greek Revival style.

When we arrived, the sanctuary was nearly filled with sedate and friendly people, perhaps twice the number expected at my church that same morning. Seating was by family unit instead of gender. The white pews and padded seats seemed very dignified. I sat up straight and imagined that people sitting behind us were wondering how it came about that the Engle family had a Mennonite girl wearing a covering on her head with them this morning. One more time, I felt an invisible finger pointing at my head, and I gave myself far too much credit for being interesting.

The service itself has long since evaporated in my mind except for one detail. I remember singing my usual alto during the first hymn (which I was happy to recognize as one we also sang at my church), but feeling a little strange while doing so. Jeanette, who also sang alto in our high school choir, was singing only melody in this setting. Evidently breaking a song into parts was unseemly to these well-dressed people sitting around me in a quiet dignified sanctuary, unmarred by the sounds of babies and toddlers and boisterous teenagers. By the third or fourth verse of the second hymn, I was singing in unison along with all the other voices.

Visiting another church gave me a new perspective on my own. Ours was an informal "low" church. We had few rituals and creeds binding us together. Instead, we had rules and discipline. But the rules didn't hold the church together; only the people could do that, helping each other, weeping with those who wept, rejoicing with those who rejoiced.

Shortly after my visit to the Presbyterian church, I tested the boundaries of the love that marked Lititz Mennonite Church.

One night in the middle of a week of daily revival meetings at Lititz Mennonite Church, the youth were asked to meet in the church basement before the service began. The painted cement floor extended to a kitchen in the rear. Along both sides of the lengthy rectangular space were a series of little Sunday school

Doris, Sue, me, Henry, Linda, Daddy, Mother. The only family picture we took in a studio in the 1960s. Probably 1965.

rooms. Each room had a bulletin board for Sunday school materials produced by the Mennonite Publishing House. Low tables and chairs designed for young children took up the rest of the space.

I found myself sitting there on a tiny chair wondering why we had been called. I don't remember who said what, but I do remember the message: we would all be asked to rededicate our lives to Christ during the service. When the sermon ended and we heard the familiar hymn "Just as I Am," we were supposed to come forward to declare ourselves as sinners saved by grace. Again.

I received this information with some shock and a little dread. I had wrestled like Jacob for several years before raising my hand in 1960. And I had often been scared by subsequent revival sermons (was I really saved?) even after that momentous evening, but now I had to face a new possibility—that the revival beast might need to be fed every year. Like the beasts of Revelation 4:6, the revival beast was "full of eyes before and behind." It could tell if you had unconfessed sins since the last time the invitation from a revivalist was given.

When I heard what we were expected to do, I looked at my shoes rather than at my youth leaders or the other young people. I decided I would let my conscience be my guide when the time came. I felt anger, confusion, and fear. What would I do when the altar call hymn began? I sat on my little Sunday school chair not knowing the answer but battling hard inside.

Not one word of that sermon has survived in my memory. Yet I can still summon up the image of all of us youth trudging up from the basement, entering the sanctuary from the front, and taking our seats. Usually we sat in the back, but on that day the first four rows on the left had been reserved for our group.

Oh no, I thought. All eyes will be on us at the altar call.

Sure enough. As verse one of "Just As I Am" ended, the first row of youth started to go into the center aisle to stand before the pulpit. Then the second. Then it was time for our row to empty out. I was sitting next to one of the younger girls, perhaps Ann

Mosemann, who was at the end of the bench. The others in our row got up and waited for us. I remained seated. So did Ann. I motioned for the others to move past us, which they did. My face burned.

Mother is sitting a few benches away on the right, I thought. What will I say to her when we get home?

Why didn't I just go with the others? Why did my soul seem to adhere itself to that bench? When Henry, too young to be in the youth group, got up out of his seat behind me and joined the throng in front of the pulpit, I felt chastened. Henry had joined the church the year before, but apparently felt no dissonance in coming forward again. Well, at least Mother had raised one of her children right, I thought, feeling slightly less pressure to conform myself.

We were on verse three now:

Just as I am, though tossed about
with many a conflict, many a doubt,
fightings and fears within, without,
O Lamb of God, I come, I come.[48]

This verse was the hardest of the six to resist. The music was so beguiling, almost like a snake charmer's flute. It was sung softly, and the verses were so accurate in describing the inner state of the soul after a revivalist's sermon. It was tempting to say to myself, Yep, I've got doubts. Think I'll walk down this aisle for that reason. But I just couldn't make myself do it. If walking in a state of doubt was the same as walking in a state of grace, wasn't it clear that no one actually cared what the walk meant so long as you moved yourself physically to the front of the room to be counted on some celestial scoreboard? I stayed right there on row three, seat two. Ann stayed with me.

After the service, I tried to act nonchalant and sweet to anyone whose eye caught mine on the way out of church. Did I imagine it, or did some of them avert their gazes? The tension in the car

---

48. From the hymn "Just as I Am" by Charlotte Elliot, 1834.

going home felt like nuclear fallout to me, as I sat in the back seat next to the window behind Daddy in our '57 Dodge. The younger children chattered sleepily when we got home, blissfully unaware of their older sister's spiritual obstinacy. I hurried to bed without any conversation.

The next day, as Mother and I were doing dishes together, I finally spoke.

"I guess you want to know why I didn't go forward last night," I said, feeling as though I were plunging off a twelve-foot-high diving board.

"Yes, I'd be interested," said Mother, with remarkable restraint.

"Why didn't any of the adults walk down that aisle?" was my first volley.

Mother didn't have an answer, but I could tell she was thinking. I simply knew in my heart it felt more honest *not* to go forward than to follow the crowd. If I had been clever, I would have pointed out the Mennonite teaching that we are supposed to be nonconformed to the world. Being herded into my behavior felt like conformity instead of nonconformity. I had not yet learned to turn the language of the powerful ones back to them, however. Mother stayed neutral, not showing her hurt but also not endorsing me. We finished the conversation when we finished the dishes.

Looking back, I see this "no" was part of a dance I was doing between trying to find an authentic individual self while also saying yes to my 450-year-old religious tradition. I really loved the ideas of nonconformity and nonresistance, but I would have to find ways to embrace them from within myself, attached by the roots to who I was, rather than have them imposed from the outside for the benefit of revivalists, parents, youth leaders, peers, or anyone else whose anxieties about change in the church needed assuaging. In March 1960, I said yes. In March 1964, I said no.

Fortunately, I soon had another opportunity to answer in the affirmative. What saved me? Bible quizzing! It came into my life at just the right time—at once public, competitive, collective, and individual. I had been prevented from playing sports for

Warwick High School, mostly because I was needed at home to help milk during the practice and game hours. Organized sports were frowned upon by the church, also. They fell into the "such like" category of the rulebook because, like clubs, they created an allegiance or loyalty to causes or groups outside the church. The church found it helpful to offer competitive activities of its own. I was encouraged to find my place in the starting lineup of the Lititz Mennonite Church Bible Quiz Team. We had no uniforms, but we did have coaches, judges, and a buzzer.

In vacation Bible school, which I had attended every summer of my life, we had been prepared for a combination of Bible knowledge and competition through something called "sword drills" based on Hebrews 4:12: "For the word of God is quick, and powerful, and sharper than any two-edged sword, piercing even to the dividing asunder of soul and spirit, and of the joints and marrow, and is a discerner of the thoughts and intents of the heart." If the Bible was like a sword, went the reasoning, how can we make memorizing the names of the books of the Bible as exciting as a battle? When the teacher announced that we would end with a sword drill, everyone cheered and sat up straight, cradling their Bibles in their laps, as fireflies started to gather outside and mothers were setting out Kool-Aid and cookies.

"Isaiah 39:8!" called out the adult at the microphone in the front of the church. All of us on the team held our Bibles—our "swords"—lightly on our laps and flipped about one-third of the way through the text. If we lucked upon the chapter of Isaiah quickly, we jumped up, knowing that by the time the teacher acknowledged us, we would be able to locate the 39:8 verse as well. If you were the first, your reward was to read the verse out loud. In this case, it was "Good is the word of the LORD which thou hast spoken." We spoke loudly and clearly, so that a hundred or more Bible school students could hear it. Elaine Wenger was the wizard of the sword drill, but I often got my share of answers right, too.

The adrenalin rush flooding small bodies and brains was almost palpable in the room. Little boys with teddy bear haircuts buzzed close to their scalps, clutching Bibles so big they could hardly open them, stood next to little girls wearing crisp cotton dresses ironed to a sheen by their mothers. As in any sport, during sword drills, the bigger children had an advantage. Everyone seemed to get into the spirit of the game, however. By the time a child left sixth grade and graduated from Bible school, he or she got to be very fast at locating a verse.

I chuckle now when a biblical passage is presented as a mere page number instead of being written out as the entire text. Page number? Are you kidding? Who needs a crutch like that? Having sharpened our mental swords, we were all henceforth expected to bring our Bibles to church and find the passage based on the text being read. Following along, praying, singing, and listening were all ways to participate in worship. We were expected to do them as soon as we outgrew the little Scottie dogs and handkerchief pigs in the blankets carried by our mothers and grandmothers.

Bible quizzing was to sword drilling as high school was to elementary school: an advanced program of biblical literacy with real study required, producing even more adrenalin. The hidden weapon of the Lititz team was a short, powerfully built woman with an intellectual intensity I had not seen before in church. Janette was married to Mel Wenger, a laid-back man with blond hair and a wide smile. She had a natural gift for organization, detail, and helping others succeed. Though she had four children herself, she and Mel volunteered their time with those of others. When the church called, this couple almost always said yes.

Janette was a born leader and a very good teacher. She loved to learn, and her enthusiasm was infectious. When the Lancaster Conference sent out information to all youth leaders about a new kind of activity known as Bible quizzing, the perfect medium had met the perfect coach.

Janette took volunteers from the sixteen- and seventeen-year-olds. I was fifteen at the time, so I had to wait my turn. I watched as Janette turned my older peers into a lean, mean, Bible-memorizing machine. At season's end, they brought back a big banner that said "Conference Champions," hanging it in the anteroom for everyone to see. I was eager to join the team when my turn came in 1964. Janette was good at picking the people most able to memorize and eager to work, and she motivated them to work hard for her. Glenn Thomas taped his Bible verses to the tractor steering wheel so he could learn while he plowed, cut alfalfa, and baled hay. Tom Brubaker did the same while he painted houses, pinning verses to his extension ladder high off the ground. I memorized, too, but not as much, because we could count on Glenn to know any questions requiring verbatim answers. I specialized in the kinds of questions that required deduction more than memorization. And I was ready to pounce on the buzzer as soon as I knew the answer or was sure someone on my team knew it.

Janette spent hours trying to think like a quizmaster, devising the kinds of questions we were likely to get when we faced the real competition from other Mennonite churches. Her combined study and intuition meant she could create study-question sheets very much like the ones we would actually hear the night of the real quiz. When Janette had not forecast the question we were given at a meet, she anxiously observed how we handled the situation.

"Name two examples of the use of contrast in the book of John" was a question that shot fear through her. She had not prepared us for that one!

BUZZ! My whole team and my coach looked at me with wonder. Had I been trigger happy or did I really know the answer? All of a sudden, I realized I only knew *one* example, the obvious one from the beautiful prologue in John 1. "Light and darkness," I said. My teammates, indeed the entire room, held their breath as I scanned through all the other verses I had memorized. Then I lit on one.

"Abraham and Jesus," I said, tentatively, at first. Then, to clinch it, I quoted John 8:58: "Before Abraham was, I am." I looked the judges right in the eyes. Evidently that was not the answer printed on the page, but the two judges conferred and agreed it should count. We won the match.

Quizzing highlighted a lot of the tensions inherent in Mennonite youth culture in the 1960s. In some ways, it was a capitulation to the exciting tonic of competition, something that church league softball also fueled. The Bible might instruct us to help each other more than compete with one another, but it also told us to strive, and strive we did. Pacifists are always looking for the moral equivalent of war. Maybe this was it! The method was nonviolent; what harm could it do? Match the desire to win with a good cause like learning the Bible, and you could drum up enthusiasm for your team the way the Phillies did in 1964—by winning—until those last terrible ten games of the season. We at Lititz were not going to choke, however!

Another highlight of my two years of Bible quizzing came in 1964 when we were entering the playoffs held at East Chestnut Street Church in Lancaster. Since Lititz had won the championship the previous year, our team was now gunning for a repeat. We sprinted up the stairs in high spirits. A member of another team, a girl about my age who did not have the good fortune to have Janette Wenger in her congregation, felt it necessary to remind us as we were stepping upward, "Pride goeth before a fall." There was that pattern again: Feel good. Be reminded of pride. Feel bad.

During one of the early quiz matches, I was one of four members representing our team. The buzzer rang. The other team answered the question incorrectly. The quizmaster went to the next question, which we answered correctly.

BUZZ! I hit the buzzer and said, "I believe the rules state that if a team answers incorrectly, the other team should have the opportunity to answer the question (or another question if the answer to the first has been given) before the quiz continues."

The quizmaster turned red and started to sputter. You could see the wheels spinning in his head as he said, "I believe you may be right." After consulting the rulebook, the quizmaster gave our side the opportunity to answer—which we did, correctly. Chalk up another point for Lititz.

Before we could go on, though, the quizmaster needed to take a seat on the bench behind him. He was feeling faint. That's how seriously people took Bible quizzing. And that's how seriously a male leader took a challenge from a teenage girl. Lititz won the whole match that day.

Two weeks later, our team returned to play another challenger. On the sign outside East Chestnut Street Church was a Bible verse. Our coach has never forgotten it. She remembered the words and then I remembered the laughter that erupted in the car as the rest of us saw the sign: "And let us not be weary in well doing: for in due season we shall reap, if we faint not"[49] In 1964, we won the championship for Lancaster Mennonite Conference and got to hoist a banner in our church another year.

All of my experiences in church, both positive and negative, however, paled in comparison to the melodrama that took place in our church during my last two years of high school. Like all melodramas, ours had a damsel in distress, a villain, and a hero. Let me introduce the cast:

Damsels: all the young women of the church.

Villain: the bishop who tried to make the damsels conform to a stricter dress code than the men and to a stricter dress code than the previous bishop had required.

Hero: the role I picked for myself at the age of seventeen.

Backstory: The role of bishop went far back into Anabaptist history. The Dutch Dordrecht Confession of 1632 established the authority of leaders, including bishops, specifying the need to "appoint faithful men who would be able to teach others also, as elders, ordaining them by the laying on of hands in the name of the Lord, and provide for all the wants of the church according to their ability; so that, as faithful servants, they might husband well their Lord's talent, get gain with it, and, consequently, save themselves and those who hear them."[50]

49. Galatians 6:9.
50. Article IX, The Dordrecht Confession of Faith. http://www.bibleviews.com/Dordrecht.html#IX.

200 • Blush

The role of bishop had been long established, but in my childhood during the '50s and '60s, it was becoming more "executive" in its function: "An idea of a 'board' of bishops grew, which was more and more polarizing as cultural change had to be dealt with. At ordination by lot the shocked bishops had to promise 'on bended knee' to keep rules that more and more of their flock were no longer inclined to honor."[51]

Usually I saw bishops only on the two communion Sundays and preparatory services of the year. Prior to 1962 or thereabouts, I paid no attention whatsoever to the visits and ministrations of these officials who presided over our minister, our deacon, and our whole congregation. When I was fourteen and our new bishop began injecting himself into the lives of the congregants in ways previous bishops had not, I started to take notice. The first bishop of my lifetime was Amos Horst. Mahlon Zimmerman was the bishop who baptized me in 1960. Then along came Isaac Sensenig, and the troubles began.

Bishop Sensenig's calling by lot in 1962[52] was a mismatch of Mennonite root systems from the start. One of the dynamics of Mennonite life throughout more than four hundred years of church history was the perennial question: What does it mean to be Mennonite? With two centuries of persecution as a backdrop for all arguments, the stakes were high. Remaining faithful to the vision of a free church for which the martyrs died turned seemingly small issues into huge ones. Conservative churches looked more like those of their cousins, the Amish, who split from the Mennonite Church in 1693 to continue the practice of shunning as a way to maintain church discipline.

Our new bishop had felt the limitations of the church in which he grew up. He wanted a more spiritual church. His previous group was called Martinites (for the leader Jonas Martin), or Old Order, because they were more conservative in dress than

---

51. John L. Ruth, correspondence, December 27, 2012.
52. Both ministers and bishops were selected by lot, a biblical method of selecting leaders. See glossary on page 255. See also this entry in the Global Annabaptist Mennonite Encyclopedia Online by Harold S. Bender: http://www.gameo.org/encyclopedia/contents/L67.html/?searchterm=the%20lot.

Lancaster Conference Mennonites, but less so than the Amish. Sometimes they were called "Black Bumpers," because they drove cars (but painted the chrome bumpers black) rather than horse and buggies like the Amish. These black bumpers indicated their desire to separate not only from the world but from other Mennonites.

Even though Isaac Sensenig had no prior relationship with our congregation, he was appointed our bishop. According to the grapevine, our beloved minister, Melvin Lauver, had been nominated for the spot, but some of the other bishops vetoed his nomination. Melvin had walked a fine line with the bishop board. He refused to wear a frock coat, deemed proper wear for a minister. The coat was worn by most bishops and ministers to show, paradoxically, both their august station and their humility.

Melvin had been quoted as saying, "Since the frock was designed to allow men's coats to cover the saddle while riding a horse, and since I don't plan to ride a horse anytime soon, I don't see the need to wear a frock coat."

Rev. Melvin Lauver and his wife, Mary, a leadership team before women were ordained in the Lancaster Conference. Both Lauvers gave themselves selflessly to the congregation and were loved by all. Photo taken in the 1960s. From the collection of Barbara Ann Hershey Becker.

On another occasion, he confessed the sin of pride from the pulpit. Everyone perked up. "I am proud that I have the oldest car in the parking lot," he said. His congregation loved this kind of wit and gutsiness, but evidently his superiors did not.

At any rate, all other candidates for bishop were moot once Isaac Sensenig stood in our pulpit. While in the outside world Lyndon Johnson was conducting a war on poverty, our bishop waged a war on worldliness. Where was the devil hiding? Sensenig saw him under any covering that didn't hide all the hair on a woman's head. Certainly the devil was sewn into short skirts and sleeveless blouses. It was clear that women and girls bore the brunt of the bishop's scrutiny, much more than men and boys. In school my brother and all his Mennonite friends looked just like the other boys. They didn't part their hair in the middle like some of the Church of the Brethren boys did. Nor did they button the top button of their plaid shirts like the very conservative Mennonite boys did. They looked as all-American in their flat tops as Jeff, the kid on the *Lassie* show. Some of the boys in my youth group attended school dances and took worldly girls to the prom. None of us girls could get away with such behavior, though. Thus, the bishop ironically made feminists of us all, at least when it came to gender equality regarding the rules.

It was communion in the spring of 1965 when the alarms sounded for me. During the preparatory services the preceding week, it became clear that what we wore for communion would be of utmost importance to the bishop. Still, we weren't prepared in the least for what would happen in the communion service that Sunday.

Lititz Mennonite Church practiced a "common cup" form of communion that meant all church members (all of whom were baptized) filed down the center aisle, pausing before the minister or the bishop, who extended the cup. The minister served the men, all of whom sat on the left side facing the pulpit, and the bishop served the women, seated on the right.

We girls, ages fourteen to eighteen, sat toward the back, watching carefully as the older women moved toward the center and then the front, eyes on the ground. Deadly serious. We all had just heard again the words in 1 Corinthians 11:29 that link communion and fear: "For he that eateth and drinketh unworthily, eateth and drinketh damnation to himself, not discerning the Lord's body." I had no idea what that last part about not discerning the Lord's body was all about. I could picture the body on the cross, bleeding for me, like the revival songs said. What I really pictured, however, was a yawning mouth at the entrance to hell as I stumbled unworthily, after drinking the grape juice and eating the bread. The reason we held preparatory meetings was to prevent such a destiny.

The preparatory meeting had taken place the Thursday evening before. This was the bishop's opportunity to lay down the law, instructing all of us. It was also our responsibility to search our hearts. In two tiny rooms off the front of the sanctuary, women hidden behind doors to the right and men to the left of the pulpit, we met in groups of about a dozen to solemnly confess that we were at peace—or else announce our intention to abstain. If we were not at peace, we were at risk of eating and drinking unworthily. We formed a circle around the minister and deacon. If we were at peace, we answered yes.

When it came my turn to speak, I reviewed my relationships at home, school, and church. They all seemed peaceful enough to me. Would God see them that way? Actually, most of the people in the church were beginning to develop a distaste for the bishop. His sermons were not warm and inviting, like Melvin Lauver's, and he didn't seem to care about knowing us as individuals. He gave no indication of having a sense of humor. We were not used to his obsession about clothing and visible signs of separation from the world; he seemed to think these were matters of eternal life and death. The wiser elders sensed that he was working out his own identity issues through the Mennonite Church. The younger people just saw strictness.

When the time came that Sunday morning for the young women in the back of the church to go down the center aisle, I was among the first. In the eleventh grade with only one more year in the youth group, I was above the average age. I felt the laser gaze of the bishop's eyes traverse my body, starting from my head to my toes. Were my head covering and bun large enough? My hair pulled back severely enough? I was not wearing a cape. I only owned one cape dress, made by my grandmother for my 1960 baptism and seldom worn again. I wore a dark sweater over my dress, like the one I wore in our family picture, which could serve the same modesty purpose of disguising my breasts. I knew that I would pass inspection, but the fact that I was scrutinized so carefully on the outside made my insides buzz with indignation.

Brother Sensenig held out the pewter cup to me. I gazed inside so I didn't have to gaze upon him. The scent of the fragrant purple juice took me to Jesus on the cross, and I wondered if it was for this kind of scrutiny that he had died.

As I rounded the corner on the way back to my seat, I caught a glimpse of the girls coming up the aisle after me. Joyce Snader, a girl whose family had rather recently joined our church, now stood where I just had stood in front of the bishop. Was it her skirt that offended him? Or her hair, which may have been too short to fit underneath a full covering? Whatever the cause, instead of holding the cup out to her, he clutched it to his chest. She didn't protest, just continued walking. The other women started to breathe in rhythm, their eyes wide. I knew the phone lines would be busy by afternoon.

Sure enough. This kind of judgment based on observation alone and at the last minute sent shock waves through the community. Without knowing it, we were participating in a crisis of leadership larger than our own congregation. The church's visual separation from the world had been slowly eroding over decades as the culture around us became harder to resist. What had been taking place in an evolutionary manner for a long time only became obvious because of many who wanted to reverse the trend.

If the bishop could refuse the cup of communion to a baptized member of the church, what would come next? Lititz was a town church. There had never been such strict enforcement of the discipline there as in the country churches surrounding it. Our minister, Melvin Lauver, focused on the theme of love in most of his sermons, making discipline subordinate to that theme in hopes people would voluntarily submit to the conference discipline if allowed a little longer leash. After the bishop withheld communion from Joyce Snader, the adults had many conversations with one another, with the minister, and with members of other congregations.

For me, though, the melodrama played out mostly at home. One Sunday afternoon, after a dispirited worship service in anticipation of another communion, my father stood in the living room across from the open staircase and said to Mother, allowing the children to hear, "My mother and father worshiped at this church all their lives. Before that, their parents. My great uncle was the minister for many years. I feel like I'm being forced to forsake my own church."

The alternative for people who wanted to stay Mennonite but didn't want the strict rules was to go to Neffsville, a Mennonite church affiliated with the more culturally assimilated Ohio Conference. Women had short hair there. Most people owned television sets. They sat in church by families rather than by gender. And they had a piano and organ. I would have liked all those things, so secretly I had been hoping the situation would get bad enough at Lititz just so we could go to Neffsville.

Something in my father's voice arrested me, however. He sounded like he really cared, even though he usually slept through part of the sermon and didn't do all the things Mother would have liked the spiritual leader of our home to do, such as read religious books, hold family devotions, or sing on key.

Therefore, knowing how much all the congregation wanted to stay, how loyal they were to each other and to the minister, I began to think differently. Instead of leaving, perhaps we could somehow see a miracle at work here. Perhaps there was a way God's grace could break through, like it did in Galatia, Ephesus, and Corinth in the New Testament. Perhaps the bishop's eyes could be opened and he would see us as we were.

That thought ignited my fantasy life, which had begun in childhood when I dreamed up ways to save the marriages of the estranged husbands and wives whose stories were told on *Backstage Wife* and other soap operas. I would turn my pillow into one of the characters in the story and develop dialogue that brought the conflict to a head and then to a halt. I also had a dream about Mother dying, which put me in charge of the children. The dream involved solving many problems along the way, while driving a large motorcycle with a side seat for the younger children. You might say my imagination tilted toward the miraculous. Instead of Mennonite martyrdom, I saw myself as a mild-mannered Mennonite problem solver and peacemaker by day, ready to transform into Wonder Woman by night.

That background from my younger years had worked its way pretty deeply into my psyche. I had a more recent experience from which to draw however: my study of the book of John. Because of my quizzing experience, I actually knew one book of the Bible from the inside out, and it just so happened that the book was the most eloquent expression of Jesus' ministry of love and outpouring of devotion to his disciples. I went to my room, picked up the leatherbound book my parents had given me six years earlier, and reread many passages I had underlined.

Then I went to my closet and pulled out the Olympia typewriter my parents had given me for Christmas. The gift was a concession to the idea that I would go to college in another year and that I needed a typewriter for academic work before and during college. I inserted a piece of paper and began to type:

"Dear Members of the Lancaster Conference Bishop Board," or was it "Dear Brothers in Christ"? The words were aimed squarely at the hearts of the bishops as they convened their monthly meeting. I had heard Uncle Paul Landis, who was a bishop, talk about these meetings. So it seemed natural to want other people in the church with authority to know how bad things were at Lititz. Our former unity had been rent asunder. I talked about how Jesus pleaded with his disciples to be one "as thou, Father art in me, and I in thee."[53] I noted that our Bible quiz

---

53. John 17:21.

team had become one and cited the verse that meant the most to me: "By this shall all men know that ye are my disciples, if ye have love one to another."[54] I didn't give examples of our bishop's insensitivity, but I did have both Joyce Snader's shame and my parents' tearful fears of having to leave their church deeply etched on my own heart.

I took the letter to Mother, who shared it with Daddy. They said, "You spoke the truth of your thoughts and feelings. You showed how much those verses in John have entered into your life. What harm can come of that?" I sent the letter.

No harm came. The letter was received by the moderator Bishop David Thomas and entered into the March 15–17, 1965, minutes by the secretary, Bishop Paul Landis: "A letter was read from a teenage girl who is a member of the Lititz Congregation expressing concerns for our church. It was agreed to accept this letter and to ask the moderator to reply to the letter."

Evidently I shared this letter with some other members of the congregation. Jane Herr, a friend of my mother's who had three daughters and wanted all of them to join this church, approached me in the women's anteroom with tears in her eyes. She had read my letter and wanted to tell me how deeply it touched her. She said I had expressed her own feelings. I remember standing in the women's anteroom, looking straight into Jane Herr's eyes, realizing "so this is the power of language."

The other outcome of the letter was that Bishop Isaac Sensenig himself called, asking to visit me. The man arrived wearing a black frock coat with no lapels. He came into the formal entrance, the same door where my various boyfriends had come. We sat in the formal living room my parents had remodeled in anticipation of their daughters' courtship years. Bishop Sensenig's visit certainly did not feel like courtship.

After saying that he and all the other bishops had read my letter, he had a question for me. I wondered how he would respond to my analysis of the book of John.

"I want to know," he said, "have you cut your hair?"

---

54. John 13:35.

I was shocked. I must have lied by saying no, because I don't remember a long conversation. I had shoulder-length hair I pinned up in a bun, but I was hoping to roll it in giant rollers like the other girls before long. I knew I would do that in college. Yet, because I hadn't cut my hair recently, I chose to interpret his question as though he meant, "Did you cut your hair last night?" And so I answered in the negative, remembering the example of my mother's conversation with her bishop before her wedding.

Did my fantasy of saving the congregation come true with my letter? No. The bishop did not miraculously see the light just because I wrote from my heart and pointed out Scriptures he should care about. In a way, though, love triumphed. The bishop was so dismayed by our worldliness and his inability to stop our train speeding to destruction that he left *us* instead of the other way around. In 1968 he and other ministers seeking a purer church started the Eastern Conference and left the Lancaster Conference. A milder bishop was appointed who was embraced and loved. No one celebrated the bishop's leaving. It seemed a sad day because it showed us how hard it is to "be ye therefore perfect, even as your Father which is in heaven is perfect."[55]

There was one moment in the four years I sat in the pews under Bishop Sensenig when I felt something other than fear or anger. It was during a sermon he preached about the importance of discipline. He quoted Hebrews 13:17 about being responsible for the souls of the congregation, saying he would have to give an account for every one of us on the day of judgment. He called for us to kneel in prayer.

I turned, knelt, and faced the back of the walnut bench, as I had hundreds of times before, often inattentively. This time was different. I listened hard to the bishop's prayer, not just to the words but also to the voice saying those words. I heard a leader's pain. I heard the throat clench and the voice grow husky as the

---

55. Matthew 5:48.

bishop whose authority I had challenged prayed for his sheep. I was glad I had challenged him. Yet for the first time, I believed he did actually care for our souls. His magnification of strictness gave him no joy. He was suffering, too! I had met my first paradox of leadership.

Though I was no longer poised at the Bible quiz buzzer, I had discovered one more contrast, this one not confined to the book of John.

Eighteen

Courtship and the Farmer's Daughter

There be three things which are too wonderful for me,
yea, four which I know not:
The way of an eagle in the air; the way of a serpent upon
a rock; the way of a ship in the midst of the sea; and the
way of a man with a maid.

—Proverbs 30:18-19

*L*ook at this beauty! Red roses on a pink velvet wrapping. Whew! Looks like Valentine's Day." The 4-H Club auctioneer was growing excited as he moved around the room. "What you say, fellas? Do I hear two bucks? I've got two. Who'll give me three?"

I was nervous listening to the bidding during my first box supper social, the most exciting event of the year. All the other boxes seemed so much more spectacular than mine. Boys and girls were seated on opposite sides of the auditorium at Fairland Elementary School. Boys raised their hands to bid on their favorite boxes, but had to wait until the end of the bidding to find out whose boxes they had purchased. Then each claimed his reward, eating supper in a corner of the room with the no-longer-mystery girl who had brought the box.

I was about twelve years old, one of the younger girls in the room that evening. Mother, who knew what box socials were all about, had gotten a brilliant idea earlier in the afternoon as we planned for the event. Necessity was likely the mother of her invention, since we didn't stock lots of glittery wrapping paper or bows at our house. Presents often came inside a plain box or a paper "toot" (bag).

So, how to make a box that would sell and attract a good buyer? Mother decided to go against the grain and turn our sow's ear of ordinary wrapping materials into a silk purse. I watched in awe as she spun magic out of words, like she had done many times before.

"Shirley, take a grocery bag and open it up at the seams, laying it flat. Then wrap up your box."

As I wrapped, she wrote, pausing to read aloud her words and getting me involved in choosing them. I had to admit it was a great idea, but it was risky, too.

Here was a plain little girl with her plain big box. What if people laughed at me?

While I had doubts about Mother's idea, I had no experience with what might entice a boy to pay good money for a shoebox wrapped in grocery bag paper.

Mother said, "Let's catch his imagination. Help me write a poem."

I can still see the four-by-six-inch card with my mother's distinctive handwriting—printing with a certain flair that looked almost cursive—in blue ink on white paper. I made several little Scotch-tape circles and affixed the poem atop the box. To emphasize the counter-glitter point, we may even have used bailing twine as string instead of ribbons.

Voilá! My box and I were ready for the social.

With trepidation, I carried my brown rectangular representation of self into the social, where a small mountain of colorful paper-wrapped boxes with carefully curled bows was already growing on a table next to the door.

When the time came to bid on the boxes, the auctioneer started at one end of the lineup and worked his way through, holding each lovely box high: "Some young lady in this room must have put a lot of time into this. Don't let her down. What am I bid?"

"Fifty cents," cried out a freckle-faced sixth grader.

"That's what I like," said the auctioneer, warming up his rhythm. "A big spender starts us off. Glad you dumped out that piggy bank before you came!"

As the bidding and kidding continued, I grew increasingly uneasy. What kind of wisecrack would the auctioneer make about my box, such an easy target for a joke. My mind worked overtime, until I saw the auctioneer reach for the lone brown box.

"My, my, my, *ach du lieber*, what have we here?" he asked, as he turned the box to read the attached card. Stalling for time, he pulled a pair of glasses from his shirt pocket.

"Why, fellas, it's a poem," he said. "Want me to read it?"

"Sure!" cried one potential bidder who had already lost to a few of the high rollers in the crowd, thus getting a little edgy. The boys were under their own form of pressure.

The auctioneer cleared his throat, paused for dramatic effect to scan the poem, and then began reading my mother's writing:

I know that I'm not fancy
I can't be very proud
Among these other pretty ones I'm quiet, not so loud.
I hope you'll like me anyway
I hope that you'll agree
My plain outside may not compete;
But inside out I'm very sweet.

"Okay, boys!" said the auctioneer, warming to the challenge. "Just think of what's *inside* the box. Poetry! Must come from a pretty sweet girl, don't you think?"

Evidently the idea of hidden beauty appealed to some of the farm boys in the room. A little kidding ensued. With each bid, I felt my cheeks get hotter. My heart beat faster. Finally, the gavel came down when the price was just under five dollars, one of the higher bids.

"Sold," the auctioneer cried, "to Tom!"

Now my anxiety shifted to the other extreme. Before, I worried that my brown-bag box would make me a laughingstock.

Now, however, the stakes had been raised by the price. Could the inside live up to its promise? Tall, brawny Tom was one of the oldest and most respected of all these earnest youth. I guessed he might be a senior in high school, since I didn't know him.

What would he do when he found out he paid five dollars for a sixth grader's box? Suddenly I saw the real question: It was not whether the food would be good enough, but rather would *I* be good enough?

Thoughts like these traveled through my mind like milk through a pipeline as the auction came to an end. Each boy paid for his box and then looked around the room to locate his supper partner.

Tom appeared hopeful as he scanned the crowd of girls in front of him. I took a step forward, trying to act confident. Then I saw his face fall. If he had been in a cartoon, the balloon over his head might have said: "What a sucker I was even to bid on this box. I wish I had stopped at $4.75 like my gut instinct told me to. Not only did I buy a plain box, but here is a plain girl— and she's only a sixth grader. Geez!"

I tried to pretend I hadn't noticed my supper partner's glum demeanor. I let him scout out a place for us to sit down, which turned out to be as far away as possible from the other high school boys.

I waited while Tom opened the box, eager to dig into what I thought was an outstanding supper: cold fried chicken, pickles, buttered bread, chips, pretzels, apples, and sugar cookies (Grandma Herr's recipe).

Tom's eyes did not light up, though. He picked at the food in front of him. I offered him his choice of drumstick, thigh, or breast, carefully inquiring, "White meat or dark meat?" Then I began gnawing on a drumstick.

I asked him a few questions such as what grade he was in, what school he went to, and where he lived. He answered politely, but his eyes roved the room. We both listened to the laughter of some of the happy couples who had arranged to beat the box social anonymity through some kind of secret language on the box itself to assure their pairing. The more they laughed, the more Tom and I felt the dead silence between us like air in a coffin.

Finally, I couldn't stand the quiet, so I rushed in to fill the vacuum. I told Tom about each room in this building, how if he walked down this hall, he would find all my teachers' rooms: on the right were Mrs. Gibble, Mrs. Rothenberger, and Miss Frey, while to the left were Miss Gibble, Mrs. McCardle, and Mrs. Lochner. I talked about the assemblies we had in this room, how I loved the smell of the white paste we used for all our art projects, and how much fun it was to be on the safety patrol. Blah, blah, blah.

Tom's eyes never landed on mine, and his ears seemed otherwise occupied, too.

When the 4-H sponsor stood up, signaling the end of the social, Tom quickly did the same. Visibly relieved, he couldn't wait to mumble thanks, get into his car, and drive off into the darkness.

When I returned home, Mother was all ears, and I was eager to release the pressure of all that adrenalin by telling her the story. She smiled as I described how the brown bag box had started a bidding war and that the buyer was a tall boy. Mom loved tallness. Then I told her about the look on Tom's face when he saw the box belonged to me and how he hadn't talked except to answer questions.

"Is this how dating is going to be?" I asked, fear creeping into my voice.

"No, not if you like each other," she answered. "It's never easy getting to know someone new, but I'm sure you'll be ready when your time comes."

I looked down at the box in my lap. There were two pieces of chicken, two slices of bread, and two apples left inside. My cheeks flushed one more time.

"Oh my goodness," I said. "Tom paid five dollars for this box, and I forgot to give it to him before he left! He only ate bread, chips, and cookies. What do you think I should do?"

"Just put the food in the fridge," my wise mother counseled, "and take the leftovers in your lunch box tomorrow. I don't think Tom will mind. It won't be the last time he pays too much for a meal."

The word that best describes my dating experience is *courtship*. Such an old-fashioned word. It conjures up blurry images of a horsedrawn carriage with fringe on top, long strolls in the moonlight, and bashful young men wearing seersucker and standing at the door with flowers and hats in hand. It's a nineteenth-century word that dates back to the courtly love tradition during the Middle Ages when longing itself was exalted, and consummation, devoutly to be wished, was a kiss or a stolen embrace rather than full sexual union.

I first saw how courtship worked when I watched Lois, a hired girl who helped Mother with household chores for several months after the birth of my baby sister Sue. Lois, who was single then, was even "plainer" than my mother (i.e., she wore a large hair covering, long dresses, and dark stockings). The neighbor's hired man, Levi, who used to be Amish but had left his church at the risk of excommunication was also single. Both Lois and Levi were a little older than the average age for dating, so anytime they came in close proximity to each other, we would tease them. Lois blushed whenever we used Levi's name. Thus, we did it as often as possible. She once sat outside with her Sunday school quarterly on her lap, reading it upside down. We suspected she was hoping to see Levi going down the road. She ended up marrying someone else, but she nevertheless showed me the connection between blushing and courtship. Even thoughts could turn your cheeks red!

Mother, of course, was my best source for courtship education, with lots of stories in her vast repertoire. And, as always, she turned what might have sounded like ordinary encounters to worldly-wise listeners into exciting ones to my inexperienced ears.

Mother loved to talk about her favorite teenage outfits—a yellow dress, cameo jewelry, a sailor suit, a coatdress—and the attention she got when she wore these. Being in plays, 4-H, and church afforded her interactions with *prospective beaus*, a term girls actually used in her day.

That same year the homeliest and most awkward boy in our class developed a crush on me. I asked Mother, "Why is it that boys I don't like like me, and the ones I like don't seem to know I exist?"

For a while, Mother just thought, her hands in the suds. Then she laughed.

"I asked my mother the same question when I was about your age."

"What did your mother tell you?"

"She said, 'You have eyes, don't you?'"

"That's all?"

"No. She told me, 'Well, use them.'"

"Did Grandma show you how?" I asked.

"No. She just smiled," said Mother as she smiled at me.

"Tell me about when you and Daddy met."

"Well, there was a tradition of having 'singings' for young people on Wednesday nights. They were held in homes. Once the singing was held at Paul Hershey's house [the Home Place]. I was standing at the mirror in an upstairs bedroom where we all laid our coats. In the reflection I saw a very handsome young man looking at me, smiling. I turned around and smiled back."

"Did you know he was the one then?" I asked.

"No," said Mother. "But your daddy later told me that *he* knew then. After we were married I asked him whether it was my eyes that attracted him that night. 'No, silly,' he said. 'It was your smile.'"

Courtship, of course, plays an important role in rural communities, which depend on young love leading to marriage and then to children as part of the economic as well as social arrangement. Without a new generation to share in the hard work of making a hundred acres pay for themselves, a farmer simply could not run a farm. Today it takes a thousand acres and a million dollars or more. For generations before this one, however, it took children, the more the merrier. The sex drive and the farm drive were in alignment with each other.

Farm folks often referred to courtship as a time of "running around." The Pennsylvania Dutch[56] expression *rumspringa*[57] means literally jumping or running around and refers to a period of relative permissiveness before joining the church and settling down into marriage. Since information about Mennonite practices is often confused with Amish ones, and because practices differ widely *within* both groups, it's sometimes difficult to sort fact from fiction. My own *rumspringa* was very tame, but it served an important purpose.

One of the practices I heard about, and we sometimes joked about, was the "blue gate" signal: a father painting his front gate blue as a sign that he had an eligible daughter within. Whether or not real fathers did this, the story that it was an Amish or Mennonite custom persisted.

At the Home Place, Daddy did not paint the front gate blue, but we had our own ways of getting the word out.

If you were in high school, as almost every young person was, people could assume you were eligible by the grade you were in. "Sweet sixteen" was the usual age at which dating began; if you were fifteen, you risked the reputation of being "fast." But there were also other ways to send out the signal. The first was to buy a huge class ring with a large red stone and the school's name inscribed around it. This glittery object was off limits for the hands of Mennonites, of course, although I often gazed longingly upon the gems worn by some of my classmates.

The other way, however, was to purchase a big, bulky class jacket. On the back of the black wool garment, an arc of bright red letters—W-A-R-W-I-C-K—formed an umbrella over two numbers: the year of the wearer's high school graduation ('66 in my case).

---

56. See glossary, 255.
57. Ibid.

My class jacket had "Shirley" embroidered on the front left side and the oval Warwick logo on the right. The jacket cost more than any other one in my closet, and I probably paid for part or all of it with my own money. I'm sure, however, that I was pleased with the investment. I loved the cool feeling of slipping my arms into the jacket's warm wool arms with their quilted satin lining. On fall evenings my friends from Warwick '66 and '65 and Conestoga Valley '65 always hoped we would run into a group of boys wearing Garden Spot '66 or Manheim Central '65 jackets.

Another way to prepare for dating was by sending one of your individual class pictures off to one of the addresses in little ads found in the backs of magazines such as *Ladies Home Journal*. You could order twenty wallet-sized pictures for only a dollar and then trade them with friends. Long before Facebook, inventive youth had created a low-tech version.

Every girl owned a wallet with many transparent picture holders. A really popular girl's wallet bulged with a trove of photos, all with messages autographed on the back. Collecting these photos took courage because the unspoken rules of social hierarchies applied. It was much better to be asked than to ask for a picture.

As I approached the normal dating age of sixteen, I hoped to find just the right glamor shot that would make me irresistible to some handsome young man gazing at my face in the wallet of a friend. I wanted that effect so much that I drove myself to the Olan Mills Studio and sat for a portrait instead of simply waiting until time for my usual school picture.

The results were disappointing, no matter which of three separate takes I chose. None was pin-up material, but I got copies made anyway. After all, I had paid good money for them, and I must have given them away successfully, because I collected a modest number of other photos in my own wallet. I still have three different headshots taken at this photo shoot. I can't believe I didn't throw them away. The eight-inch-by-twelve-inch photo apparently never made it into a frame, judging from the

Not exactly cheesecake. The Olin Mills Studio picture taken about 1965.

crease along the edge. And the outfit? Even the bishop would have been impressed by my buttoned-up modesty.

I began my courtship earlier than many girls did. The summer I turned fifteen, I went to Black Rock Camp for a week, along with about forty other Mennonite youth. There I met a young man named Paul Kennel at the first mixed-gender camp I ever went to. There were only a few boys and about twenty girls that week. Paul was the only boy who interested me, and I was thrilled when he started to talk to me. Both of us loved baseball. Both of us had ruddy cheeks. Somehow I was the lucky girl who got to hold hands with Paul and then write letters back and forth for quite a few months afterward. Maybe it was my eyes.

Timing is everything though. Somehow the letters became less frequent. About the time the letters ended, our family was invited to the home of a family we didn't know very well. They lived close to the town of New Holland, went to Groffdale Mennonite Church, and did not live on a farm. We enjoyed getting to know them better one Sunday over dinner, followed by a little socializing when the kids retired to a game of foosball in

Paul and me at Black Rock Camp, 1963.

their family room. Nelson Wert and his younger sister were the
only children in the family. Nelson was a year older than I was
and planned to go to college to become a veterinarian. That fact
alone made him devilishly handsome to me. By the time we left
the house that afternoon, I was hooked. When he called to ask
me out on my first real date, I was thrilled. Since I was still only
fifteen, I wasn't sure if my parents would allow me to go, but they
must have seen how much I wanted to. Since they had already
met and approved of the whole family, they said yes to our date.

I have a foggy recollection of wearing a polished cotton dress
with a large floral print. I think we may have hiked, a good
excuse for holding hands.

What I remember most was being ready for my first real date
fifteen minutes early. I had taken special care with my hair, having learned a trick from other Mennonite girls. When you wear
a bun, the only staging area for creating anything like a hairdo
is the hair that surrounds the face. If you washed your hair and

then used bobby pins to hold it in place, you could crimp your hair like a pie crust. When dry, the hair would fall into a set of waves around the face. I looked in the mirror and was pleased by the result.

I paced nervously in the kitchen, waiting, until I heard the sound of stones crunching in the driveway as Nelson drove his family's sedan (proof he was not a farm boy!) into our lane. That sound, one I had heard thousands of times before, sent a shock through my body. Sound reverberated under the earth, connecting through my feet to something beyond. I felt like the invisible world was speaking to me. The stones themselves whispered, "You will leave this place, and this is the beginning."

One night, around 9:30, after the rest of my family had gone to bed, Nelson and I were sitting in the living room next to the open staircase. We were trying to find subjects that led to natural, relaxed conversation—difficult to do since both of us were so young and nervous and inexperienced. Suddenly, a little brown mouse darted out from under our legs and skittered across the wide wooden floorboards of the old house. Neither of us laughed as we both pretended not to notice. I blushed right red. Soon it was time for Nelson to go. When he left, would my chances to date a Mennonite boy on the way to college, such a rare creature, also disappear?

Shortly after the mouse episode, my parents decided it was time to make the parlor more suitable for dating. My father probably wished he could have bought just one bucket of blue paint for the gate. Instead, he had to cough up a lot more for some serious remodeling. We needed a room that could be made private instead of a room that led upstairs and was easily accessible to the curious eyes and ears of younger brothers and sisters on the second floor. Fortunately, the Home Place farmstead was a "double" house with an apartment on the other side. We could enlarge our space by reclaiming one of the two living rooms from that area. The door next to the rental space was closed and locked, and another door opened into the living room with the staircase. The crucial point about that new door was that it could close again, and it was well away from the staircase, so family members could come and go even if I were entertaining a boyfriend in the now-private new parlor, resplendent in its makeover: new wallpaper, paint, carpet, and an accent wall sporting real walnut paneling, the latest in farm interiors.

When the workers peeled away old wallpaper and plaster, they had encountered a surprise. A rugged wooden beam emerged with a black bell attached to one end. The beam still carried rough hatchet cuts made in 1735. Now I would have something to talk about on awkward first dates. The room had a story. Maybe this was the very place where Count Zinzendorf preached in 1742. I noticed most of my boyfriends were not as impressed by this fact as I thought they should be, however.

Now that we had a room and I had turned sixteen, I was ready for the phone to ring again. Despite my fears of rejection after the mouse incident, Nelson did call again, but I wasn't allowed to go with him on his youth group's trip. Some other girl took that space, a disappointment to me. But soon I was back playing my favorite game of Walk-a-Mile[58] with our youth group, open to using my eyes on other boys.

By the age of seventeen, I had reached the flagging-interest stage of courtship. I had been with one boyfriend, John, all though the winter of Bible quizzing in 1965. He had learned about me from his sister, my camp counselor. I adored her because she made me laugh. So I looked forward to dating her brother. When he showed up driving a convertible, I was even more interested. After several months of double dates with other friends and their dates, however, we got to that fork in the road: Either get more serious or get going. So we got going . . . in different directions.

Soon thereafter I had a bright idea. Why not start an Old Maids Society? A group of girlfriends pretended along with me

---

58. Walk-a-Mile was a popular rural mixer in Lancaster Conference Mennonite youth groups. First, select a country road with low traffic. Then, girls line up on one side, boys on the other. Hold hands. Walk. Try to say something interesting. Walk and talk until one boy taps another boy's shoulders and takes his place. You might call it Mennonite speed-dating.

that we would never marry and therefore had no more use for courtship. Shades of the Hikta Stikta Club!

We even crashed Joe's Diner one night. Curious about what Mennonite guys found so appealing in this steel-clad diner, we drove there ourselves, sat in a corner booth, and observed the scene—more like anthropologists than frisky cats on a hot tin roof.

All around us was classic Americana. A waitress wearing a cute little apron ambled over to our table.

"Hi there, gals. What can I get for you-uns?"[59]

We studied the plastic-coated menus carefully, always conscious of our pennies yet eager for a treat. We all asked for milkshakes and split an order of fries and a hamburger.

The jukebox in the corner almost always had several platters ready to drop down onto the turntable: "Peggy Sue," "The Little Old Lady from Pasadena," or "Itsy Bitsy Teenie Weenie Yellow Polka Dot Bikini." We knew the words to all of these tunes. We loved pretending we could dance and for a little while were just another bunch of teenyboppers. Except for those prayer coverings on our heads.

In the spring of my junior year in high school, with Mother and Daddy's approval, I planned a visit to Eastern Mennonite College. I was stepping out in the direction of my dream. For Mother the trip was exciting in another way. Her mentor in combining writing and speaking with traditional roles in the home was Ruth Brunk Stoltzfus, *Your Friend Ruth* on the radio. Ruth lived just a few miles from the college.

Ruth and Grant Stoltzfus lived in a big white house overlooking the western mountains of the Shenandoah Valley in Virginia. Mother contacted Ruth to see if she, Daddy, and I could stay in their home while I attended special events for prospective students during the college's homecoming activities.

At breakfast the next morning, Daddy, Mother, and I joined their family of five children and two parents for breakfast. The

59. See glossary, 255.

food was simple and the table unadorned. What mattered more than food, to the whole family it seemed, was conversation. I was used to chatter at family meals, but not this kind! No one talked about the weather, the list of chores, or what the neighbors were up to. The talk was about books, music, art, and any interesting ideas in what they were reading and experiencing. The Stoltzfuses didn't always agree. In fact, the point of the conversation seemed to be trying to view the same object or idea from as many different vantage points as possible.

If this was the kind of family life produced by college, then I was all for it! When I returned to my high school classes after my visit to EMC, I doodled in the edges of my three-ring denim binder. I wrote "Allen Grant Stoltzfus" along the edge of my binder, using the oldest son's full name, positioning it north-south like a lighthouse, not east-west like a field. The very name sent a powerful beacon to my future, which I was sure now would be large with energy. I continued the Old Maid Society halfheartedly, had a few more local dates, and began to focus not only on my academic plans but also on my social ones for the four years ahead. I hoped to spend them at that magnetic place far away in Virginia called Eastern Mennonite College, where I was destined to find some intelligent, good-looking Mennonite man looking for adventure. The name I wrote in my binder was a placeholder. The man himself was a mystery, but one thing I knew. Our conversations at the breakfast table would be brilliant.

How exactly were my future children, the offspring of a former Old Maid and a Future Intellectual of America, going to come into the world?

Courtship and sex were not designed to travel the same road, according to my parents and the books they gave me about Christian dating. I knew the basic facts of life and understood how a woman could become pregnant. I had often seen my little brother taking his bath, but from the time I was ten until the time I got married at twenty-one, I never saw a naked man. The closest I came to such a sight was observing my father exit the bathroom wearing only jockey shorts.

Our sex education in public school health class consisted of a little section about the reproductive organs and menstruation. But sex, of course, is always the subtext of any high school. There were the boys with tight jeans, combs in their back pockets, side-burns, and ducktail haircuts. At school, however, I hung out with the bookish kids who liked to talk about politics and literature, which saved me from too much envy of the popular crowd's social scene.

So it was that I moved all the way through high school just as pure as Mother and Daddy expected me to be. I never thought of myself as a virgin. I was just a girl. I knew my body was full of energy. I loved the feeling of waking up in the morning firm and strong in every muscle, ready to tackle the world.

Years later, when I eventually wrote a dissertation on women authors born in the nineteenth century, I knew exactly what Willa Cather meant as she described her main character Thea's emerging sexuality:

> She used to drag her mattress beside her low window and lie awake for a long while, vibrating with excitement, as a machine vibrates from speed. Life rushed in upon her through that win-dow—or so it seemed. In reality, of course, life rushes from within, not from without. There is no work of art so big or so beautiful that it was not once all contained in some youthful body, like this one which lay on the floor in the moonlight, puls-ing with ardor and anticipation.[60]

In fact, I could see my own body stretched out on the double bed that had been in the Hess family for three generations. The wide and deep windowsill beside the bed led out to the starry night. The long body pillow I hugged every night stretched diag-onally across the quilted cover on the bed.

My joy in my own body led me to curiosity about sex, and then to literature for clues about what the connection between sex and joy might be. I had gone out of my way to try to locate a sex scene a friend told me about in one of Pearl S. Buck's books,

60. Willa Cather, *The Song of the Lark* (Boston: Houghton Mifflin, 1915), 177.

but I never did find it. I also begged my father to stop the car whenever we went past a drive-in theater so that I could study the huge faces on the screen. I longed to see the faraway dreamy people kiss in Technicolor. My father, however, never stopped the car—merely slowed it down.

Mennonite prohibitions included dancing, television, and movies. When my gym teacher taught a class unit on dancing, I had to turn in a note sent by my mother excusing me for religious reasons. Those classes spent with one other lonely Mennonite classmate on the wooden bleachers were some of the longest fifty minutes in high school for me.

Back at the Home Place, one would think I would have gotten a sex education by watching all those animals. However, even our pets did their mating out of sight. The suckling of their young, however, was a very public act. Our dogs and cats were

My sisters, Doris and Sue, with our dog, Nellie, and her puppies. At the Spahr farm, about 1960.

prolific, spawning brood after brood of helpless puppies and kittens clamoring over each other for time at their mothers' breasts.

My mother was rather prolific also. Six live births. Five different times in my life I was presented with a new baby sister or brother. I loved smelling the tops of their heads, kissing the napes of their necks, even sucking their earlobes or toes. Whenever I had a new sibling, my mother's discrete breastfeeding was both an embarrassing reminder of her sexuality and a good memory of the perfect union of mother and child. Someday, perhaps, I would want to become a mother, too. But not yet.

Part of the lack of visual sexual instruction on the farm stemmed from the fact that my father was a member of the Dairy Herd Improvement Association and owned registered Holsteins. He no longer left breeding to Mother Nature. Science had entered the scene and spoiled the sex. In contrast to the old way of allowing a bull to jump the cow when she went into *estrus,* or "heat," the scientific way is not to call in a bull but rather a professional with the unromantic title of Artificial Inseminator (AI). This person (always a man in my experience) has to arrive soon after the heifer goes into heat, the signs of which are extra vaginal lubrication and her attempts to mount another heifer.

The AI would arrive with a vial of semen procured by duping a bull to have sex with a reasonable facsimile of the back end of a cow. One ejaculation produces over a billion sperm cells, which means that the owner of a quality bull can freeze the semen and sell it to farmers all across the world. Ivanhoe was the great Holstein bull of the 1960s and the daddy of most of our best-producing milk cows.

On several occasions I was allowed to watch the amazing process of insemination. The inseminator put on long rubber gloves and then used both hands, one in the rectum to guide and the other in the vagina, to deposit the semen. Then he pulled off the soiled glove, washed his arms in a bucket of hot soapy water, filled out his invoice, and headed up the road to insert his arm into the next cow. Fortunately, artificial insemination bore no resemblance to my later sex life, but it certainly was amazing to watch.

The church made its own contribution to my sex education. A doctor and his wife delivered the formal instruction at Lititz Mennonite Church. They were missionaries returned from Africa, now on a mission to help American youth avoid temptations of the flesh until their passion could be consummated in marriage. The doctor talked to the boys in the main auditorium, while his wife talked to the girls. My friends and I mostly made fun of "Mrs. Doctor" because the approach was so serious, and, like so much other cautionary education, this talk exaggerated even the slightest danger. It was like a *Reefer Madness* film for the Mennonite world.

Mrs. Doctor exhorted us not to wear high heels because they thrust the body, especially the breasts, into prominence in such a way that a young man might not be able to control his carnal urges. Having worn heels from the age of twelve without provoking any danger worse than wobbly walking, I felt free to disregard this advice.

My mother saw the humor in the Byzantine lecture after a group of my girlfriends and I did a satirical rerun of the event in our kitchen. Mother's own advice was based on a similarly respectful view of the power of male sexual urges, however, along with confidence that a young woman who knew how to protect the boundaries of her bra straps could keep not only herself pure but her boyfriend also. When I was ten, Mother told me my body would soon be ready to have babies. This information alone was reason to guard oneself, wear modest clothing, and be careful around men both young and old.

The most instructive story my mother ever told me was about one weekend she and Daddy went to the beach together before they were married. She said that weekend had taught her how hard it could be to save sex for marriage. I had seen pictures of the two of them in their bathing suits, with my father's muscular torso, long arms, and handsome features next to my mother's curves, curls, and full breasts only partially covered by her two-piece bathing suit.

I never got the message that sex was dirty or unpleasant. Quite the contrary, actually. I sensed that sex was dangerous precisely because it was *so* pleasurable and could burn you up unless the institution of marriage protected you. My parents often held hands in front of us to display their affection, and my mother loved to brag to us about how handsome daddy was. She even hinted how much she enjoyed sex by saying with great emphasis and a beatific smile, "Your father is a *man*."

My mother bought me a book about dating, sex, and marriage within a spiritual context. The gift vanished long ago, but I still have her accompanying letter, written in 1961. I was thirteen then, and she was only thirty-four herself—and very respectful of the power of passion. The letter reveals her struggling to offer both guidance and freedom to her daughter: "I should have liked to have underlined some truths that I think are especially important, but I guess it would be better to let these truths stand out themselves without my assistance."

I began to notice other nuances. We had gender segregation in church—with men sitting on one side and women on the other. Teenage girls sat in one or two rows near the back, while the teenage boys were on the opposite side. We ogled each other across the center aisle, whispering to our friends, and barely contained our voices well enough to prevent a disturbance in the Sunday service.

One of our favorite frivolities was to go through the hymnbook index and add the words "under the bed" to various titles. Sometimes the hilarity of this juxtaposition would send us into silent paroxysms of laughter that shook the whole wooden bench, producing glares from the sedate matrons in front of us.

Another activity we girls enjoyed in church was faintly, and gently, stroking the tender insides of each others' arms. This touching was innocent, intended as a diversion from the boredom of sermons or even as aids to keeping us quiet and apparently attentive. Later, when I read that the skin and the brain for women are the two most important sexual organs, I smiled.

When I was thirteen, I learned about the subtext of danger firsthand. As luck would have it, another farm family we knew included two good-looking sons just a few years older than I was. Their mother invited our family to come to their house for lunch one snowy Sunday. Following a big meal that afternoon, someone suggested the four oldest children might want to go sledding. I eagerly buttoned up my coat; put on hat, gloves, and boots; and hurried to join Henry and the two older boys.

There were only three sleds. Henry joined the two older boys on the first ride, which left me standing alone at the top of the hill. My intuition told me that something was not right. Below me in the distance, the two older boys started whispering something in my little brother's ear. Obediently, he yelled out the letters they dictated: "F" and then "U" and then "C" and "K." The big boys laughed. Suddenly, the fun of sledding was all gone for me as I watched the older boys take advantage of my brother, who had no idea what he was saying. I never went down that hill. Instead, I ran back to the house, tears streaming down my face. I made up some lie about being too cold and never told anyone what had happened.

I would later recognize this event as an awakening into the power of the patriarchy. The boys were not threatening bodily harm. They were trying to shock me with the worst bad word they knew. But behind their taunt was warning. The wrong man, the wrong sexual act, could scar me forever.

After that, I examined every boy and man I met with a little more care and a little less trust. In the 1960s that was not necessarily a bad thing. I lost a piece of innocence on that snowy hillside at age thirteen.

As a teenager, I wanted to postpone marriage, to avoid marrying a farmer and having babies until I had discovered on my own what courtship would be like in an altogether different place: a college nestled among the purple mountains of Virginia. It had not escaped my notice that the sports teams at Eastern Mennonite College were then called the Courtiers.

SILVER SUMMIT FARM

REGISTERED HOLSTEINS

H. RICHARD HERSHEY

Leaving Home

Whatsoever thy hand findeth to do, do it with thy might.
—Ecclesiastes 9:10

While I was losing interest in the dating game, I turned my attention to my senior year of high school. My boyfriend crushes were often less intense than my teacher crushes. Ever since Mrs. Lochner in sixth grade had consumed my imagination, I always had a role model, male or female, whose very existence plucked some inner heartstrings within me. There was Miss Riehl, my guidance counselor, formerly the physical education teacher who nicknamed me "Rosy Cheeks." And my favorite English teacher, young Miss Ringlaben, who had started out as a student teacher. Most beloved of all was my history teacher, Mr. Price. In the presence of all of them, I wanted to shine. Often, I did. Just as often, I stumbled and blushed, trying so hard to be whatever it was that I thought they admired rather than simply being myself.

Once, as I was walking down the empty hall after the dismissal bell had rung, I spied Miss Ringlaben's reflection in the window to her classroom. She was looking down on the students boarding the school buses below, and I could tell she was crying. The moment was brief but vivid. Her pain seared me. Like all undeserved suffering, it reminded me of love. I both loved her for those tears and took away a warning. The calling to be a teacher wasn't some magic wand of authority one waved. Like all callings, it would be a spiritual journey. In the words of one of my favorite poems, it would be no "crystal stair."[61]

Mr. J. Lorell Price was a young, single teacher with short-clipped hair and an athletic build. His wardrobe ran to tweeds and plaids, quite fashionable yet understated. His shirts were Oxford weave and usually included a little snap collar, one of those '60s fashion "improvements" designed to make the knot of a skinny tie stand out. He had a way of holding his tie in front of him like a wand or antenna as he paced around the classroom.

Mr. Price taught political science my senior year, and I excelled in this class out of a strong motivation to work hard. Mr. Price attracted the best and brightest students to his elective classes, mostly boys, all of whom were smart, nerdy, and much more aware than I was of current events, including the Vietnam War. Bill Pezick wore glasses and, rumor had it, size fifteen shoes. He was a National Merit Scholarship winner, a status I hardly understood except that I knew it was related to the SAT test that I had also taken in my junior year in high school and that I had a letter somewhere telling me I was "commended."

The SAT and the college application process can seem like a totally new language, even gibberish, to the student whose parents never went to college. Fortunately, I had Miss Riehl, now my guidance counselor, to help guide me.

Out of three Mennonite girls in a class of 144 students, I was the only one who planned to go to college, even though the other two were excellent students. Without Mennonite role models, I wasn't sure how to combine academic ambition with the church's teachings. I knew that the Lancaster Conference Mennonites had not encouraged higher education for reasons having to do with the potential for pride and independence from God and the community. Would education give me a "big head"? Would it destroy my faith? I wanted to find biblical courage as I prepared to leave home.

---

61. Langston Hughes, "Mother to Son," *African-American Poetry: An Anthology, 1773–1927* (Mineola, New York: Dover Publications, 1977), 76.

I had read in the *Saturday Evening Post* or *Look* that Ecclesiastes was John F. Kennedy's favorite book. So, of course, I devoured it and thought of it in a new way as a book that is older and wider than Mennonites. Reading that book as a young woman set off chimes in my soul. From there, I read all the wisdom literature I could find. My black leather-bound, Christmas-gift Bible contains lots of passages in both Proverbs and Ecclesiastes that are underlined with pink and red pens. Later, I would learn that John's gospel, the one I nearly memorized, was built on the late wisdom literature of the Hebrew Bible, and that the Sermon on the Mount, the very heart of Mennonite theology, also shared this same ancient source.

Occasionally, the Scriptures I was reading and underlining connected to the frenetic pop culture surrounding me. In 1965, The Byrds transformed Ecclesiastes 3:1-8 into a hit record with Pete Seeger's song "Turn, Turn, Turn." As the song climbed to No. 1 on the Billboard Hot 100 chart, it reached me in Lititz. I drove to school in the little black convertible, turned up the volume when I recognized the words, and sang along. The idea of "crossover" between faith and folk music appealed to me. Could God be present in some of the very places, such as pop culture, I had been most warned about? I didn't assume the answer was always yes, or that all uses of the Bible in public life were good, but I did sing even more lustily, "There's a time to every purpose under heaven."[62] I knew I was driving toward it.

Mr. Price inspired me to think that intellectual life and spiritual life might actually go together. He believed politics should be about justice and compassion. I was sitting in his class when the news that President Kennedy had been shot came over the public address system. All of us sat staring at our desks in disbelief. I felt sick. Mr. Price's instant grief quickly translated into an angry outburst about the assassination: "This must be the work of those Goldwater people!" Our class had been having vigorous debates between Barry Goldwater supporters who were already emerging in late 1963 and supporters of President Kennedy's

62. Ecclesiastes 3:1.

"New Frontier" vision that favored welfare state solutions to such issues as poverty, racism, and crime.

I was on Mr. Price's and Kennedy's sides (in that order) of these arguments, partly because I was attracted to the youthful, handsome president and his equally charismatic supporter, my teacher. I also sensed here another "crossover" opportunity to connect the Mennonite values with the speeches and proposals of John F. Kennedy.

So when Kennedy was shot, I wanted to run to Mr. Price and hug him. Instead, I watched him collapse on the classroom windowsill. Then I walked home across the fields, wondering what would happen to America now.

Mr. Price later apologized to the Goldwater supporters in the class for his hasty judgment. His outburst had been an anomaly, and though his philosophy of reason and debate buckled briefly under the weight of trauma, his apology restored him. In front of me I saw an example of unforced humility, and I loved it deeply.

I dealt with my own grief by constructing a book made out of oversized construction paper. It contained newspaper clippings and an essay I wrote about my generation and our great loss. I didn't do it for a grade. Or for a contest. I don't think I even showed it to Mr. Price, although I would have loved to lift his grief. Like my mother before me, I turned to writing when I could no longer make sense of the world. Without John F. Kennedy in the White House, how would I keep learning about what inspiring things I should do with my life?

For a girl who had always loved competition, I had a good playing field during my senior year of high school. Warwick High School gave the largest monetary reward in the nation to three students at commencement each year. Or so we were told. Our teachers voted for the students they thought best exemplified courtesy, dependability, initiative, honesty, tolerance, leadership, punctuality, self-control, and appreciation of teachers.

The teachers also consulted church and youth group leaders and employers.

The philanthropist behind this gift was Elmer Holmes Bobst, a man who grew up in Lititz and went on to become a pharmaceutical company magnate at Warner-Lambert. Even more important for the welfare of his hometown, Bobst established a pharmaceutical manufacturing plant in Lititz, first called Warner-Lambert, then Parke-Davis, and finally Johnson & Johnson. The plant still stands—testimony to a homeboy's respect for the work ethic of his childhood friends and neighbors.

I wondered what it would feel like to be one of the three winners of this award. I wanted very much to be one of those people. I needed the money, since my parents were not able to pay for my college, and $500 (the first prize) would cover one-third of my bill for tuition, room, and board for the first year. More than that, I sought a blessing from the biggest stars in my universe—my teachers.

At home, our family had expanded to five children. Sue and Doris had both been born during the Spahr farm years. Sue's birth a year after the death of Mary Louise brought joy into our grief, and Doris's birth three years later gave us a new playmate. A few months after we moved back to the Home Place, Mother started wearing maternity tops again. I was not happy about that. Enough already! The new gravity of our financial burdens and my own emerging sexual maturity made it hard for me to accept a new baby. Once I was even mistaken for my baby sister's mother in Dr. Hess's waiting room! I thought that blush would never disappear.

I tried to harden my heart permanently against the new baby, Linda, born the same day John Glenn went into space. But, of course, that was impossible. Her bright smile, blonde hair, and dark eyes soon captured me. And her love for farm animals, which appeared as soon as she could chase after them, endeared her to all of us. The three younger girls created a unit a little like the one Henry and I had earlier forged. As the oldest, I was called upon to babysit my sisters. I used the opportunity to practice my dream of becoming a teacher even though the setting was often the hay mow or cow stable.

"Doris," I would call out to my four-year-old sister. "What is the highest mountain in Africa?"

She would jump up and down and shout, "Mount Kilamanjaro!"

We took that show on the road, starting in the kitchen with Mother and the rest of the family and sometimes performing for cousins and friends.

My high school years were hard ones for Henry. Unbeknownst to us, he had injured growth cells when he broke his leg back at Fairland Elementary. When his leg began growing crooked and causing him pain, he had to have surgery. When that surgery failed, three others followed. During the summer of 1964, Henry lay in a hospital bed in the living room, a body cast encasing his lower body. He managed to maintain good cheer, but he and I were no longer able to continue our adventures together.

My sister Sue stepped into the void left when Henry could no longer help on the farm. She was a passionate, determined child who, like my mother, loved the farm and farm work, becoming a rock of stability for my parents after Henry's surgeries and my eventual departure.

Money was very tight at our house in the mid-1960s. Drought threatened many of our crops, and milk prices did not make up the losses. Several capital outlays were needed, however. One was a new tractor. "That tractor would pay for four years of college!" I lamented to Mother while we washed and dried dishes together. I was using my teenage gift for transforming a business decision into a drama that revolved around me. I didn't have the courage to complain to Daddy, however. Mother defended his decision, and I continued to plan for how I would pay for college without a lot of parental help. I would get a job!

I found work as a cashier at Stauffer's Market of Kissel Hill. This job not only supported me before and during college, but it also taught me some lessons. Stauffer's began as a small fruit stand, selling Florida oranges to the citrus- and sun-starved Lititz residents in the winter. The original entrepreneur, Roy M. Stauffer Sr., had a daughter Rhoda who, along with her husband, Jay Oberholtzer, was a lay leader in our church, another speaker like my mother and a force in the family business.

By the time I applied for a job at Stauffer's, it had grown into a sizable chain of meat and cheese markets, with fresh fruits and vegetables in all seasons, dried and silk flowers for arrangements, and a nursery for annuals and perennials. At Christmas, trees and wreaths made the whole place smell like a pine forest.

I enjoyed my work. I wore a white cotton jacket or white apron not only to protect my clothing, but also as a badge of honor, as my safety patrol belt had been in elementary school. I wanted to serve the public. The job at the cash register required me to stand all day and took its toll on my legs and feet. It could also get boring after a few hours. Usually I took my mind off the monotony by chatting with customers. If one of my teachers happened to come through the line, I felt my heart race. I always tried to think of some witty comment but often felt tongue-tied, hoping I wouldn't blush.

Even brief encounters at the cash register with teachers, who seemed to speak from thrones in the classroom, would bring them down to earth for me as they placed tomatoes and eggs on the conveyor belt just like any other ordinary person. When it occurred to me that they were also human beings with bodily needs and functions like my own, I was so shaken by the revelation that I packed Mr. Anchak's bags with the soft items on the bottom—a big no-no. When the customers weren't my teachers, I could converse much more easily.

I also developed a game when making change. In those days before credit cards, everyone paid by cash or checks—usually cash. The register tallied the change so that both the customer and the cashier could see the amount due, eliminating the need for any mathematical calculations. I decided to challenge the machine. As a customer handed me the money, I'd look at the bills, then at the customer, and announce the amount due back in change. In short order, I had memorized all combinations of amounts up to $100. If the customer's bill was $5.64, for example, and the person offered a $10 bill, I'd say $4.36 immediately, and then turn to the drawer to withdraw that amount, looking up at the numbers on the register only as confirmation.

This practical skill has proved to be quite handy. It affirmed my capacity to perform lower-level calculations in my least favorite subject, math. Depending on my mood, I could do this either perfunctorily or dramatically and playfully. There's more than one way to find a stage, even when you are wearing a hair covering.

My job at Stauffer's was my first experience working for people other than my parents. I had to learn not only how to make change and handle what seemed like large sums of money, but also how to listen to customer complaints respectfully while also thinking about my responsibility to my employer. In addition, I had to get along with my peers and the middle managers. Once, the head cashier became very angry with me. She had just replaced the food-stained table covering in the lunch room with a new white cover, made of the kind of cardboard we used to make signs indicating prices for the produce. I enjoyed making those signs, and I did so whenever the head cashier, whose job it usually was, allowed it.

So, when I saw the white cardboard, my first instinct was to begin drawing faces on it, something I loved to do. Doodling, it was called. But I would actually begin to think of these faces emerging under my hand as characters. In the back of my diary, I created "families" of characters, all of whom bore a resemblance to the comic strip character Mark Trail, whose adventures I followed in the Lancaster *Intelligence Journal*.

To say that the head cashier was unhappy was a vast understatement. She went directly to my boss. I was chastised and I apologized. Later, I learned to look at the situation from the manager's perspective, but at the time I just saw an empty canvas.

I had thought others might enjoy my decorations and fascinating characters. My idea of beauty was that a blank slate was an invitation to become an artist myself. When I realized that my participation was viewed as desecration, I blushed.

One encounter with a customer stands out in my memory: I was helping a woman choose a watermelon, using the "plunking" method for detecting ripeness. She told me that previous employees had not found her "good" ones. I tried to lighten the mood by asking what she did, noticing her professional dress. When she said she was a teacher, I brightened, and said, "Oh, I'm going to be a teacher, too!"

The woman looked me up and down from head covering to white apron to my denim skirt and dirty Keds sneakers. Her mouth drew up like a little brown fig.

"I see," she said, obviously not seeing a future teacher.

My cheeks stung as I returned to the cash register. Mennonite bishops were not the only people who judged only on the basis of externals.

I made other mistakes while working at Stauffer's. I was an honest employee and would never have taken money from the till. But a few times I stuck stray cherries and grapes in my mouth, and, at least once, when I went into the refrigerated storage room and saw a particularly delectable peach, perfectly round with a rosy glow on each side, I took a bite. Then, of course, I had to consume the evidence of my sin. Like Adam and Saint Augustine, I was tempted by a piece of perfect fruit, and I yielded.

This one job, at $1 per hour and increasing to $1.25 by 1966, granted me my first taste of financial independence. I spent a little of my earnings, gave some of the money in church, but most of it I saved. I worked part time during the school year and thirty-six to forty hours per week in the summer. In two years, I saved $1,500. Along with scholarships and campus jobs plus $1,000 from my parents, I earned enough to pay for my own college education, something nearly impossible to do today.

Working was just a part-time effort. School, especially that last year, took my full-time energy. As one of the editors of the student yearbook, I had eagerly supported my friend Jeanette's suggestion that we adopt the Shakespearian theme "The Past Is Prologue." Like Wordsworth, I developed a nostalgic view of my childhood even before I left it. All through the summer months I tried to imagine what lay ahead.

On parents' night at school, Mr. Price asked for a private audience with Mother and Daddy. I blushed at hearing that request, disappointed that I couldn't hear what he had to say and even a little worried about why he wanted me to leave. Afterward, my father, in his gabardine overcoat, stood with his gray hat in his hand. He was looking serious and a little misty-eyed. Mother sat with her own light blue cloth coat and her black bonnet over her covering, smiling. When I asked why I had to leave, Mother said, "Mr. Price told us that if he ever has a daughter, he hopes she will be just like you." Only if he had asked for my hand in marriage, one of my fantasies in tenth grade, would I have been happier.

My yearbook (*Warwick Warrian*) picture, 1966. This was my second photo. The first one featured the same covering on my head, but my hair was "down" and curled. To please Mother, I went back to the studio for a retake. In truth, it represents well my last days as a "plain" girl.

When graduation came, I had not achieved the goal of becoming valedictorian or salutatorian of my class, coming in fourth. At commencement I received two awards. I felt happy and rewarded for my hard work. But one more event remained.

All of us had been trained to focus on the alumni banquet held on June 11, because that's when the three coveted awards would be given out. When the night came and the chicken had been consumed, all eyes were on Dr. M. H. Yoder, whose job it was to announce the winners. The third prize of $200 was given first to Dawn Ketterman. The second prize of $300 was given next to Joyce Nauman, our valedictorian and my Sunday school classmate at Lititz Mennonite Church. I felt proud of her, but also possibly a little jealous, depending on what happened next. All the students held their breath for the last chance at the $500 prize.

"Shirley Ann Hershey" said the speaker.

I had imagined this moment. I thought it would be the ultimate in big events. I would feel as tall as a silo and as wide as a wheat field.

Instead, I felt a new kind of smallness. Did I deserve this honor? What if my parents hadn't dreamed me into existence and told me stories and painted my bike with such care? What if I hadn't moved to Warwick and accidentally become a "brain"? What if Janette and Mel had never encouraged me to think on my feet and hit the quiz team buzzer? Faces of all my family members, mentors, and friends flooded my consciousness. Compared to all these people and to the huge fabric that connected them to my life, I felt small and grateful. Very grateful.

I also felt a new kind of big. Joining the church had taught me that submission to God and community could expand, not contract, my vision of my own life. Now, being rewarded for values others had taught me made me feel all the more eager to fulfill the dream of becoming a teacher myself. It was the right dream for me. It united the passions I carried forward from Mother and Daddy; it connected me to a long tradition both inside the church and outside the church; and it was, in fact, the way God made me before the earth was born.

I knew that everyone at Lititz Mennonite Church would calmly but warmly congratulate both Joyce and me, among them my employers, Jay and Rhoda Oberholtzer. Directly in front of me sat Mother and Daddy, cheering me on, even if they were sad and fearful about the endpoint of this prize—to usher me out of the Home Place and on to an unknown destination. They had lived their dreams. It was my turn now.

Mother and Daddy's graduation present, a set of three blue canvas suitcases, signaled that I would be leaving for college in the fall. I spent the summer planning how to pack up my entire wardrobe into those suitcases. I also took one piece of furniture with me. No, it wasn't a stuffed chair or a refrigerator or a stereo. The one indispensable piece of furniture was a bookcase Mother had brought from her parents' home. I had used it in my bedroom to collect all the 25- and 30-cent books I had bought in my English classes from Scholastic Book Club. I took a set of three matching clothbound books that included Homer's classic tales, *The Odyssey,* and *The Iliad.* Jean Paul Sartre's *The Reprieve* was on the shelf also. Many of the books, like Hegel, were a little above my ability to comprehend, but none was beyond my yearning to become wise.

As I packed my suitcases, patted my brother and sisters on the backs, and smiled at them a little more than usual, I looked around me and tried to see my home one last time before I went off to my new home. There it was: the big white barn with its limestone foundation; the springhouse with its cool limey smell and white walls; the garden with tomatoes, corn, and beans ready to harvest; the kitchen—always the hub, always a little disheveled; and my bedroom, all clean and ready for my sister Sue to claim when I left. Outside my bedroom window, acorns in the oak trees were almost ready to rain down. The curtains next to my bed moved ever so slightly in the breeze.

I looked around and finally saw that it was good.

Then the day came I had dreamed of since Mrs. Lochner's

class in sixth grade. I said goodbye to Henry, Sue, Doris, and Linda. I promised to write often.

Daddy lifted my heavy bookcase and put it in the trunk of our '57 Dodge. Then he picked up the three suitcases, my hockey stick, my guitar, and some posters. Everything I would wear and use to decorate my dorm room was in the trunk.

The three of us, Mother, Daddy, and I, climbed into the car and headed it toward U.S. Route 11 south to Virginia and Eastern Mennonite College. Our ancestors had arrived in boats two hundred and fifty years earlier. Some of their Mennonite kin had invented the first moving van, the Conestoga wagon. There we were, setting out in a modern version of that wagon. I was the one blazing a new trail, but I was glad I didn't have to travel the first miles alone.

I waved out the window to my brother and sisters, then turned my eyes to the road ahead. The last sound I heard on the farm was gravel crunching under our tires as we drove away.

Epilogue

After the Glitter, the Gold

What we have loved, others will love and we will teach them how.
—William Wordsworth, *The Prelude*

As I left the Home Place for college, I was convinced that life was just beginning for me. And in some ways it was. I was leaving behind the cows, the fields, the garden, the tobacco worms, and the hours of toil they required. Goodbye to all that.

I sincerely hoped no one would call me "Rosy Cheeks" in the years ahead, so that I would never again feel the heat begin at the base of my neck and then move up my face until I glowed crimson.

I was leaving Lancaster Conference and its bishops and rules forever, which meant that I would cut and curl my hair and drop the prayer covering as soon as another Mennonite church permitted it. In college I would read books all day long and have long talks about how to help create peace in a time of war and what to do about racial injustice and poverty. I would connect my faith anew to the issues of my own time.

At Eastern Mennonite College I would share a dorm room with Tina Hess, who would turn out to be as fun and smart and funny as one of my short-term boyfriends had said she would be. And we would find other friends, especially Mary Bender and Gloria Horst, who would share popcorn and Sara Lee treats and their *Mamas and Papas* record albums. In the privacy of our rooms, we would practice "spontaneous foot movement," since the college rules disallowed dancing. Like others of our generation, we would place candle after colorful candle in the neck of a Portuguese wine bottle. The provenance of the bottle would be a mystery to me, since I had not consumed any of the original contents. However, I would learn to say the word *Mateus* knowingly and to enjoy a special brand of ignorant sophistication that comes from a sheltered childhood.

We four would also pray together and argue theology and current events. We would tell stories about our respective Lancaster County Mennonite pasts, all of them a little different. From our own circle, we would expand into the rest of the campus, each making different friends and each finding young men we would marry.

Mother had heard a good idea for how to stay in touch while I was in college. She sent me off with a loose-leaf notebook and a pack of lined notebook paper, keeping an identical one for herself. She wrote me a letter on a few sheets of hole-punched paper. I read it, answered it, and then stored her letter in my notebook. She did the same with my letters. By the end of the year, we each had a full notebook recording the happenings at both the Home Place and Northlawn residence hall. I still have four full notebooks from those years.

I wrote my letters home while seated at my small wooden dorm-room desk and thought about each of my four siblings, Henry, Sue, Doris, and Linda. For their sakes and to entertain and reassure Mother and Daddy, I described the food, the dorm room, my new friends, and my professors. For the first time in my life, I had nothing to do but study, except for five to ten hours a week helping a professor for wages. When I read about Lewis and Clark mapping the land west of the Mississippi, I identified with them. The purple mountains of Virginia were my version of the Rockies, and I had my own discovery expedition underway. The vistas ahead were large but indistinct. The only thing I knew was that I would become a teacher.

I would meet and fall in love with Stuart W. Showalter. He would break his vow not to date any freshman girls (the phrase "first-year women" was not yet in vogue). The editor-in-chief of the student newspaper would become the editor-in-chief of my life. He and I would "go west," choosing the image of the Pennsylvania Conestoga wagon as our guide. In Goshen, Indiana, we would find a calling to sculpt a new kind of Mennonite life— two-career family with both parents teaching in a Mennonite college.

Becoming a professor, a college president, and a foundation executive . . . none of these were planted in me as goals while in college. Like my experiences at Fairland and Warwick, however, my years at Eastern Mennonite would give me plenty of opportunity to observe the kinds of people I admired most. College had given me a way to combine the glittering world away from the farm with a new understanding of what it meant to be Mennonite. We could be activist, not passivist, pacifists. Our bumper stickers declared that "Peace is Patriotic," and we students collectively rallied the whole local Harrisonburg and larger Mennonite communities to save a library building project on the EMC campus.

Several times a year now I walk the old meadow on visits to my sister Doris, who lives in the home my mother built with limestones from the old barn. I can stoop and pick up a clod of earth, remembering Daddy's lecture about the beauty of limestone soil.

I now know something about my ancestors I didn't know when I was young.[63] I'm connected to a limestone trail that leads back not just to Germany and Switzerland, to mountains and caves and cowbells and memories of martyrs—but also to Celts who found God in trees and skies and all living things. My ances-

---

63. Thanks to DNA test results of my male (Hershey) ancestry, I have a June 20, 2012, report on the migration patterns prepared by Darvin Martin and sent from the Lancaster Mennonite Historical Society: "The story progresses as follows: East Africa>Arabia>Iran>India>Central Asia>Caucasus Mountains>Turkey >Balkans>Eastern Europe>Alpine Europe>Continental Celts>Gallo-Roman Culture>Benedictine Catholic>Bernese Swiss>Anabaptist>Pennsylvania Mennonite."

tors' path leads all the way back to Africa and there connects to all other lives in the birthplace of the human race.

As for becoming big? I've had a lot of what the glittering world calls success, and I am grateful for that. But I would not be my ancestors' daughter if I didn't know that "the grass withereth, the flower fadeth: but the word of our God shall stand for ever."[64]

The closer I get to the day of death, the day I have known about since the age of six, the more I go back to the wisdom in the old books and the more I remember dear faces. What I seek in both are glimpses of glory; what my ear wants to hear is eternal music. When I hold my grandchildren, I relax into the light we share, coming from and going back to God.

Death will be my last great adventure. Like always, I'm both excited and afraid. My family, my church, and my vocational calling have prepared me. I turn toward the morning and face again the great unknown.

When I learned, on a trip to England two decades ago, that my name, Shirley, means "bright meadow," I felt a thrill of recognition. Of course, I thought of the Home Place and Mother's magic elevator story. What is life but a journey one takes walking barefoot along a stream, woods on one side, pasture on the other?

I now live next to a Virginia meadow and look out to the Allegheny Mountains where the sun sets every night. My new landscape takes me back to the old.

Beyond the mountains lie more mountains. Beyond the meadows, another Home Place.

Beyond everything visible, all things invisible.

Beyond everything known, the glittering unknown.

Beyond the glitter, the gold.

---

64. Isaiah 40:8.

Acknowledgments

I developed an interest in spiritual autobiography while a senior fellow with the Lilly Fellows Program for Humanities and the Arts at Valparaiso University, 1993–94. While there, I published my first personal essays and felt called to explore what it means to transmute experience into wisdom via the writing process. Special thanks to Mark Schwehn, who agreed to weekly mentoring conversations, and to all other participants in that intense, profound year of spiritual and intellectual exploration. Walter Wangerin Jr. critiqued one of my first essays and encouraged me to continue.

My colleagues in the English department and all the faculty and staff of Goshen College became both audience and source for many stories that eventually found their way into this book. Thank you for calling me into leadership and for honing my inner ear for the good, the true, and the beautiful. Goshen College, ever singing!

Likewise, my colleagues, partners, and friends at The Fetzer Institute. Thank you for helping me better understand the power of story to nurture love and forgiveness in the emerging global community. I will be forever grateful for the six years I spent with you and for the confirmation that my purpose in life is to be a witness for love and forgiveness.

The *Kalamazoo Gazette* ignited my interest in memoir by holding an annual literary awards contest. I took a weekend at Gilchrist Retreat Center and invited my memory to speak. Three stories flowed out, including "The Fresh Air Girl" that won first place in the contest, giving rise to the idea of an eventual book. Thanks especially to Joyce Pines for the vision and stamina to keep a contest like this going and to the amazing literary community of Kalamazoo for supporting it.

"Daddy's Girl," the story of the tobacco worm challenge was published both in the *Kalamazoo Gazette* and online at the Center for Mennonite Writing, sponsored by the English department of Goshen College, where Ann Hostetler, Ervin Beck, and others have created a wonderful resource: www.mennonitewriting.org.

I had the good fortune to have novelist Bonnie Jo Campbell as my first writing coach and to attend the Santa Barbara Writers Conference twice, the Bear River Writers Conference, and Mennonite/s Writing Conference VI.

While living in Brooklyn, New York, in 2012 I benefited from the coaching of novelist Christina Baker Kline and the gracious critique of writers Deborah Siegel, Jessica Saffron, Heather Hewett, and Kibum Kim.

Readers of complete drafts included Carolyn Yoder, Janette Wenger, Barbara Ann Hess Hershey Becker, Henry Hershey, John L. Ruth, Tom Beech, Bill Stott, Jean Engle, Ann Peters, and Ervin Stutzman. Others read draft chapters: Bill Pezick, Ann Mosemann Overly, Joyce Snader Sauder, Jane Tompkins, Joanne Gabbin, and Gloria Diener.

The Language and Literature Department at Eastern Mennonite University, chaired by Vi Dutcher, cohosted a reception and reading and assisted me in many ways, as did my students in the fall 2013 honors course I taught at EMU.

Editors are a writer's best friends. I thank Lanie Tankard and Amy Gingerich who guided me skillfully through several drafts. I'm grateful also to author Darrelyn Saloom, who steered me to editor Dave Malone, who helped me whittle and prune the text. From there, Byron Rempel-Burkholder and Nancy Klemm of Herald Press provided many helpful edits and suggestions.

Herald Press has proved to be an extraordinary partner in this enterprise. Thanks, to Amy Gingerich for encouraging a proposal and to Russ Eanes for approving it. To Ben Penner for weekly phone calls during the last four months prior to publication and Evan McCarthy for great marketing ideas along the way. Merrill Miller designed the cover and scanned innumerable photos, some of which are published here. Dorothy Hartman helped connect me with early readers and endorsers. Together, we extracted a lot of wisdom from experience and enjoyed the benefits of community with online friends.

I met many other memoir writers in the National Association of Memoir Writers and numerous other groups on online social media. I am especially grateful to those who "liked" www.facebook.com/shirleyhersheyshowalter and gave me great advice on everything from title to photos to recipes as I wrote this book.

In addition to my uncles, aunts, siblings, and cousins who love the Home Place, I want to thank the Mennonite Foundation, who helped our family preserve a precious legacy, the Home Place house. Dale and Suzanne Groff purchased the house from the Foundation and turned it into the bed and breakfast now known as Forgotten Seasons. Dale curated family photos, researched the history of the house, collected memorabilia about the colonial period, and cared for the memory as well as the buildings. Kathy and Jay Wenger continue the stewardship of place, restoring the house to its original condition, one stone at a time. Kathy opened all the doors of the house to me and to my niece Joy Rittenhouse for two photo shoots. She and Jay always welcome guests with the kind of hospitality that exudes their quiet, deep, simple faith.

I am deeply grateful to my literal and figurative Mennonite ancestors. To early martyrs, brave pioneers, and simple, devoted farmers who tended their farms and contributed time and talent to their churches. And to new generations of Mennonites who used education as a way to find their own deep joy and serve the needs of the world. Also to many Mennonites of many races and cultures around the world who do not share my Swiss-German ethnicity. I rejoice in a goodly heritage.

I also want to thank the critics of my faith: the artists who had to leave the church in order to survive as individuals. The business people driven away by lack of understanding or jealousy. Those who tried to live up to Mennonite perfectionist standards and failed. And those who simply stood outside and pointed to hypocrisy and paradox. You have been my teachers and mentors, too.

I am grateful to all my teachers, from Mrs. Gibble to my most recent writing coaches. You led me into a sacred calling. Then, my students also became my teachers, and I thank each of them. What could be more gratifying than a life lived in school?

My family matters most of all and was more than incidentally involved in this project. Son Anthony started me off with a WordPress blog as my birthday present in 2009. Daughter-in-law Chelsea offered ideas from her many years of experience in the publishing industry, and grandchildren Owen and Julia lifted my spirits over and over as I sat in my chair and tried to write the stories I want them to have after I am gone.

My daughter, Kate, a writer, speaker, and blogger herself, was my personal marketing director. She knows how to live life like a party, a skill that turned out to be helpful many times. Son-in-law Nik contributed his web design skills and helped solve many technical glitches along the way.

Finally, my husband, Stuart, my life partner and dearest friend, has been there for me through every mountain and valley of my life since 1969, the year we married. He read draft after draft, cooked, and drove the car—whatever was needed at the time. He's the first person I want to tell when there's something to celebrate, and he holds me safe in hard times. I could say more, but then both of us might blush.

Glossary

Amish (pronounced Ah-mish)—an Anabaptist group that separated from other European Mennonites in 1693 to follow their leader, Jakob Ammann, from whom they get their name. The Amish are known for uniformly plain dress, nonresistance (see below), simple living, and reluctance and sometimes refusal to adopt modern technology. Their wish to separate from the world is so strong that they practice the ban, excommunicating members who refuse to repent, sometimes shunning them. Amish and Mennonites have traditionally farmed in many of the same places, with Lancaster County being a focal point for both groups.

Anabaptist—a Greek word meaning rebaptizer and, since the sixteenth century, referring to a group who withdrew from both the Roman Catholic Church and the newly Protestant churches. The practice of rebaptizing adults and of refusal to baptize children was seen as a threat to both the established church and the state. Some defining characteristics put emphasis on "discipleship as the essence of Christianity, on the church as a brotherhood, and on an ethic of love and nonresistance." For more, see http://www.gameo .org/encyclopedia/contents/A533ME.html.

Arch cellar—named for the shape of this underground vault dug deep under the house at the Home Place. Sometimes called a root cellar in other places. Used for storage of meats and vegetables before freezers and canned goods. Cool in the summer, warmer than outdoors in the winter. The arch cellar of the Home Place was probably dug soon after 1735.

Fraktur—a Pennsylvania German folk art that is both a style of lettering and an elaborate manuscript illumination practiced most widely in Pennsylvania, 1740–1860. The cover of the *Mennonite*

Community Cookbook pays homage to this tradition. Mennonites may have fraktur pieces as family heirlooms, and a few artists keep the tradition alive today.

The lot—a method of determining leaders in two stages. First, all adult members of a congregation (or bishop board) are invited to nominate candidates whose character is examined on the basis of biblical descriptions of the requirements of the roles of the office. In the second stage, in the presence of the congregation a slip of paper is placed in a set of hymnals or Bibles, whose order is shuffled so that no one knows where the marker lies. Each candidate is then asked to come forward and choose a book. The one whose book contains the marker is then immediately ordained. The biblical precedent for using this method to fill leadership positions is found in Acts 1:15-26. "We believe the ministry is called by the Holy Spirit . . . we believe the use of the lot is a scriptural way of finding God's will and promoting peace and unity in the church." *Statement of Christian Doctrine and Rules and Discipline of the Lancaster Conference of the Mennonite Church*, July 17, 1968, 27–28.

Mennonite—the name for the followers of Menno Simons (1496–1561), a Dutch priest who joined the Anabaptist movement and became a leader in the first years of its history. In opposition to violence-condoning Anabaptists such as those taking over the German city of Münster, he maintained the position of biblical nonresistance and thus was essential in the formation of the identity of the church. "Mennonite is the most common designation since the mid-17th century for the largest continuing Christian tradition rooted in 16th century Anabaptism." From the Global Anabaptist Mennonite Encyclopedia Online (GAMEO). Here is a link to an entry titled "Mennonite (The Name)": http://www.gameo .org/encyclopedia/contents/M4673ME.html.

Nonconformity—one of the twin pillars of Mennonite faith as I was taught it. The other was nonresistance. "We recognize that Christians are in the world but not of the world, and that this separation unto God must be expressed in all of life." From *Statement of Christian Doctrine and Rules and Discipline of the Lancaster Conference of the Mennonite Church*, July 17, 1968, 18.

Nonresistance—one of the twin pillars of Mennonite faith as I was taught it. The other was nonconformity. "We recognize the place of government in God's order. However, government's methods of maintaining order in society differ from scriptural teachings for the Christian, which teach love and overcoming evil with good. Therefore the doctrine of nonresistance makes it inconsistent for Christians to become involved in areas such as political offices, military services, lawsuits, and jury duty." From *Statement of Christian Doctrine and Rules and Discipline of the Lancaster Conference of the Mennonite Church,* July 17, 1968, 22.

Ordinance—a practice ordained by Jesus or the apostles and prescribed for believers. Very close in meaning to "sacrament" but preferred by Mennonites in the twentieth century because of the implied closer connection to the idea of order rather than to holiness or the Roman Catholic tradition. In years following the 1890s until the 1970s, the time period relevant to this memoir, it was common among Lancaster Conference Mennonites to speak of "the seven ordinances."

Pennsylvania Dutch—Pennsylvania Dutch is not Dutch at all, but rather a dialect of German spoken by the Swiss and brought to America with the first Mennonite and Amish immigrants in the eighteenth and nineteenth centuries. The confusions between German and Dutch arose because the German dialect word for German, *Deitsch,* sounds so much like Dutch. See http://en.wikipedia.org/wiki/Pennsylvania_German_language.

Plain—this word referred to a style of unadorned dress and architecture common to most Lancaster Conference Mennonites until rules began to relax in the late twentieth century. In dress, women wore their hair long and under prayer coverings (see below). They wore modest skirts and dresses, sometimes with special "capes" to disguise their breasts. Men had more latitude in plainness. Some of them wore special coats without lapels called plain coats (ironically similar to both Catholic priest attire and the Nehru jackets made popular by the Beatles). Others buttoned up their long-sleeved shirts, but most wore pants and shirts similar to non-Mennonites. The degree of plainness in clothing resulted either from the strictness of the bishop in one's district or from the desire of the individual to show how serious his or her faith was. (In other words, even in the same church, some people were plainer than others by choice.)

Plain Mennonites are still numerous in Lancaster County, though not among the members of the group called the Lancaster Conference. A merger occurred among Mennonite denominations in 1995. Today Lancaster Conference congregations affiliate with Mennonite Church USA, which does not require plain clothing as an expression of faithfulness.

Today many Mennonites, both conservative and liberal, seek their own version of plain-ness. The phrase I like to use to describe my own preferred style is one I first heard from Evelyn Kreider, who, as Dean Carl Kreider's wife, presided over many meals in their home at Goshen College. When it was time to instruct the architects planning the new Music Center at Goshen College, I gave a two-word directive borrowed from Evelyn: "simple elegance." I much prefer such elegance to the glitter that first caught my eye as a child, and I like to think that I am choosing my own form of plain-ness today.

Plain architecture—Churches and homes were plain and utilitarian. No spires, stained glass, sculpture, padded benches, or thick carpets. Beauty could be cultivated in lovely gardens and flower beds but not in costly, showy, elaborate, and non-utilitarian design. Whenever possible, scraps or old items would be recycled into new ones. Quilts and rag rugs are good examples of how frugality, utility, and craft could create a distinctive style.

Prayer covering—In Lancaster Conference Mennonite practice, the covering, or veiling as it was sometimes called, was a particular type of stiff, white netting sewn so as to conform to the shape of the head in sizes large, medium, and small. The larger the covering, the more conservative the woman. The most conservative Mennonites wore black or white strings on their coverings. These began disappearing in the 1950s. Wearing the covering was required of all women members as an ordinance (see above) based on 1 Corinthians 11:4-16 wherein women are commanded to wear their hair long and to have their heads covered when they pray, to indicate the order of God-man-woman.

Quaker—the popular name for members of the Religious Society of Friends, a group that emerged in England in the middle of the 1600s. Quaker leader William Penn brought Quakers and

Mennonites together in Pennsylvania when he invited Mennonites and Amish to join him in his quest to establish a peaceable kingdom in the new world. Although Quakers and Mennonites came from different historical periods and different countries, and developed different practices, the emphasis on peace and simplicity in both faiths brought them together. They cooperated in seeking exemption from military service, for example.

"Redd up"—a Pennsylvania Dutch term meaning to clean up, rearrange, straighten a room, usually before guests arrive. This is just one of a group of words or phrases that survive in Lancaster County, even after people no longer speak the German dialect. Other examples: *schtrublich* (messed up hair), *rutsch* (move around with too much energy—often applied to children), and *schushlich* (random rather than graceful in movement).

Rumspringa—literally means "running around." Rumsprings refers to a period (adolescence) when Amish youth are encouraged to court each other. A certain amount of misbehavior may be tolerated during this period, and the punishments are lighter for youth who have not yet joined the church. The hope is that the good times enjoyed in youth will lead to romance with a good partner, then to joining the church, when behavior comes under the strict discipline of the bishop and list of rules known as the Ordnung.

Rumspringa has been explored in American popular culture partly because extreme instances of Amish rebellion in the form of drunkenness or drug use or sexual activities have made the news and partly because such images contrast so sharply with the much more dominant ones of plainness, humility, and highly disciplined behavior enforced by the church. See http://www2.etown.edu/amishstudies/Rumspringa.asp.

Shoofly pie—a traditional "sweet" often featured in Pennsylvania Dutch restaurants. The basic ingredients are flour, molasses, brown sugar, lard, one egg, and soda. The pie tastes like coffee cake with a gooey, sweet bottom. These ingredients formed the staple diet of the first immigrants to this hemisphere. Clever cooks created the recipe, baked the basic ingredients in outdoor ovens, and also cooled the sweet pies outside, attracting flies. As they shooed them away, they developed the name. Or so the story goes.

Susquehannocks—The name of a group of Indians living south of the Five Nations (Iroquois) in what would become known as Lancaster County. These people shared much of Iroquois culture, including the Seneca language and the construction of longhouses. Their grandparents had been defeated in warfare in the 1670s by the Iroquois, who had earlier obtained guns. When William Penn received his enormous land grant from King Charles II in 1681, he was aware of Indians inhabiting the land and arranged to "buy" it via peaceful agreements with them. Since, as remnants of the Susquehannocks, the so-called Conestogas remained tributary to the victorious Iroquois, Penn had to purchase the Susquehanna claim from both the Five Nations and a governor of New York who had paid them earlier. See John L. Ruth, *The Earth Is the Lord's* (Scottdale, PA: Herald Press), 2001.

Despite Penn's pledge that the Conestogas would be esteemed by him as his own people, he could not sustain the promise into the next generation, and tragedy ensued after his death. The last of the Conestogas came to a tragic end at the hands of the Paxton Boys in a 1763 massacre.

The world—refers to numerous passages in the Bible that warn of misplaced love, especially 1 John 2:15: "Do not love the world or the things in the world. The love of the Father is not in those who love the world" (NRSV). The world is another name for the shadow side of creation or evil. The Lancaster Conference Mennonite Church's twentieth-century focus on nonconformed externals like dress was a way to remind the believer that the world and the Father are in conflict with each other and that Christians are called to stand apart from the love of power and pleasure.

You-uns—a local expression in eastern Pennsylvania; the plural of you equivalent to *y'all* in the South or *yinz* in Pittsburgh.

Recipes

Two favorite family recipes I still make on special occasions and have passed along to my children:

Great-Grandma Herr's Sugar Cakes

Cream together:
> 2 cups sugar
> 1 cup lard
> 3 eggs

Add:
> 1 cup sour milk (Pour 1 tablespoon white vinegar into a measuring cup, add milk to reach 1 cup, and wait a minute until thickened.)

Sift together and add to the above:
> 5 cups flour
> ½ teaspoon lemon juice
> 3 teaspoons baking soda
> ¼ teaspoon nutmeg
> 1 teaspoon cream of tartar
> 1 scant teaspoon salt
> 1 teaspoon vanilla

Chill dough for 2 hours and then drop by teaspoon on cookie sheet. Bake at 350 degrees until they begin to turn light brown, about 10 minutes.

This is a hearty cookie that is delicious with coffee or other hot drinks. Feel free to decorate top with sugar, walnuts, raisins, etc., before baking.

Steamed Cherry Pudding

Cream together:
  2 cups sugar
  6 tablespoons butter

Sift together:
  4 cups flour
  2 teaspoons soda

Add alternately with
  2 cups milk

When batter is smooth, remove from mixer and add the following:
  2 cups canned or fresh sour cherries (if canned, you can substitute cherry juice for up to 1 cup of the milk). Pour into a greased 9x13-inch pan.

Bake at 350 degrees for 40–45 minutes. Top should be brown, and knife inserted into the middle should come out clean.

The following recipes are from *The Mennonite Community Cookbook*, by Mary Emma Showalter, first published by Herald Press in 1950.[65] Page numbers below are from the 1957 edition. Following each recipe are the names of the Mennonite women who supplied the recipe from their family recipe collection.

SWEETS

Cherry Pie (pp. 364–365)

2½ cups sour cherries	3 tablespoons minute tapioca
⅓ cup cherry juice	1 tablespoon butter
⅓ cup brown sugar	⅛ teaspoon almond extract
⅓ cup granulated sugar	Pastry for 2 (9-inch) crusts

Combine cherries, juice, sugars, flavoring, and tapioca.

Let stand 15 minutes.

---

65. Reprinted here with permission.

Pour into pastry-lined pie plate. Dot with butter.

Place crust or strips on top as preferred.

Bake at 425 degrees for 10 minutes, then in moderate oven (375 degrees) for 30 minutes.

Makes 1 (9-inch) pie.

> *Mrs. Fannie A. L. Gable, York, Pa.; Mrs. Ira Eigsti, Buda, Ill.*

Shoo Fly Pie (p. 380)

Bottom Part:
¾ cup dark molasses (sorghum or dark Karo syrup)
¾ cup boiling water
½ teaspoon soda

Top Part:
1½ cups flour
¼ cup shortening
½ cup brown sugar
Pastry for 1 (9-inch) crust

Dissolve soda in hot water and add molasses.

Combine sugar and flour and rub in shortening to make crumbs.

Pour one-third of the liquid into an unbaked crust.

Add one-third of the crumb mixture.

Continue alternate layers, putting crumbs on top.

Bake at 375° for approximately 35 minutes.

Makes 1 (9-inch) pie.

> *Mrs. Arthur Ruth, Chalfont, Pa.; Mrs. Roland Detweiler, Souderton, Pa.; Mrs. C. R. Ebersole, La Junta, Colo.*

SOURS

Beet Pickle (Cold) (p. 394)

1 gallon beets, cooked	2½ cups brown sugar
⅓ cup prepared mustard	3 cups vinegar
⅓ cup salt	½ cup cold water

Cook beets until tender. Skin.

Slice and place in a stone crock or jar.

Mix mustard, sugar, and salt, and add vinegar and water.

Pour mixture over beets and keep in a cool place.

These are ready to use after 24 hours.

Mrs. Earl Brenneman, Lima, Ohio

Pickled Red Beet Eggs

After the pickle is complete above, drop hard-boiled eggs into the brine. In one day the eggs are pickled. In two days, the color purple penetrates the entire egg white.

Potato Salad (p. 182)

(Grandma Hershey was renowned for her excellent potato salad. She probably used this recipe or a variant of it. Mother thought her secret was dicing the potatoes into small rather than large squares.)

8 medium-sized potatoes	1½ teaspoon flour
4 hard-cooked eggs	2 eggs
1 medium-sized onion	½ cup sugar
2 small carrots, ground	½ cup vinegar
1 cup celery, diced	1 teaspoon mustard
1½ teaspoons salt	1½ cups water
2 tablespoons butter	

Cook potatoes in jackets until soft.

Cool and peel.

Dice potatoes, eggs, onion, and celery.

Grate carrots.

To make dressing, mix together the dry ingredients; add eggs, vinegar, and water.

Melt butter in saucepan and add dressing.

Cook until thickened.

Cool and pour over potato mixture and mix lightly.

If desired, ½ cup of sandwich spread or mayonnaise may be added to dressing before it is poured over vegetables.

Serves 6.

Mrs. Richard Danner, Hanover, Pa.; Mrs. G. P. Showalter, Broadway, Va.

Coleslaw (p. 179)

   4 cups finely shredded cabbage
   3 tablespoons sugar
   ¼ cup sour cream (or cream or milk)
   1 teaspoon salt
   ¼ cup vinegar
   ⅛ teaspoon mustard (optional)

Chop or shred the cabbage.

Mix together the sugar, salt, mustard, vinegar, and sour cream.

Pour over cabbage and mix well.

Garnish with green pepper rings.

Serves 6.

Stella Huber Stauffer, Tofield, Alta., Can.

Bread and Butter Pickles *(pp. 394–395)*

30 medium-sized cucumbers (1 gallon, sliced)	5 cups sugar
	5 cups vinegar
8 medium-sized onions	2 tablespoons mustard seed
2 large red or green peppers	1 teaspoon turmeric
½ cup salt	1 teaspoon whole cloves

Slice cucumbers in thin rings. Do not pare.

Slice onions in thin rings.

Cut peppers in fine strips.

Dissolve salt in ice water and pour over sliced vegetables.

Let stand 3 hours and drain.

Combine vinegar, sugar, and spices, and bring to a boil.

Add drained vegetables and heat to boiling point. Do not boil.

Pack into sterilized jars and seal.

> *Mrs. William E. Martin, Wellman, Iowa; Mrs. Edna Newcomer, Dallastown, Pa.; Mrs. Amos Leis, Wellesley, Ont., Can.*

Deviled Eggs *(pp. 176–177)*

4 hard-cooked eggs	2 teaspoons vinegar
½ teaspoon salt	1 tablespoon mayonnaise
⅛ teaspoon pepper	1 tablespoon cream
¼ teaspoon mustard	

Cut eggs in half lengthwise.

Remove yolks and mash until smooth.

Add other ingredients and mix well.

Refill the whites and garnish with paprika or parsley.

Serves 4.

> *Mrs. Samuel Ramer, Versailles, Mo.*

Finally, another "recipe" from the *Mennonite Community Cookbook* (p. 455)

One of my favorite "recipes" isn't a recipe at all. It's merely a list, an entertaining list. But it's also a list that spells out the nature of community itself. Food comes from the land and returns to the land through the acts of kindness and nurture that make all living things grow.

If you saw the movie *Witness*, you can imagine the Amish workers relishing this lunch. Notice the heavy emphasis on sweets, meats, and sours. Nothing in this list except sugar and flour ingredients was processed.

What is harder to describe is the effect of all that food, prepared by the women for the men, the children, and for each other, as a symbol of community itself. The prayer would be simple, the conversation quiet and hearty, mostly about people. Who died? Who was born? Who is ill? Who will be married?

Thus, the rhythms of life follow the rhythms of the land—creation, birth, death, and resurrection.

Food for a Barn Raising

115 lemon pies
500 fat cakes (doughnuts)
15 large cakes
3 gallons applesauce
3 gallons rice pudding
3 gallons cornstarch pudding
16 chickens
3 hams
50 pounds roast beef
300 light rolls
16 loaves bread
Red beet pickle and pickled eggs
Cucumber pickle
6 pounds dried prunes, stewed
1 large crock stewed raisins
5 gallon stone jar of white potatoes and the same amount of
    sweet potatoes

Enough food for 175 men.

Why I Am (Still!) a Mennonite

One generation passeth away, and another generation cometh:
but the earth abideth for ever.

—Ecclesiastes 1:4

*B*ecause one early morning outside of Abidjan, Cote d'Ivoire, West Africa, I walked down a dirt lane and heard the distant sound of music. It was a group of young Mennonite Central Committee volunteers singing "For God So Loved Us." I cried as I drew near them, both for the beauty of their four-part harmony and the dedication of their lives to the cause of peace and justice.

Because when I was a young faculty member at Goshen College, still uncertain about whether to stay or leave that Mennonite college, a student from Cambridge, Massachusetts, said she came to Goshen because if a religion has lasted among a small group of people for almost five hundred years, she didn't want to be the one to break the link.

Because I went to Eastern Mennonite College where I met and married Stuart. We established friendships there that have lasted a lifetime, even across thousands of miles and over more than forty years. We chose to spend our lives in Mennonite higher education because of the transformative impact it had on us.

Because I memorized most of the book of John, where I met Jesus as a real presence and where his radical belief in love laid a claim on my heart. The prayer of Jesus for his disciples in John 17 has kept me in the church, believing in the unifying power of love, even when particular people or decisions disappoint me.

When I think of Jesus, I think of the faces of people who carried his image into my life: Anna, Barbara, Emma, Mary and Melvin, Janette and Mel, Jay and Rhoda, Roy and Martha Jane, and, of course, my parents and grandparents, my aunts and uncles, cousins and siblings.

Because the congregation I joined in 2012, Community Mennonite Church in Harrisonburg, Virginia, has brought new faces into my life whom I connect with Jesus. Every week I hear stories and sing songs that give me hope for this troubled world. I feel inspired and encouraged on Sunday mornings to take my faith into the rest of my week.

Because, in an era of acrimonious rhetoric, I can still come to the communion table with my political opposites and turn my anger and fear over to the One whose perfect love casts out fear.

Because my dreams are now for the biggest kind of happiness, the kind Willa Cather described first in her novel *My Antonia* and later requested for her tombstone: "This is happiness, to be dissolved into something complete and great." I'm Mennonite because I have dissolved often over the years while sitting in church, while placing grout around new floor tiles for victims of Hurricane Katrina, and while kneeling in prayer and meditation.

I'm Mennonite because I choose to be. I am free to join any Christian denomination, any other religion, or no religion. I have learned a lot from members of these groups. To be rooted in the faith of my fathers and mothers *and* to link arms with the rest of God's children moves me as much as the old time religion that's still good enough for me.

I'm also glad to be walking the "lonesome journey" home to be with God in the company of the people who first saw me and called me by name. I realized by writing this book that one of my first names for love was Mennonite.

The Author

*A*fter graduating from Eastern Mennonite University in 1970 and following two years of teaching high school English at Harrisonburg (Virginia) High School, Shirley Hershey Showalter entered graduate school at the University of Texas at Austin, from where she received the PhD in American Civilization in 1980. She joined the Goshen College faculty in 1976, becoming professor of English in 1989.

In April of 1996, Showalter was named the fourteenth president of Goshen College and served there until November 2004, when she joined The Fetzer Institute in Kalamazoo, Michigan.

She is now a writer, blogger, and consultant living in Harrisonburg, Virginia. Shirley and her husband, Stuart, spent the 2011–12 academic year taking care of grandson Owen while living in Brooklyn, New York. Most of her memoir was written in Brooklyn.

Shirley enjoys public speaking, teaching, and storytelling. She can be reached through her website, www.shirleyshowalter .com, where other material (for individuals, book clubs, Sunday school classes) related to this book can be found.